Police and

Crime Control

in Jamaica

Police and Crime Control in Jamaica

Problems of Reforming Ex-Colonial Constabularies

Anthony Harriott

THE UNIVERSITY OF THE WEST INDIES PRESS
Barbados • Jamaica • Trinidad and Tobago

The University of the West Indies Press
1A Aqueduct Flats   Mona
Kingston 7   Jamaica   W I

04   03   02   01   00   5   4   3   2   1

CATALOGUING IN PUBLICATION DATA

Harriott, Anthony
    Police and crime control in Jamaica : problems
    of reforming ex-colonial constabularies /
    Anthony Harriott.

    p. cm.
    Includes biographical references.
    ISBN 976-640-076-8

    1. Jamaica Constabulary Force. 2. Police –
    Surveillance operations – Jamaica. 3. Crime
    prevention – Jamaica. 4. Police corruption –
    Jamaica. 5. Police administration – Jamaica.
    I. Title.
    HV8173.A2 H38 2000   363.206'8 dc-20

    Set in 10/13 Atlantix SSi x 26 text
    and Myriad Roman display
    Book design by Karen L. Collins
    Cover design by Robert Harris
    Cover art: drawing by Safi Harriott, depicting
    a Utopia where the police are able to arrest
    criminals by the force of their moral authority.

For Safi
and
a safer and more just society

Contents

Section III – The Reforms

Tables

Figures

Acknowledgments

This work was hardly possible without the assistance and encouragement of colleagues and friends and, of course, the cooperation of many police officers who were the research subjects of the project. I wish to thank former Commissioner of Police Colonel Trevor MacMillan for readily approving the project and giving me the opportunity to present my ideas to audiences of police officers at the Staff College of the Force, and members of the other ranks at the Police Academy. I must also thank the present commissioner of police, Mr Francis Forbes, who has afforded me the opportunity (immediately on the conclusion of this study) to more carefully think through some of the policy implications of this study by recruiting me to participate in the development of a strategic plan for reforming the Jamaica Constabulary Force. The interaction with the members of the Force in many different work settings – from discussions at the Staff College to exchanges with the leadership of the Force on immediate problems of policing – has contributed to my understanding of the field and that institution.

I owe a special debt of gratitude to Dr Donald Robotham for his encouragement of this work from its inception and for prodding me to apply to the University of the West Indies (UWI) Foundation Endowment Fund for the research grant that allowed me to complete the study, and later for critically reading the draft report. I owe a handsome debt of gratitude to him for his insightful and incisive comments. I thank the foundation for allowing me to benefit from their generosity and the Institute of Social and Economic Research (ISER) staff, especially Ms Judith Tavares who administered the project. The report on this research project should have been submitted in the summer of 1996, but instead it was not completed until 1997. The ISER was very understanding and supporting.

I must express my sincere appreciation to my reviewers for their kind remarks and useful critical comments and suggestions. I am indeed grateful to my colleagues at the UWI, Professor Rupert Lewis and Dr Tony Bogues for the collegial spirit displayed in finding the time to comment on a lengthy monograph somewhat beyond their immediate field of interest. Mr Richard Quarless and

Dr Sunday Iyare made useful comments on chapter 6. Professor Basil Wilson and other members of the faculty at the John Jay College of Criminal Justice were kind enough to read the manuscript and I thank them for their supportive and generous remarks. Thanks also to Karen Collins and the staff of the UWI Press, and to Mr Lloyd Waller, who assisted with aspects of its presentation. I hope that all this effort was worthwhile.

Abbreviations

ACR	Attitudes to citizens' rights
ALE	Attitudes to law enforcement
APS	Attitudes to police style (style of policing)
ARJCF	Attitudes to reforming the JCF
ASC	Attitudes to the sources of crime
ASP	Assistant superintendent of police
CBP	Community-based policing
CIB	Criminal Investigations Bureau
CJS	Criminal justice system
CP	Commissioner of police
CPO	Community police officer
DC	District constable
DCP	Deputy commissioner of police
DEA	Drug Enforcement Administration
DSP	Deputy superintendent of police
ESS	*Economic and Social Survey*
GDP	Gross domestic product
IMF	International Monetary Fund
ISCF	Island Special Constabulary Force
ISER	Institute of Social and Economic Research (at UWI)
JCF	Jamaica Constabulary Force
JCFHQ	Jamaica Constabulary Force Headquarters
JDF	Jamaica Defence Force
JLP	Jamaica Labour Party
KMA	Kingston Metropolitan Area
KMO	Kaiser-Meyer-Olkin
KRC	Kingston Restoration Company
NCO	Noncommissioned officer
NDM	National Democratic Movement
NIC	Newly industrialized country
PACE	Police and Criminal Evidence Act (UK)

PNP	People's National Party
PSC	Police Services Commission
REM	*Report on Election Malpractices General Elections* (JLP)
RIC	Royal Irish Constabulary
RPD	Revenue Protection Division
SACTF	Special Anti-Crime Task Force
SAP	Structural Adjustment Programme
SF	Security forces
SSP	Senior superintendent of police
STATIN	Statistical Institute of Jamaica
UNDP	United Nations Development Program
UNIA	Universal Negro Improvement Association
UWI	University of the West Indies

Introduction

Crime control has become a central developmental issue and an important public policy concern in most Caribbean territories. These tourism-dependent economies have become more vulnerable to violent crime, yet more criminogenic. In the case of Jamaica (which is perhaps the most problematic), the high rates of violent crime and insecurity among all segments of the population are matched by declining public confidence in the criminal justice system and growing cynicism among its functionaries.

There is a greater recognition of the negative impact of crime on these economies in reducing their attractiveness to investment capital, increasing the proportion of the public resources spent on treating the victims of violent crimes and its potential for frustrating broader development goals. For example, it is estimated that the developing countries spend between 9 and 14 percent of their national budgets on crime prevention and criminal justice. This contrasts with the developed countries, which spend 2 to 3 percent of their budgets for similar purposes [United Nations Commission on Crime Prevention and Criminal Justice 1992]. In many developing countries, the capacity of the state to provide for the physical security of its citizens, as well as effectively maintain order and a social environment conducive to development, is increasingly being questioned.

This has helped to induce a shift in the political agenda from concerns with change and social justice to the preservation of order. The movement away from social reformism, as well as the use of social policy as a prophylactic rather than a developmental instrument, is accompanied by a more punitive approach to crime control. Consequently, the state control agencies have been put under greater strain, at the same time as there has been greater élite commitment to improving the efficacy of the police, as evidenced by the number of state commissioned reports [cf. Teten 1991; Herst 1991; Wolfe 1993].

Despite the transformations in the society, the basic patterns of policing have, in essence, remained unchanged since the reforms of the 1950s that were designed to prepare the Force for Independence, and arguably since the formation of the Jamaica Constabulary Force (JCF) in 1867. The dynamic of the interactions with the citizenry and the logic of power on which these interactions are based have not been fundamentally altered. Thus unjust, rights-disregarding, partisan security policing, pervasive corruption, and incompetence are all part of the popular reputational imagery of the Force [cf. Stone 1995]. This is not peculiar to the JCF. Within the Commonwealth Caribbean, the Royal Bahamas Police Force [Ehrenfield 1992], the Trinidad and Tobago Police Service [Ali 1992; O'Dowd 1991; Scott 1987], the Antigua Police Service and Army [Blom-Cooper 1990], the Guyana Police Force [Danns 1982; Liverpool 1995], the St Kitts and Nevis Police Force [de Albuquerque 1996], among others, are all mired in similar difficulties. Even the reputedly pristine Royal Barbados Police Force has in recent times faced concerted public calls for a public enquiry into its conduct.[1] The universality of these problems, as reflected in their near global scope and their persistence in the face of public exposure and popular pressure, suggests that perhaps the challenge in reforming particular police forces ought to entail (as a condition for enduring success) fundamentally reforming policing as we now know it.

Reforms designed to improve the effectiveness of the police are a limited, but important, element of any programme of crime control. Unlike other state functions, however, crime control and public safety, which are universally accepted as core responsibilities of the state, cannot be "solved" by privatization. At the time of writing, the Jamaican government was seriously considering investing private security guards with police powers[2] [Miller 1997].[3] This would add another dimension to private corporate power and perhaps create a dual system of policing on class lines without proper mechanisms of accountability to the mass public, which would lead to even greater abuse of the citizenry. It would seem to reflect a tacit acceptance of the failure of the police to adequately protect the citizenry. However, the imperative of reforming the state security establishment and the wider criminal justice system can hardly be avoided.

Reform efforts in the Caribbean, and in particular Jamaica, have been piecemeal, truncated, internally inconsistent, and are too often exercises in symbolic manipulation and image reconstruction rather than substantive problem solving. They have been unduly influenced by the agendas and policy objectives of foreign agencies (the source of funding for some of these reform projects) or, where internally energized, tended to be simply knee-jerk symbolic responses to public criticisms and moral panics. While a complex of factors account for this record, too often these reform efforts are divorced from research or are based on research conducted in alien environments.

This study seeks to examine the extent and sources of police ineffectiveness in managing and controlling crime and the impact of this ineffectiveness on the patterns of reproduction of order, the methods of law enforcement, and the quality of justice. It critically analyses the existing reform efforts and examines the extent, character and bases of police support for reform. In a highly politicized organization such as the JCF, the outcome of the reform process will be determined by the balance of power between the different advocacy coalitions. The study therefore maps this configuration of power within the JCF, including the extent and quality of the commitment or resistance to reforming the JCF in more socially responsive and democratic ways. In so doing, it attempts to ascertain the extent to which these attitudes to reform are anchored in coherent beliefs about criminal justice and deeply held political values. In general, it seeks to analyse the interaction between the important policy actors and how this affects the outcomes of the reform process. In pursuing these objectives it is hoped that the study will illuminate aspects of state-citizen relations and thereby stimulate the elaboration of a more just and effective security policy and democratic reform of the police force. The policy implications of the analysis are not always made explicit, however.

It is argued that the ineffectiveness of the police has at its source a deep legitimacy crisis of the mode of reproduction of order, the nature of the social and political relationships that circumscribe its behaviour (an exclusionary social structure and gross social inequalities which are seen as the outcome of a zero-sum game among the classes – made more acute by a protracted economic crisis), an overloaded and lagging criminal justice system, and its response to these conditions. This is depicted in its style of policing, which is characterized by the low value placed on adherence to law and routine resort to illegitimate means and differential treatment of citizens on the principle of status congruence rather than equality before the law. It is a nonintegrative rather than consensual style of policing. It is therefore suggested that a radical change in the "model" of policing is required and that the JCF ought to reinvent itself along more democratic lines.

This crisis of policing is compounded by the development of a thriving underground economy, the consequent social embeddedness of crime in Jamaica, and an incongruence between social and legal definitions of some categories of crime. The effective repression of crime would therefore entail considerable economic and social dislocation and resistance. The police force is thus increasingly faced with a tension between the twin objectives of maintaining public order and controlling crime.

This problem is even more complicated. If effectively controlling white-collar crime contributes to a "lack of confidence" among corporate executives, this could lead to disinvestment and economic dislocation (as some active players in the financial sector have argued their case for impunity). Therefore, controlling disorder, those targeted for police action (such as illegal vendors) similarly argue and even threaten, would lead to increased street crime. The reason for this is that much of the disorder is associated with independent survival initiatives. These dilemmas perhaps partly explain why crime control has been such a politically sensitive issue in Jamaica. This is particularly interesting as Kelling and Coles, in a further elaboration of the "broken windows" theory, posit a strong relationship between disorder and crime. They therefore advocate, not without stirring some controversy, a kind of zero-tolerance of disorder in order to better control crime [Kelling and Coles 1996].

The crisis of the JCF, it is here argued, is but an instantiation of a more general legitimacy crisis of policing and of the Jamaican state. It is suggested that state-police repression in support of the existing model of development is not (ultimately) a viable option for resolving this crisis. Such an approach carries the likelihood of a descent into greater disorder (rather than an Asiatic newly industrialized country [NIC]-type state disciplined accumulation process) as the weak repressive capacity of the state security establishment could not ensure its success. More inclusive, democratically oriented solutions are not only morally more desirable, but also more viable. The imperative of reform is thus to move from the colonially inherited state-politically managed form of social control, to more police-citizen interactive and socially managed forms, and to develop a model of policing (within the framework of this new citizen-state, citizen-police power relations) that is oriented more towards crime control and less towards state security.

Basic research on crime and crime control in the Caribbean is still in its early stages. Twenty years after an attempt by Pryce [1976] to examine the theoretical implications of the unique features of the Caribbean and the need to create an independent space for a Caribbean criminology, and thirty years after similar debates in Caribbean economics [see Beckford 1984; St Cyr 1983; Brown and Brewster 1974] and sociology [Robotham 1984], this discussion has been renewed, but in a tentative and task setting, rather than reviewing, mode [see Bennett and Lynch 1996; Cain 1996].

Research on the policies and institutions designed to control crime has pursued three aspects:

- The legislative responses by governments [McCalla 1974; Sutherswaite 1975]. These adopted a legal perspective and have been mainly postgraduate theses in law.
- Sentencing policies. With the exception of Chuck [1980], these studies have focused narrowly on the effectiveness and justifications for specific

instruments such as the death penalty [cf. McIntosh and Ghany 1996] and the Gun Court [Lewin 1978].

• The putative rehabilitative policies of the state [Allen 1980].

Policing forms an important aspect of the crime control strategy of the state. In the developed countries a massive volume of literature in police studies has been accumulated, although systematic academic work in this field did not begin in earnest until the early 1970s [Reiner 1992]. Reiner associates this explosive growth in police studies with three factors: the sharp increases in violent crimes and the drug epidemic; police repression of the mass protests of the 1960s and 1970s; and greater fiscal constraints on the state. These factors, he argues, have provided the impetus for an official charge and public demand for increased police effectiveness and greater police accountability [Reiner 1992].

Cain [1979] and Reiner [1992] have provided valuable reviews of the English and North American contribution to this literature. Reiner identifies three thematic "traditions" in the literature: first, research aimed at explaining police behaviour (including the politics of the police) and its relationship to state and society [cf. Brogden 1982; Hall et al. 1978]; second, evaluations of the impact of policing strategies on the control of crime [cf. Kelling et al. 1974; Sherman 1992]; and third, concerns with internal administrative forms and defining the functions and structure of the police [cf. Goldstein 1979; Buttler 1992]. The relationship between the police and community may be regarded as a fourth theme, where the concerns have been primarily with external modes of accountability and police styles [cf. Leighton 1991; Melchers 1993].

In contrast, the literature on policing in the developing states, and in particular those of the Commonwealth, is sparse. The early excursions were mainly amateur histories which, with few exceptions [Jefferies 1952], were limited to country specific accounts of policing during the colonial era, such as Curry's [1932] account of policing in India. In the Caribbean, these histories took the form of autobiographical works by former members of the Jamaican [Thomas 1927], Dominican [Richards 1940], British Guyanese [Orrett 1951], and Trinidadian police forces [Otley 1964].

These autobiographies, written by Caribbean nationals or English officers who had served long tours of duty in the region, while giving useful insights into the daily routines and styles of these police forces, nevertheless tend to reflect the biases of police insiders and were, in the main, written from a colonial perspective.

More recent research on the police has been mainly state commissioned evaluations, but there has also been some independent scholarly work. The former have been either narrow management audits [cf. Herst 1991] or evaluations of much broader scope which have only skirted aspects of police policy as part of wider treatment of the governance of crime and problems of the criminal justice system. The reports which offer some comment on policing, with the possible exception of Wolfe [1993], suffer from three major defects. First, they have all been done by foreigners who simply transfer the current thinking and their specific applications in the metropolitan centres to Jamaica. The Herst report, for example, draws heavily on those aspects of the Scarman report that were implemented in the UK. It largely reflects the British (police) concern with narrow managerial issues of efficiency rather than the more foundational normative issues associated with effectiveness. This orientation is the outcome of the internally focused organizational approach of these studies and their ignoring of the societal matrix within which the Force operates. Second, these reports are usually written by, or under the direction of, senior professionals in criminal justice. They therefore, like the police biographies of the earlier period, tend to reflect an insider bias and a taken-for-grantedness of the basic principles on which the criminal justice system operates. Finally, they tend to lack methodological rigour and to rely heavily on anecdotal evidence.

If the state commissioned reports have been preoccupied with the mana-gerialist discourses of efficiency and the effectiveness with which the coercive power of the state is employed, the academic literature, on the other hand, has been largely concerned with the normative discourse of human rights, with the repressive abuse of this power [cf. Chevigny 1991; Danns 1982].

Various factors account for the sparsity and direction of the literature. These include attitudinal variables associated with the society, the police, and academia, such as a strong but declining anti-intellectualism among some members of the police force. The undeveloped character of civil society and, consequently, the facility with which issues of public policy and the performance of state institutions are party politicized allow the police considerable latitude in its treatment of citizens, and retards the fashioning of proper instruments of police accountability. Associated with this, public demand for research on the police and wider criminal justice system has historically been low. The closed nature of the police force and criminal justice system also presents considerable difficulties for researchers in gaining worthwhile access [cf. Lacey 1977; Danns 1982:26]. National security is still considered to be the exclusive domain of the small group of state officials at the apex of the security establishment. For example, calls for a public inquiry into the Barbados Police Force in 1990 were (in a style typical of most Caribbean governments) rejected on the ground that it was "a very dangerous thing to expose the Royal Barbados Police Force to public review".[4] The anti-intellectualism of the JCF and a generally hostile internal environment towards researchers are born of an occupationally ingrained suspiciousness and an experientially grounded fear of exposure of the poor human rights record of the Force. A factor of no less significance has been the preoccupation of Caribbean academic researchers with treating the "root causes" of crime, which has meant that crime control and issues in policing have been neglected as cosmetic and ideologically suspect concerns.

Evaluations of the governance of policing need to go beyond simple moral condemnations, on the one hand, and the usual concerns to make existing systems more efficient, on the other, to an examination of prior issues, including the functions and role of the JCF, its powers, and the nature of the fundamental relationship in which the Force is enmeshed (police-government, police-community and police and the law) in order to explicitly harmonize the model of policing and approaches to crime control with greater developmental opportunities and more rights regarding polity.

Police forces tend to resist internal change [Ortiz 1994; Sparrow, Moore and Kennedy 1990:31; Skolnick and Bayley 1986:81–116].[5] Reforms are therefore usually externally imposed and managed in a top-down mode. This contributes to making the change process even more delicate. Reform strategies that are anchored in a solid information base are better able to negotiate the inevitable difficulties and resistance to change. The significance of this project lies in its attempt to begin to unveil the police force and to provide policy makers and reform minded police managers with the kind of analysis of the reform process needed in order to aid more successful outcomes.

In so doing, it serves to reduce dependence on foreign experts, who tend to perpetuate the slavish imitation of inappropriate reform packages that are often the outcome of ideological-political battles fought at a different time and place.

More significantly, the perspectives on police reform reflect the differing approaches within the élite on how to treat with the more general legitimacy crisis of the state. The experiences of police reform are likely to inform (and anticipate) the approaches to wider state reform.

Conceptual Frame

Policing is the exercise of state power for constraining social and political action. The defining feature of the police is its institutional claim to the right to use legitimate force within the sovereign territory of the state [Klockars 1985:10; Manning 1977:10]. Societies, particularly their élite, may shape the definition of crime by treating behaviours as deviant and imposing social sanctions on them, but it is the state that ultimately defines and prosecutes criminal behaviour [Hagan 1994:11–13]. In the case of ex-colonial societies, there are numerous instances of socially approved behaviour (including religious rituals) being legally proscribed, thereby reflecting a divergence between state and society, élite and mass public. In such societies there is greater dyscensus, and the reproduction of order tends to require greater resort to state coercion.

No state can effectively govern, or even rule, primarily by force. To be functionally effective, the police must be legitimate. In using force in legitimacy-seeking ways, the police must ensure its protective rather than repressive use. With an eye to police legitimacy, Marenin distinguishes between repression and protection: "not [in terms of] the politicized exercise of coercion nor in coercion itself, but in the distribution of interests which are served by the actions of the police – that is, the degree to which the police protect and promote their own or the general or particular interests" [Marenin 1990:124].

This point emphasizes the legitimacy of ends. The more universal and just the ends or interests served, the greater the legitimacy of the police. However, in the exercise of their function, the police are subject to tests of legitimacy related to both the ends pursued and the means used to achieve those ends. The former (the nature of the interests served) does not necessarily legitimate the latter, which is subject to authoritative procedural codes and processes that need not always be located in law, but may also be derived from popular sources of authority.

The problem with ends as a legitimating principle is that they are not simply abstract political values, neither are they (particularly when applied to the police) usually conceptualized as positively protective (such as ensuring the freedom of movement of females rather than apprehending rapists). The primary universal value associated with the police role in ex-colonial societies is that of order (not justice), which is interpreted in its concreteness as defence of the existing order and thus of the special interests dominant in that order. In this regard there is an interactive effect between state and police legitimacy. The narrower the interests served by both police and state, the more repressive the police will tend to be.[6] Repression of crime is not to be equated with political repression. However, maintaining order in an unjust society is problematic for the police and compromises the legitimacy to be derived from ends served.

A peculiarity of the police is that all of its relationships are shaped by the means it is authorized to use, that is, how and why it applies coercive force. Brutality and disregard for procedural law are indicators of repressive means; endemic brutality is indicative of gross power imbalances in state-citizen relations and undemocratic modalities of policing.

The liberal tradition emphasizes the protective function of the police. It justifies policing (in liberal democracies) as being protective of the universal value of individual freedom by creating an orderly and law-governing framework for the pursuit of the individual good [cf. Nozick 1974; Hayek 1960]. This provides philosophical justification for traditional reactive (and nonintrusive) policing which simply provides support for negative freedoms. From this perspective, policing is, and ought to be, equated with law enforcement, and crime prevention is seen as being properly beyond the scope of police responsibility. This view rests on the dubious assumption that law enforcement provides an effective deterrent to crime or, worse, treats law enforcement as an end in itself rather than a means of managing crime.

In this perspective, the repressive potential of the state and its expression through policing ought to be limited to ensure that the police force does not subvert its mission. This is informed by a well-grounded fear of state power. But limiting the power of the state and its institutions also limits their constructive problem-solving potential. Consistent with a minimalist notion of the role of the state, any proactive or positively interventionist approach to policing (as in the case of community policing) and socially engaging crime control is abjured as too intrusive. In a socially unjust society with a colonial legacy of exclusion, such an approach, in effect, necessitates the use of repression to maintain the existing structures.

Unlike the liberal consensus perspective, the repressive function is emphasized by conflict perspectives. Social inequality and skewed distributions of power are seen as sources of conflict. Policing is seen as the disciplining and controlling of subordinate groups. For example, Foucault (whom we must locate in a poststructuralist framework, but whose work approximates conflict theory in important respects) regards policing as a functional response to the expansion of capitalism and the need to discipline the poor for the labour market [Foucault 1977]. He directly links policing and the spread of the disciplinary power of states with the needs of the economy. In ex-colonial societies, policing has most definitely been about patrolling the social (including ethnic) boundaries within these societies [cf. Cain 1996; Enloe 1976]. It is about control, in the more profoundly political sense of controlling the large number of marginalized poor who permanently reside outside the labour force. Danns, for example, argues that the role of the police in ex-colonial societies is largely to protect the interests of the élite and to maintain the system of colour-class domination [Danns 1982:4–10].

There are strong experiential foundations for this view. The truth that the law is downwardly directed is most evident in ex-colonial societies. Consistent with this, policing (in the more segmented Caribbean societies with high concentrations of wealth and power, as in the case of Jamaica) tends to be even more sharply downward-directed. This type of policing is nonintegrative, helps to reproduce an unjust social order associated with an oppressive past and, ultimately, undermines the rule of law.

Central to either perspective is the issue of legitimacy. From the notion of legitimacy of ends discussed earlier, it is evident that this work departs from the Weberian notion of legitimacy, which regards a structure as legitimate if the ruled believe in its right to rule – leading to conforming behaviour anchored in a notion of obligation. In a sharp critique of this Weberian view, Beetham [1991] argues that to define legitimacy as belief is to ignore how it comes about and to ignore those aspects of legitimacy that have little to do with beliefs such as conformity with the law. For him, a structure or power is legitimate if it meets the following conditions:

- Power must be exercised according to established rules, which may be legally codified or informal.
- These rules must be justified in terms of the shared beliefs of the government and the governed.
- Legitimacy must be demonstrated by the expression of consent on the part of the governed [Heywood 1994:96].

As with Habermas, both means and ends, or interests served, are necessary conditions for legitimacy. The consent of the ruled (in relation to both) is a necessary condition, even if this consent is manipulated from above. On a *hard definition* of legitimacy, a system is legitimate if and only if the consent of those subject to it is overtly demonstrated. A *soft definition* of legitimacy would simply require the active consent of the élite or main power holders and the socially influential bystander groups (such as the middle strata) that are not usually the targets of police power. In this case, unlike the hard definition, the consent of the mass public and the policed is not regarded as a necessary condition for police legitimacy. Indeed, the soft definition suggests that legitimacy may be maintained even in the face of substantial popular dissatisfaction from below. A condition for this, however, is that the lower social classes take their social cues from the groups that legitimate the system.

These social cues and core values on which the authority structure is based are increasingly being subjected to considered behavioural criticisms by the mass public. Recognizing this, various researchers of differing perspectives have characterized the present moment in Jamaica as "a power disequilibrium" [Stone 1992:6], "hegemonic dissolution" [Meeks 1996:130–34], or one of "dual social power" [Grey 1994:186–88]. Stone describes the situation as one in which "old and new ideologies, core values and norms compete for ascendency" [Stone 1992:6]. Difference on grounds of race, colour and class, associated with the acceptance of notions of social place inherited from the colonial order, are being replaced by assertiveness, aggression and new notions of egalitarianism [Stone 1992:7]. This has weakened authority in all domains of social space and hastened a legitimacy crisis of policing.

By legitimacy crisis is meant an inability to continue with the existing mode of policing without further decline in public confidence and a growth in social tensions. Policing events, rather than resolving and controlling conflicts, become regular conflict points in the society. It need not signify imminent collapse of the institution or even the existing mode of policing, but rather, as Habermas [1995] suggests, indicates an inability of the institution to self-correct and thus the necessity for change. It is used to describe a critical juncture that marks either a positive programme of adaptation and reform or a qualitative turn for the worse.

This crisis of the JCF and policing is expressed in:

- The high rate of violent crime, and particularly of murder, and the routine, flagrant and remorseless violations of the laws of the country. These violations are at times carried out in full view of the police and relevant policing authorities and may be taken as evidence of a breakdown of the system of formal social control. Indeed, it reflects a more deeply held attitude to the law. Further empirical research on this is required, but the existing evidence from survey work conducted by Stone [1991a] suggests that respect for the law is not anchored in a general normative agreement that it is right but rather a (much reduced) fear of sanctions.

- The existence of whole urban communities living beyond the state and law. These have been characterized as "garrison" communities [see Figueroa 1994; Chevannes 1992].

- A generalized ineffectiveness of the police in controlling crime. This is indicated by sharply and consistently increasing rates of violent crime, accompanied by falling solution rates.

- Prevalent and highly intense fear of crime often leading to an apocalyptic view of the future whereby the high rates of violent crime are seen as a harbinger of a more general social meltdown of Jamaican society.

- A generalized decline of public confidence in the police and, most importantly, increasing doubts regarding its commitment to democratic values.

- Popular withdrawal of participation in policing – as expressed in the reluctance to provide the police with information, to act as witnesses and so forth. Citizenship is certainly not seen as entailing a sense of duty in this regard. This is an important indicator of legitimacy, as participation in the criminal justice system implies not just passive consent but active approval. And as will be shown later, active participation, not simply the tolerance of the police as a necessary evil, is required for an effective system.

- Political conflicts over the police. These and the associated efforts to gain party control of the police have been most intense during periods of divergence and popular mobilizations by the two major political parties, but have persisted since Independence.

- Greater resort to violence and its manipulation by the police force without regard for the law, that is, a lawless law enforcement.

- The growth of a range of new, but perhaps more ineffective, state and nonstate policing institutions designed to shore up the system of formal social control. These state agencies include a forest and national parks police (1993), a resort patrol to deal with tourist harassment (1993), an antisquatting and land occupation police under the Ministry of Housing and the Environment (1993), the Ports Security Corps (1989), a parks and markets police under the direction of the Metropolitan Parks and Markets (1985), agricultural wardens (1974), and traffic wardens (1974).

- As noted earlier, the emergence of elements of an alternative informal criminal justice system in some of the communities of the urban poor where crimes are investigated, suspects tried and punished by "jungle courts" controlled by so-called community protectors.

Using even the soft definition of legitimacy described above, 1991 marked the recognition of a deep legitimacy crisis of the JCF. The upper and middle classes, whose level of direct contact with the police is very low, registered negative appraisals on a broad range of measures of police performance on specific issues regarding the management of particular types of crimes and on value related issues as revealed in the nature of police-citizen encounters and the treatment of the various target populations. On some indicators they returned even more negative evaluations of the JCF than the high-contact, urban, lower-income groups. Disaffection with the JCF had become uniform throughout the society and its isolation nearly complete [see Stone 1992].[7]

This legitimacy crisis of the police is mediated by a wider crisis of governance and state. Its delegitimation is associated with a more general discrediting of the state and its capacity to lead the developmental process, to fairly allocate the social goods and to deliver the services associated with its core functions. Indeed, the police had become deeply integrated into the discredited political structures and party machines in particular.[8] The expressions of this crisis of governance and incapacity to ensure social compliance includes pervasive, morally indigent (yet indignant) tax evasion and system circumvention;[9] routinized electoral fraud (often with the aid of senior police officers);[10] the negative, at best indifferent, attitude to state symbols; and distrust of its institutions, including the law and the courts.

More than three decades after Independence, it could be plausibly argued that party, racial and perhaps class identities are still stronger than a common national identity. An enduring lack of confidence in the capabilities of the system of governance is reflected in the willingness of the majority of Jamaicans to migrate [Stone 1992]. Its most profound manifestation is, however, its general inability to ensure social and legal compliance, despite the efforts to extend and strengthen the capacity of the state for surveillance and control of the people. These efforts are evident in the development of new information systems designed to improve tax compliance and compliance with traffic ticketing by the police and so forth, the projection of force via joint police-military operations, extending the legal powers of the police and setting up special police squads, and other ways that will be discussed later.

In the context of this intractable crisis, the sharp class divisions and strength of group identity make it difficult to aggregate the interests of the different social groups in nationally integrating consensus-building ways. It intensifies the partiality in the allocation of goods, thereby inhibiting state legitimacy. Moreover, given the character of the Jamaican economy and social structure, it is difficult to create greater opportunity and economic access without redistribution. Élite support for redistributive policies is unlikely, as the experience of these policies in the 1970s (when the creation of opportunities for the poor involved a redistribution of resources at the expense of the rich) led to fierce resistance and class mobilizations.

The legitimacy of the state, like the police, is linked to its *raison d'être*. In the case of an ex-colonial state such as Jamaica, a mission of social reform was essential to the postindependence project. This middle class–led project served to strengthen their social power (via control of the expanding state bureaucracy and growth of the professions) and that of the local economic élite, which (with the assistance of the state) displaced their foreign counterparts, but the society remains poorly integrated.

One outcome of this process is the tighter integration of the economic and political élite, or at least a reduction of the historical disjuncture between these two groups identified by Stone [1980:93–110]. Given the reluctance of the economic élite to support reform, it was this disjuncture and the downward alliance of the middle strata and working classes that in the past contributed to the reformism of the state.

Since the mid 1970s, the Structural Adjustment Programme (SAP) intensified the historically high concentration of wealth in the society, facilitated the convergence of economic power and political influence in the society, and in the process enfeebled the political influence of the poor and other power centres associated with lower status groups such as organized labour.

This process was deepened in the 1980s as the idea of the developmental state was ditched and replaced with an equally strong neoliberal commitment to a minimalist state. The state was discredited as being inherently inefficient, given to corruption, and irrational in its allocation of social goods. As an enemy of the social good, it was thus considerably downsized and weakened by the main policy initiatives of the decade. By the end of the 1980s, on most indicators this process was considerably advanced. The proportion of the labour force contracted to it was reduced from 16 percent in 1981 to 8 percent in 1996 [*Economic and Social Survey Jamaica* (*ESS*) 1981, 1997]. Similarly, public expenditure as a proportion of gross domestic product (GDP) was reduced from 43 percent in 1980 to 32 percent in 1996 and with 56 percent of total revenue being siphoned off to service the growing debt [*ESS* 1997]. The capability of the state to aid the development process and to protect and enable the more vulnerable in the society has thus been considerably reduced.

Under the SAP, the process of encouraging private capital formation was profoundly state aided. State enterprises were privatized, with access to these resources often determined by corrupt influences or, at best, a dubious and translucent process. The deregulation of the economy, which accompanied privatization, energized the general tendency towards upwardly redistributive or rent-seeking rather than wealth-creating activity. The consequent increased inequalities and marginalization of the poor have generated powerful, socially destructive tendencies and induced the use of greater (but ineffective) coercive force by a weakened state in support of this mode of development.

Such a developmental project thus poses a greater difficulty in masking the particular interests of the economic élite as universal or coinciding with the good for the society. Its minority racial character, predatory rent-seeking behaviour and lack of national commitment further complicates the project. It is this process that accounts for what Meeks describes as "hegemonic dissolution".

There is an apparent consensus on the comprehensiveness and multi-dimensional character of the crisis, extending beyond the economic to social and political expressions. However, this need not take a cataclysmic trajectory, for while the lower classes are generally locked out, they enjoy greater social mobility via nontraditional avenues. Their social mobility tends to diffuse rather than concentrate resistance to the system and, indeed (as has happened in the past), offers prospects for it to be co-opted by reformist movements within the established channels of political participation. This is the background to the policing crisis and broader crisis of governance as it took shape in the late 1980s and early 1990s.

Both Meeks [1996] and Stone [1992] suggest three possible outcomes or change initiatives in resolving the crisis. These are:

- A drift toward social anarchy. This drift may proceed at an imperceptibly slow pace, allowing for constant adjustments by the population, but may accelerate at points, eventually leading to the conditions similar to that of a failed state. Such a process may alternatively give impetus to, and provide justification for, an authoritarian response.

- Political authoritarianism. Here order is restored based on naked power. As Meeks recognizes, this could come from within or outside the constitution [1996:137]. Indeed, the former is more likely and would certainly be more viable as a bipartisan or multiparty coalition government.

- A democratic renewal. As with the authoritarian solution, this is seen as essentially an initiative from above, with – for Stone [1992] – charismatic leadership being essential in aiding the formation of new legitimate institutions able to channel new forms of democratic participation and create new lines of opportunity for the marginalized poor. While Stone may be right on the importance of leadership, for such leadership to be successful it must take its cues from the profound critique of the old order from below. Democratic renewal and mass legitimacy must entail mass participation, new power relations and mechanisms of accountability, and consequently, perhaps more authentic structures and less reliance on state coercion for law enforcement and the reproduction of order.

Either project, that is, either a strong disciplinary regime (whether within the existing structures of governance or based on an authoritarian alteration) or a democratic renewal, requires radical reform of the security establishment.

With the authoritarian solution, the police and military become highly repressive and political resistance suppressed in the interest of the accumulation of capital. This has become an increasingly attractive proposition to many in the political élite and in the security establishment and indeed enjoys a wider appeal. The economic advances of the NICs of Asia, such as South Korea, Singapore and Taiwan, have made them developmental models for some countries. In Latin America, Chile is similarly regarded as the success case of the 1990s. Their economic "miracles" are attributed to their authoritarian state forms – whether of the military or civilian variety. This has cast doubt on the state form of Jamaica which, it is argued, is characterized by a lack of consensus on core issues vital to the development of the country, a destructive political competitiveness coupled with clientelism which has been labelled "political tribalism" and which is associated with over 25 years of economic stagnation and crisis. Authoritarianism is thus erroneously regarded as a necessary precondition for development or at least a speedier and more effective path to it. The cost of these successes, when measured in blood and the deprivation of basic rights and freedoms, was quite great, however. But this aside, it must be remembered that such modernizing authoritarian regimes are few; the vast majority tend to be of the type experienced in recent times by Nigeria or Haiti, that is, lawless, corrupt and parasitic regimes that tend to retard national development.

Such an authoritarian approach, if applied to Jamaica, would have some continuity with the colonial period. In establishing the JCF, the British could have opted for one of the three models of policing that existed at the time: the British home model of a highly decentralized local police service; the French dual system of centralized and highly militarized gendarmerie responsible for public order and a local general police; or the Irish model of a constabulary totally focused on the maintenance of public order. As will be developed later in the text, the British elected to adopt the Irish constabulary model in Jamaica. This was apparently better suited to security policing (which characterized the colonial situation) than the English home model of civil "consensus", highly localized policing, and the rights-protective mechanisms associated with it.

But the repressive approach is not a viable option for "soft", poorly articulated states with numerically weak and socially representative police forces that are easily influenced by well-organized popular sociopolitical movements. It is even less so in a society where the economic élite is still largely racially distinct and tends to exhibit low levels of commitment to the nation, and the élite, more generally, is viewed by large sections of the urban population as corrupt and self-seeking. Any such repression would therefore tend to be viewed not as being a necessary phase of a broader developmental project but, rather, as the protection of a corrupt system and its primary beneficiaries. For these reasons, this process would ultimately generate considerable conflict and/or the reconstitution of new socio-economic spaces beyond the reach of the state (as is already the case with the burgeoning informal and underground economy) and greater disorder.

The poor articulation of the state (and its relationship to society) has reduced its capacity to either ensure law and order via the effective application of coercive force or to police by consensus. For example, impartiality, which is cardinal to legitimacy, is difficult to attain given the uneven distribution of social power. The well-articulated networks or conduits of power link the life chances of the individual to group identity. Expectations of reciprocal favour granting also favour the powerful and "connected" and make impartiality difficult. Therefore, needs articulation and political demands from below generally take the form of resistance. It is reactive and confrontational, not definitional (that is, shaping the policy agendas) and participatory, and usually involves periodic confrontations with the police.

This is the dilemma of the police. It is not able to effectively perform its duties based on authoritative action and community support or on naked but efficiently applied coercive force. The project for a more effective and just model of policing has to be linked to a more integrated, less criminogenic society and more democratic polity.

Method

The study is based on data derived from a combination of sources and techniques, but primarily from reported crimes and an attitude survey of the JCF. The data on the JCF were collected in three phases. In the first phase, exploratory interviews were conducted with key informants within the organization and focus group discussions held; in the second, a probability survey of the opinions of the members of the first was conducted; and in the third, police behaviour in community settings was recorded.

Official police statistics are noted for their unreliability and dubious validity. Homicides are, for example, classified without any stated operational definitions of the categories used to describe the "causes" and "motives" (both are often confused and used interchangeably). Thus, for 1994, the JCF reported that 37 percent of all murders were "domestic" [Statistics Unit JCF]. As no consistent procedures were or are applied, classifications and their meanings were left to the judgement of the coders occupying the desk on a particular day. From what could be discerned from the pattern of coding, "domestic" was sometimes taken to mean a relationship (from all amorous relationships to members of household to neighbours) and at other times to be a label referring to the nature of the precipitating events (if judged by the coder to be trivial). Much of the data was therefore meaningless and had to be reconstituted from the source documents (the case files) using consistently applied definitions and independent coders.

As indicated above, data collection on the JCF proceeded in the following three phases. First, key informants were identified and a number of exploratory interviews and consultations held with them. These informants were chosen based on their experiences and postings, which made them valued sources of information. The interviews were not restricted to the first phase but were conducted at every stage of the project.

As a preliminary to the development of the survey instrument, four focus groups were organized in order to identify the central issues from the viewpoints of the police. Taken together, the groups were composed on the principles of representativeness of sex, experience, specialization and rank. However, within each group homogeneity of rank was preserved in order to ensure the free participation of all. The first group consisted of operatives (constables); the second of supervisors (sergeants and corporals); and the other two of managers (officers), with one grouping composed of junior officers, each having 25 or more years experience in the Force, and the other, of young officers who had been promoted through the ranks via the accelerated promotions programme.[11] For convenience, most of the participants were taken from the Kingston metropolitan and St Catherine areas, which are also the areas with the highest crime rates and offer the most intense experience in policing. This made it difficult to ensure anonymity within the groups, as the area represents a small section of a small force in a small country. To avoid individual bias, the panel of names selected for the groups was reviewed with the assistance of two officers. These groups provided the range of perspectives on the problems of the JCF and contributed to the development of a more effective survey instrument.

The second phase of data collection involved the administration of a probability survey of the attitudes of all serving members of the JCF. This included all recruits in training at the time of the survey, which was conducted during the period October to November 1995. From an updated sample frame provided by the JCF High Command, a probability sample of 1,036 persons stratified by rank was drawn. This constituted 18 percent of the population (5,788) and 19 percent of the sample population (5,508). This exceeds the absolute minimum sample size recommended (for factor analysis) by Gorsuch's formula, which in this instance would have been 390 [see Bryman and Cramer 1990:255]. As there is no significant difference in sample error between systematic and random samples, in order to ensure the best response rate with an economy of effort, the former was adopted. The response rate was 66 percent (684) and the sample error is plus or minus 2 percent. All interviews were conducted in the face-to-face mode in conditions free of external influences.

The survey instrument was designed to excavate the core ideological beliefs and values regarding the treatment of crime and law enforcement. Collection of attitude data on relatively stable attitude objects (equality, freedom and justice in the context of law enforcement) enabled an assessment of core beliefs, rather than topical but passing issues that simply indicate the mood of the moment (although some of this was included).

The instrument consisted of logically connected multiple-item scales designed to map attitude consistency across a wide range of related topics – from the attitudes to the sources of crime (ASC), attitudes to law enforcement (ALE), to citizens' rights (ACR), police style (APS), and to the programme and process of reforming the JCF.[12]

Reliability tests on these scales using Tucker and Lewis' Coefficient returned the following outputs: the ASC .5728, the ACR .7331, the ALE .6682, the APS .8301. These coefficients are somewhat low, but later these scales will be reconstituted in their constituent dimensions (as subscales) – with higher coefficients of reliability. To assist valid interpretations of the data and further qualitative exploration of the issues, the results were reviewed with a purposive sample of members of the JCF.

In the third phase, two research sites were selected in order to study policing in a community context. The community is the most intensive point of police-citizen contact; it is where stable relationships are formed. As any democratic solution to the problems of crime control and police-citizen relations must include people participation at the source of the problem, the community is perhaps the best unit for both understanding the problems and developing workable solutions. Since the primary interest is not in representativeness but, rather, the saliency of the processes of criminal embeddedness and police-citizen interaction, the principle of intensity sampling was adopted.[13]

Given the sensitive nature of the issues explored and the suspiciousness of outsiders common to most inner city communities, considerable time was needed to build confidence, even when entry was facilitated by contacts. The number of research communities was thus restricted to these two.

This mix of techniques ensured an examination of both attitudes and behaviour. Attitudinal and behavioural coherence is validating, and this is sufficient justification for studying them together. But more importantly, as an exploration of the prospects for reform, it allows a demonstration of the extent to which behaviour is attitudinally and cognitively entrenched.

Organization of the Study

This work is organized in four sections. The first section seeks to conceptualize the problems of the JCF. It begins with an analysis of the changes in the social organization of crime in Jamaica. This is followed by an overview of the structural features of the police force. The second section consists of three chapters, each examining one of the major problems facing the JCF – corruption, its style of work and relations with the citizenry. Against this background, the third section analyses the process of reform and the responses to it. In the final section, consisting of a single chapter, conclusions and proposals for deepening the reform process are discussed.

Section I

Context

The Changing Structure of Crime in Jamaica

The behaviour of the police is shaped largely by the sociopolitical context in which they operate. Important elements of this context include the patterns of crime and the responses of the society to it. This chapter provides a descriptive analysis of the changing structure of crime and of the social organization of criminals since the mid 1970s. In so doing, it presents the setting against which the impact of these changes on the effectiveness of the police force and the challenges facing any reform project may be better understood.

As indicated above, there are several difficulties in presenting an analysis of this nature from secondary data. It is universally accepted that reported crime is generally an inaccurate measure of the frequency of offending. However, assuming that the factors determining the rate of reporting have remained fairly constant up to 1993, then it may be taken that these data accurately depict the basic patterns and trends and are thus valid for the kind of trend analysis adopted here.

There are three easily discernable stages in the development of criminality in independent Jamaica. The first stage (1962–77) is characterized by continuity with the colonial era in terms of the structure of crime. As the central concern is with the nature of the break with this traditional pattern, little attention is paid to this period. The first turning point, and second stage (1977–87), was associated with the concatenation of three interrelated processes which have transformed the social organization of crime in Jamaica. The first of these is the Structural Adjustment Programme (SAP). In response to the deepening economic crisis, the SAP assisted in shifting the economic and social burdens of adaptation to the poor through mechanisms such as layoffs and reduced investments in social services and state programmes designed to create opportunities at the base of an already highly criminogenic society [Boyd 1988; Anderson and Witter 1994]. The second related process was the accelerated growth of the export trade in cannabis as traffickers sought to exploit the economic political crisis facing the island, and the third, the resort to organized high-intensity political violence as the country became ideologically polarized. The third stage (1987 to the present) is associated with a shift in the position of Jamaican gangs in the international drug trade. Their position in its division of labour shifted from being mere cannabis producers to distributors in the main markets of North America and Europe of a more diverse product range which included cocaine and its derivatives. This stage is consequently also distinguished by the development of a relatively small but growing local hard drug market, a more developed informal economy, and structurally embedded violence. For the remainder of this section, the features of the period since 1977 will be further elaborated.

Since the mid 1970s, Jamaica has been undergoing a protracted economic crisis reflected in high levels of unemployment, inflation, indebtedness and a steady devaluation of the currency. It is an ex-colonial society typified by high levels of socioeconomic inequality, poverty, social segmentation (as social integration was attenuated by classism and racism) and high rates of urbanization in a mode that tends to concentrate the syndrome of social problems associated with underdevelopment.

As a consequence of this economic crisis, in 1977 Jamaica entered a structural adjustment programme aimed at diversifying the economy and improving its competitiveness in international trade. The strategies for achieving this included attracting foreign investments on the basis of a cheap domestic labour market. This was not new: the process of accumulation in Jamaica has historically been based on the exploitation of cheap labour; the SAP simply intensified this process.

This strategy for achieving structural adjustment was induced by a combination of conditionalities imposed by the International Monetary Fund (IMF), and later, the influence of the globally dominant neoliberal paradigm which associates inequality and individualism with efficiency and economic progress. While a direct relationship between inequality and efficiency is doubtful, it is clear that high levels of inequality and competitive individualism are associated with high rates of violent crime [Hagan 1994:64; Haferkamp and Ellis 1992:273; Messner 1989]. The empirical evidence of this association is fairly strong, but in the Jamaican context explanation of it has been mainly in terms of relative deprivation [cf. Stone 1987:25–26].

Our argument runs in a somewhat different direction. Inequality might be criminogenic, but it is not evident why it should provide such impetus to the rate of violent crime (as it may be the outcome of just processes, although in Jamaica its grossness suggests otherwise). Its problematic nature is rooted in the reality that this inequality and the successes of those in the upper classes are not seen as the outcome of fair processes but rather are increasingly associated with corruption and criminality. This delegitimation of the class structure is coupled with another consequence of the concrete processes associated with the logic of inequality in the Jamaican context, that is, the marginalization of large sections of the population and particularly the urban poor. These two outcomes give both indirect and direct impetus to violent criminality via social modelling as well, by engendering strain and the aggressiveness born of feelings of being the victim of unjust processes of allocating social goods.

This assertion of the problematic nature of inequality in its Jamaicanness is an uncomfortable point for many as it is often taken to imply that little can be done to control crime short of radical social reform of these societies and that this kind of programme distracts from the imperatives of law enforcement. This need not be the case. In the countries where high levels of inequality are strongly associated with high levels of serious crime (such as Jamaica, Brazil and South Africa), it simply points to deeply alienating and excluding features of their social structures. These, as will be shown in the case of Jamaica, tend to lead to adaptations that in turn are strongly associated with high levels of violence and that have to be attended to in association with other levels of crime prevention and control interventions if these latter projects are to be maximally effective.

The SAP has had a profound effect on the labour market. The distinction is often made between a primary and secondary labour market based on skills level, with low skills and thus low-paying jobs being located in the secondary market [Anderson and Witter 1994]. Consistent with the strategy adopted, a major outcome of the SAP has been that the winning sectors are located in the secondary formal sector (in tourism, export-processing manufacture and small-scale service industries). This sector grew by some 80 percent during the period 1985–89 and in 1989 it accounted for 32 percent of the employed labour force [Anderson and Witter 1994:29].

Tourism was the biggest winner in this process. As a percentage of gross domestic product (GDP), tourism grew from 4 percent in 1977, to 16 percent in 1993.[1] However, it has developed on a model that in many respects typifies the changes in the political economy of the country. The growth in this sector was the outcome of a profoundly state aided process involving the privatization of state owned physical plants and state support in marketing.

The tourism sector nevertheless developed on an exclusive model of which the most acute expression is the all-inclusive hotel. This invention was clearly developed in response to the deteriorating social conditions in the country at a time when tourism was one of the few growth areas. It consequently attracted (and continues to attract) large numbers of persons to the tourist areas in search of opportunities, which resulted in the growth of squatter communities, aggressive vending of all sorts of commodities from craft and taxi services to drugs and sex, and contributed generally to greater disorder in the society. The all-inclusive "solution" to this problem, however, could only have been the product of the kind of social thinking that pervades a highly segmented society such as Jamaica. It is designed to socially exclude and tends to concentrate wealth by manipulating the fears of criminal victimization and consequently monopolizing a wide range of services offered to tourists, such as ground transportation, entertainment, food and so forth, and by offering low wages [see Patullo 1996:52–76].

This approach to development compounds the social problems of the country by concentrating wealth within the sector and excluding, stigmatizing and even criminalizing its competitors from among the excluded poor as "hustlers and harassers" who constitute a threat to the industry and, by extension, the country. This threat is based on aesthetic, environmental and physical security objections to the high visibility of the poor in the resort towns, which is seen as reducing the attractiveness of the tourism product.

More generally, the wage levels within this secondary sector were among the lowest in the region. Lower wages were compounded by high inflation rates. Thus, for example, wage rates in the "807" garment programme declined from an average of US 91¢ per hour in 1990, to US 72¢ in 1994.[2] This scenario resulted not only in increased poverty but also changes in the social character of poverty and in greater inequality. In 1994, 32 percent of the population was in poverty, with a significant proportion of the poor being located in the employed labour force [see United Nations Development Program (UNDP) 1995]. The mean consumption for the wealthiest decile was 12 times that of the poorest, and the share of the top quintile in national consumption was 46 percent [UNDP 1993:11–12].

The intensification of inequality is rooted in the logic of the process, which turned on the policy instruments of divestment, market liberalization and devaluation of the dollar. Huge state owned resources were transferred to rich insiders, the relaxation of regulations facilitated corporate crime, and the devaluation of the dollar and high inflation rates reduced the purchasing power of wage earners and hastened the transfer of wealth from the poor to the rich. Wages as a percentage of GDP declined from 56.1 percent in 1977 to 42.7 percent in 1988 [Anderson and Witter 1994:7–8]. Moreover, there has been a similar decline in the social wage. If the ratio of the summed state expenditure on health and education is taken as a measure of the social wage, then it declined from 22 percent in the 1977–78 budget to 17 percent in 1992–93. After almost 20 years of structural adjustment, the economy still remains in a profound crisis.

The upshot of the changes in the labour market described earlier was labour force withdrawal. Many of the available jobs were regarded as "unprofitable" or below the reservation wage of young males in particular. Work in the form of wage employment no longer exempted one from socially demeaning practices, such as begging, nor did it indicate an ability to fulfil the traditional male role of reliable provider or automatically confer social respectability, although it still tends to reduce suspicion and police scrutiny. The realization of manhood, in the social meaning of the word, is no longer associated with wage employment or even work but rather with access to money. This the primary good with which all social goods (power, status and so forth) may now be bought. Based on a community survey of unemployed inner city residents, Buchanan [1986:31] reported that some 53 percent were uninterested in regular employment as they found "hustling" or robbery more rewarding. Unfortunately, Buchanan did not report the proportion of young males of this orientation, but it is to be expected that this would have been significantly higher than its representation in the general population. Male labour force participation fell from 84 percent in 1985 [Anderson and Witter 1994:25] to 74.6 percent in 1993 [see *Economic and Social Survey Jamaica* (*ESS*) 1994:18.8]. This decline was much greater among the younger (less than 45 years old) male cohorts.

It is in the social organization of work that the social structure is most compressed and the self-consciousness of one's social place and apparent social worth most acute. And it is through work that a commitment to the approved means of acquiring social goods (including respect and the symbolic goods) is best expressed. Success in this process usually leads to a greater acceptance of official authority and the structures of social control. But wage employment – at the lower end of the labour market – is associated with social stationariness, the improbability of acquiring the above social goods, socially controlling and oppressive work relationships, and the expectation of patterns of deference which are no longer observed in other social spaces. This experience with and attitude to wage employment (not to be mistakenly equated with attitude to work) associates it with necessity rather than self-actualization.

For the above reasons, self-employment has tended to be the preferred mode of work. Withdrawal from the labour market was thus accompanied by the growth of an already large informal sector and a more prevalent resort to deviant adaptive strategies. The rapid growth of this informal sector served to foster and affirm the cultural traits of a fiercely competitive individualism, aggressiveness, "system beating" (as reflected in the evasion of all forms of taxes) and a general disregard for state authority. These traits have flourished, as this sector is essentially an unregulated sphere of economic activity operating beyond the reach of the state. An important component of this alternate opportunity structure and second line of response was the creation of illegal economic opportunities, mainly in the drug trade. Indeed, the rapid development of the informal economy served to stimulate and drive the growth of the drug trade as a source of foreign exchange for trade in light manufactures.

The dislocations associated with the crisis led to a third related line of response: increased migration to the USA and the growth of the Jamaican enclaves in the major cities [see *ESS* 1984]. This movement accelerated in the mid 1970s and has continued into the 1990s, with illegal migration opening up an option to criminals and young males whose illegal status, limited skills and acquisitive ambitions, coupled with a short time horizon for their fulfilment, made the opportunities in the American drug trade all too alluring. The entry of these criminals into the distribution of hard drugs in turn provided the resources, the impetus for higher levels of organization and easy access to firearms that has helped to transform the character of crime in Jamaica.

The economic crisis and its attendant social problems precipitated a deep political crisis in the late 1970s, characterized by sharp ideological polarization of the political parties and society and high levels of organized political violence [see Kaufman 1985]. This conflict has had a profound effect on the political geography of the urban areas of the country. It resulted in the reinforcement and multiplication of armed, politically homogeneous communities, which are militantly hostile to neighbouring communities that may be supportive of the opposing party and tend to be highly centralized in their mode of party political administration. Supporters of the competing party were treated as a fifth column and driven from their communities.

Eyre estimated that in 1980, a significant proportion of the population of the inner city areas of Kingston was displaced [Eyre 1984:24]. The continuing process of territorial conquest and political cleansing, or "putting out" as Chevannes [1992] appropriately describes it, helped to provide more secure conditions, indeed safe havens, for criminals who were prepared to engage in the armed campaigns of their parties, or to simply support in less militant ways the dominant party in their communities. The period of political violence served to school criminals (who doubled as party militants) in organization, extended their contacts spatially and socially, armed and trained them in the management of violence and, most importantly, resulted in the accumulation of a large blood debt between a number of urban communities. The political "war" therefore gave impetus to various forms of social violence, including the violence of ordinary criminality. This electoral effect on the rate and character of the crime in Jamaica preceded 1980, and since then it has been periodically renewed during election campaigns but with much less intensity.

While direct political violence has declined, the political infrastructure (garrison communities and a politicized police force) and the modes of managing the more impoverished urban communities (that give legitimacy to criminal local leadership), which aid the development of criminality, remain as potent as before. These are the conditions driving the changes in the structure of offending and the social organization of criminals in Jamaica.

Structure of Crime

For the period 1977 to 1993, the incidence of crime in Jamaica increased by 14 percent, but the rate declined from 2,220 to 2,156 per 100,000. In 1992 Jamaica's overall crime rate ranked fifth in the Commonwealth Caribbean [Harriott 1994]. These data may sound comforting, yet public debate in Jamaica reflects a somewhat disorienting fear and near panic with regard to crime. The reasons for this lie, to a large measure, in the startling changes in the structure of crime during the period under review [see Table 1.1]. The main change has been a sharp shift in the ratio of property to violent crime in favour of the latter.[3]

There has been a consistent decline in the rate of property crimes, but a corresponding increase in the rate of violent crimes. This has reversed the old structure of offending, which was characterized by a direct relationship between the rates of both categories of crime and a distribution skewed in favour of property crimes. Thus in 1994, only 10 percent of all crimes were violent and 78 percent were property crimes; but in 1996, 43 percent were violent and only 23 percent were property crimes [Table 1.1].

Table 1.1 The Structure of Crime (percentage)

Type of crime	1974	1984	1993	1996	change%
Violent crimes	10	41	40	43	+33
Property crimes	78	38	29	23	−55
Fraud	3	3	4	4	+1
Drug crimes	9	9	13	12	+3
Illegal possession of guns	1	3	3	4	+3
Other	0	6	11	14	+14

Sources: STATIN 1975; *ESS* 1984, 1993.

Until the end of the 1970s, the basic structure of crime in Jamaica (that is, property crimes exceeding violent crimes) was typical of the Caribbean and, indeed, most developing countries [Buendia 1989:415]. In 1977, the ratio of property to violent crimes was 2:1 [Table 1.2]. This pattern has been maintained across the Caribbean. In 1991, Trinidad and Tobago, which seems to be tending toward the Jamaican pattern, still reported a ratio of 2:1 [Trinidad and Tobago 1991], Barbados 7:1 [The Royal Barbados Police Force], Belize 3:1 [Belize 1992] and Guyana 2:1 [Guyana Police Force 1990]. In Jamaica, this traditional pattern was disrupted by the political "war" of 1976–80. However, despite the low level of political violence since 1980, this distorted pattern remains. In 1994 the ratio of property to violent crimes, which was 0.64:1, was worse than the 1980 level of 0.73:1 [Table 1.2].

The decline in the rate of property crime began in 1980 (809.2) but became more consistent after 1986 (819.5) and has continued through to 1993 (622.4) [Table 1.2]. It is not attributable to lower rates of reporting, as this trend is corroborated by victimization surveys [see Stone 1991a]. This decline has occurred despite the protracted economic crisis and the continued growth in poverty and inequality. It reflects rather curious changes in the structure of property crimes. Blue-collar fraud has increased absolutely and relatively. Between 1977 and 1993, the incidents of fraud increased by 58 percent [*ESS* 1978:22.6; 1993:23.3], and as a proportion of all property crimes the incidents of fraud increased from 7 percent to 11 percent over the same period. White-collar or corporate offending is not identifiable in the police statistics. But impressionistic evidence and case reports suggest pervasive price fixing, insider trading, over billing (especially on state contracts), and other illegal techniques designed to obviate the competitive effects of the market [see *Annual Report of the Contractor General* 1993]. The decline in household burglaries and theft of personal property, that is, the property crimes of the poor, accounts for the general decline in the crime rate. This is even more curious as it points to the qualitative shift in the illegal modes of adaptation to the crisis that has occurred. New income-generating activities in the underground economy now offer higher income and status and lower risks than the traditional forms of property crime.

The growth of the underground economy is closely associated with high levels of violent crime. Jamaica has the highest rate of violent crime in the Caribbean (857.2 per 100,000). Between 1977 and 1994, there were 9,012 Jamaicans murdered (the rate increased from 19.2 per 100,000 to 27.71 over that period); 21,374 were shot (a decrease from 55.6 per 100,0000 to 50.1); and 16,652 raped (from 86 per 100,000 to 85.1) [Statistics Unit, JCF]. In the late 1970s the rates of violent crime, particularly murder and shooting, escalated as the ideologically embittered electoral competition intensified. However, even during periods of ideological convergence, an electoral effect is apparent. This effect is evident in the peaks in the rates of these types of crimes in the election years 1976 (reflected in the "crime year" ending March 1977) and 1980 [Table 1.2]. But even when trimmed for the electoral effect, the rate of violent crimes still shows a steady increase, with a sharp upward trend since the mid 1980s.[4] By providing guns, protective organizational networks (often extending into the police force) and a measure of legitimacy for their "fighters", the political parties have helped to propel the rate of ordinary violent crime in the postelection years. However, these increases are sustained primarily by the drug-driven character of the underground economy and the use of violence to regulate its transactions and to mount competitive challenges. This level of violent crime is indicative of the more pervasive use of violence and aggression as a mode of conflict resolution [see Mansingh and Ramphal 1993; Crandon, Carpenter and McDonald 1994] and of acquiring valued social goods.

Table 1.2 Reported Property Crimes versus Violent Crimes 1977–96

	Property Crimes		Violent Crimes		
Year	Number	Rate per 100,000	Number	Rate per 100,000	Ratio
1996	13,534	541.4	24,617	984.7	0.55
1995	13,766	553.3	23,083	927.8	0.60
1994	14,353	575.0	22,394	897.1	0.64
1993	15,454	622.4	21,275	857.2	0.73
1992	14,521	588.6	20,173	817.7	0.72
1991	16,476	676.4	18,522	760.4	0.89
1990	16,158	669.0	20,698	857.0	0.78
1989	15,184	634.7	19,886	831.3	0.76
1988	15,336	650.4	19,456	825.1	0.79
1987	17,152	728.1	20,647	876.6	0.83
1986	19,301	822.6	19,228	819.5	0.99
1985	21,123	908.2	21,058	905.5	0.99
1984	19,607	853.7	21,186	922.4	0.93
1983	18,041	797.2	20,825	920.2	0.87
1982	17,592	776.6	19,867	876.9	0.88
1981	17,020	771.4	22,279	1,009.8	0.76
1980	17,602	809.2	24,201	1,112.5	0.73
1979	35,401	1,647.2	16,387	762.5	2.16
1978	33,191	1,563.1	16,640	783.6	1.99
1977	30,315	1,445.7	15,893	757.9	1.90

Sources: Statistics Unit, JCF; STATIN 1981:271.

Note: For 1977–79, the STATIN provides the best estimates. Although they are based on the financial year ending in March, its presentation of the data better facilitates definitional consistency. For these and earlier years, *ESS* aggregates minor violent crimes (woundings, assaults) with minor property crimes under the category "other crimes".

To better understand this general pattern, a more detailed examination of the structure of violent crimes is required.

Patterns of Violent Crime

The rate of violent crimes (with the exception of the shooting rate, which in 1993 was below the 1977 level) has increased significantly [see Table 1.3]. But the structure of such crimes has remained relatively stable, with the proportion of the most serious offences either remaining the same (murder and rape) or changing marginally (shooting: –1 percent; robbery: +2 percent) since 1977 [Table 1.3]. These data could, however, easily conceal the significant changes in the character of violent crime and the corresponding changes in the society that they reflect. The data on murder will therefore be used to better illustrate the nature of these changes. These data have been reworked by the author, making them more reliable and more valid than the extant data for other crimes.

Table 1.3 Rates and Structure of Violent Crimes 1977–96

Year	Murder		Shooting		Rape*		Robbery	
1996	37.0	(4%)	61.6	(7%)	142.8	(7%)	179.8	(18%)
1995	31.3	(4%)	52.6	(7%)	128.0	(7%)	177.8	(19%)
1994	27.7	(3%)	50.1	(6%)	85.1	(5%)	218.8	(24%)
1993	26.5	(3%)	45.6	(5%)	104.4	(6%)	220.1	(25%)
1992	25.6	(3%)	43.9	(5%)	90.1	(6%)	200.4	(23%)
1991	23.0	(3%)	45.9	(6%)	89.5	(6%)	204.7	(27%)
1990	22.4	(3%)	56.7	(7%)	83.2	(5%)	222.1	(26%)
1989	18.4	(2%)	49.5	(6%)	90.7	(6%)	188.1	(23%)
1988	17.6	(2%)	42.1	(5%)	94.4	(6%)	188.0	(23%)
1987	18.8	(2%)	48.2	(6%)	85.1	(5%)	208.2	(24%)
1986	19.1	(2%)	44.8	(5%)	77.8	(5%)	210.2	(24%)
1985	18.7	(2%)	49.3	(5%)	73.8	(4%)	214.5	(24%)
1984	21.1	(2%)	57.3	(6%)	77.7	(3%)	215.5	(23%)
1983	18.7	(2%)	48.5	(5%)	72.9	(3%)	176.6	(19%)
1982	18.3	(2%)	42.8	(5%)	80.0	(5%)	163.1	(18%)
1981	22.5	(2%)	63.6	(11%)	71.3	(3%)	211.6	(21%)
1980	41.5	(4%)	106.5	(16%)	72.3	(3%)	220.8	(20%)
1979	16.3	(2%)	41.6	(5%)	57.7	(4%)	169.1	(22%)
1978	17.9	(2%)	37.9	(5%)	66.8	(4%)	187.9	(24%)
1977	19.2	(3%)	55.6	(7%)	86.0	(5%)	167.4	(22%)

Sources: Statistics Unit, Criminal Investigations Bureau (CIB); *ESS* (for later years only, after 1985)

Note: The rates are per 100,000 persons in the population.

Structure is calculated as a percentage of total violent crime.

*The rate of rape is calculated per 100,000 females. These rates are thus much higher than those of the police which are based on the assumption that the entire population, regardless of gender, is at risk.

Since 1988, unlike other violent crimes, the murder rate has steadily increased. In 1990 Jamaica's homicide rate of 22.4 per 100,000 was four times above the global average of 5.5.[5] In 1996, it had risen to 37 per 100,000, that is, approximately twice the mean for the Latin American and Caribbean region, which was estimated at 20 per 100,000 in that year [Inter-American Development Bank 1997]. There is a direct relationship between the rate of murder and the rates of other violent crimes. As these crimes are increasingly executed with the aid of firearms, murder becomes an associated outcome.

Historically, most murders were crimes of passion and disputes over personal property [Johnson 1987:34]. With the development of the society, increased urbanization and, consequently, a weakening of the intensity of interpersonal ties, these types of homicides may be expected to relatively (and perhaps absolutely) decline. Thus, not altogether surprisingly, a sharp shift has been effected in the sources and motives associated with criminal homicides from emotive interpersonal conflicts, to a close association with income-generating crime.[6] In 1993, for example, in 64 percent of the cases the offender was known to the victim, but paramours and spouses accounted for only 2 percent of all cases, other family members were 2 percent, and members of the same community 15 percent. The reality is better understood by examining the homicidal motives. Here the shift is most dramatic. In 1983 sexual competition and control, loss/accumulation of face and communal conflicts (the motives most associated by the police with "domestic murders")[7] cumulatively accounted for 28 percent of all homicides, while in 1993, this declined to 16 percent.

The general direction of violent criminality has been towards greater rationality and its instrumentality as means to commonly valued ends such as wealth, power, status-respect and so forth. Since the mid 1980s, murder has been largely associated with income-generating activity in the underground economy. This is reflected in:

- Increased gang killings. As a proportion of all murders these have increased from 11 percent in 1983 to 21 percent in 1993. These are usually directly or indirectly related to turf control in order to ensure a monopoly on protection rackets, the local drug market and to enhance the political leverage of the gang. Turf control is not simply an expression of some primeval territorial instinct.

- The symbolic displays and dramatic representations associated with some of these killings. Such displays may involve the killing of unconnected individuals, who may by chance be present at the scene, and the mutilation of the victims. Such acts are designed to define the boundaries of permissible conduct in the underworld and to communicate the willingness and capability of the particular actor to enforce these boundaries. Of course, these boundaries shift with the acquisition of greater power. So stealing a gun is generally punishable by death, but in a context of an attempt to assert power, trivial issues may also result in death. The messages communicated by these displays may be intended for different audiences – the disaffected members of the gang, competing gangs, the community in which the gang operates and so forth. One cannot properly comprehend these displays without knowing the audiences for which they are intended. Some of these displays are associated with political competition or control, including garrison maintenance, and are thus calculated to deter by terror any collaboration with political competitors or the institutions of the criminal justice system, or any resistance to the internal control mechanisms. But most of these dramatic displays are drug related outcomes of intergang competition and intragang control of their operatives.

- The increasing use of illegal guns in murder. While in 1986, 46 percent of all murders were committed with illegal guns (which are hardly accessible outside the criminal networks), in 1993 this had risen to 56 percent, and in 1996 to 68 percent. This reflects a more generalized use of guns in other violent crimes. In 1993, 53 percent of robberies and 24 percent of all reported rapes were also committed with the aid of guns [Statistics Unit, JCF].

- The attributes of victims. In 1993 the majority of victims were young (65 percent were under 35 years old), urban based (70 percent), male (89 percent) and unemployed or self-employed. These characteristics clearly indicate that homicides were not primarily the outcomes of "domestic" conflicts. If they were, there would be a higher proportion of female deaths (the outcome of intergender conflict), and a more widely dispersed class and age distribution of victims and offenders.

The murder rate is no longer primarily driven by domestic, communal type disputes, or even political competition, but rather by materially acquisitive crimes and conflicts arising from various types of illegal and informal transactions. This profound change is reflected in the changing social organization of criminals.

Changes in the Social Organization of Criminals

More significant than the quantitative changes in the rates and structure of crime are the qualitative changes in the social organization of crime and criminals that became evident in the mid 1980s. The new features of criminality involve: a more complex division of labour with greater specialization of roles; the development of more intricate organizational networks; the internationalization of these networks on the basis of a changed role in the international narcotics trade; greater differentiation and integration within the underground economy; and its social embeddedness. Indeed, it is in the emergence of these features that the Jamaican underground has asserted its economic and social power and has come to be described as an "economy".

The division of labour in the underground economy has become more complex, exhibiting greater specialization and higher levels of organization. This has resulted in considerable differentiation and greater stratification among criminals. In the underground economy, specialization occurs at different levels. Among criminal networks, it may involve crime type preferences (drug trafficking and related support services, immigration rackets involving the production of false travel documents and the creation of new identities in the desired destinations for their clients, robbery, burglary, car theft, murder); target type (bank robberies, warehouse burglary); and, at the level of the individual, a multiplicity of role specializations (drivers, entry experts and so forth). There are, of course, linkages between some of these crime type specializations. For example, drug trading tends to create a greater demand for the use of forged travel documents for criminals doing international business. It stimulates, integrates and helps to sustain these new specializations.

Reflecting an advanced division of labour, some of these specializations are finely differentiated one from another. This is particularly true in the drug trade, where, for example, "pressmen", who compress cannabis for packaging, are distinguished from packaging specialists. The latter are required to keep abreast of the latest chemicals for neutralizing sniffer dogs and new innovations in concealment, waterproofing and so forth. Many of these specializations have become viable full-time occupations. For example, warehouse burglars can easily dispose of their goods in the informal retail outlets, car thieves may operate on contracts to auto repair shops, while the services of professional murderers and enforcers find employment among narcotics traders and corporate actors.[8]

This has led to greater differentiation of crime careers, which may be judged by the level of vocational commitment to crime, contribution to total income and type of activity [see Best and Luckenbill 1989]. Offenders may thus be classified into three groups: occasional, habitual and professional criminals:

- *Occasionals* are unwilling criminals for whom crime is largely a survival strategy. They tend to engage in low-risk opportunistic crimes.
- *Habituals*, though not committed to criminal careers, engage regularly in criminal activity. For this group, crime is a means of capital accumulation to enter or sustain legitimate business activity. Habituals fall into two basic categories. First, there are those involved in structured criminality but who already operate formal businesses. The financial demands of their businesses and legitimately unsustainable lifestyle, however, provide

the impulse for eventual criminal habituation. Their engagement in socially approved victimless crimes (the cannabis trade) as their favoured source of accumulation and their linkages into social networks that provide them some protection from the control agents of the state tend to assure them some measure of success. Second, there are poor, urban based habituals who engage in violent street crimes with a view to quick accumulation. The upshot of this low level of commitment to a criminal career is usually noninvestment in the physical, human, and social capital necessary for success in the underground economy. They therefore tend to be less successful as criminals.

- *Professionals* are those whose incomes are primarily derived from crime. They tend to exhibit a higher level of career commitment and they dominate the high-income, highly capitalized sectors of the underground economy.

In 1994, the JCF estimated that there were 3,000 hardened criminals or "super-predators" as they are called in the USA.[9] This is reflected in the increasing proportion of recidivists among the prison population. The proportion of prisoners serving a second period of incarceration remained stable at 60 percent between 1982 and 1992, but triple recidivism increased to over 50 percent as early as 1988 [*ESS* 1988:21.6].

The development of a critical mass of professional criminals (sufficient to alter the social organization of crime) is a post 1977 development. Safe havens, where externally directed criminality is accepted, have been in existence for some 30 years. These are the garrison communities of the Kingston Metropolitan Area (KMA) and Spanish Town, which are characterized by politically homogeneous populations, tight integration between local party structures and criminal gang organizations (which exercise a highly centralized control over social and political activity in these communities), and a fair measure of political protection from police action.[10] A new generation has grown up under these conditions, in a milieu in which the internalized moral inhibitors against criminality are considerably neutralized.

This process of differentiation at the individual level is similarly exhibited at the group level. Here, as elsewhere, there is a wide range of groups: from "crews", who may occasionally engage in criminal activity as a group but whose primary group activity is organized around sports and entertainment, to gangs, who consistently engage in violent criminal activity but whose self-identity is not decidedly criminal and who may participate in useful community activity, and finally, highly organized networks of professional criminals.

Differentiation has not only accelerated the processes of specialization and professionalization but has also resulted in the increased integration of new groups, including women and children, into the criminal enterprise. Formerly, women and children were involved in support functions, such as information gathering on prospective targets and on the activities of the police, and the provision of logistic support for criminal gangs. Females are now more directly involved in crime, particularly in the drug trade (albeit in subordinate roles), acting as couriers for drugs and guns. Consistent with this new quality of involvement, women are accounting for an increasing proportion of offenders and convicts. In 1994, females accounted for 23 percent of the arrestees for breaches of the Dangerous Drugs Law (mainly trafficking) and 34 percent of arrestees for cocaine trafficking.[11] Although in 1992 they still accounted for only 8 percent of all incarcerated convicts [ESS 1994:23.7], they represented 16 percent of all convicted violent offenders, an increase from 12 percent in 1977 [STATIN1978, 1994].

The level of involvement of children has similarly moved from support to active direct engagement. In some of the Kingston inner city communities, the process of criminal socialization of young boys begins as early as 10 years. They are gradually initiated by giving them simple tasks and small rewards. For example, from being simply "gunbags" or weapons couriers, they have now become "shottas" or gunmen. This new role has contributed significantly to the growth of violent delinquency. The rate of juvenile (aged under 17) offending, based on cases brought before the courts, increased from an estimated 332 per 100,000 juveniles in 1977, to 394 per 100,000 in 1993. The sharpest increases in juvenile offending occurred in the late 1980s, during the period of the most rapid change in the social organization of crime.

The advances in specialization, therefore, are apparent in an emerging role specialization, often along age and gender lines. This trend could develop within networks that may be identified with a particular crime-type specialization or by individual specialists who offer their skills to different groups. Formerly the same persons would try to develop the knowledge, skills and networks necessary for success in a particular type of crime, but would be involved in all aspects of that crime. With the division of labour becoming more complex, roles have become more differentiated and interdependent. Consequently, greater coordination and more complex organization are required.

Indeed, there is considerable variation in the levels of organization of criminal groups. These groups vary in the intensity of their involvement in and level of economic dependence on criminal activity, size, resources, hierarchy, coordination, spatial extension and linkages with other organizations. Many are simply community based networks with an ill-defined membership, varied levels of involvement and points of contact, but with a discrete territorial domain and often having linkages to other gangs. Others are large gangs with a well-defined membership, usually numbering between 30 and 50, a shared identity, and an established leadership; yet with a loosely configured structure allowing individual initiative and varied levels of criminal gang involvement.

Here gangs refer to groups that recognize themselves as such and that consistently engage as a group in criminal activities for economic gain. This definition does not distinguish between gangs and the more disciplined networks engaged in organized crime, it rather includes the latter. The boundaries are not very distinct perhaps because the process of differentiation is still unfolding and because the age variable is not very helpful as a principle for establishing this boundary.

The highest levels of organization and best articulated structures are to be found in the drug trade. Risk reduction is ensured by planning, which contrasts with the principle of opportunity on which the less organized habitual criminals tend to operate. These organizations, unlike the looser networks, provide regular income for their members. Drug trading and protection rackets (aimed at corporations and more recently at small community businesses) are the two most stable sources of income. In 1993 the assets of one of the better organized gangs, the Shower Posse, was valued by the US Drug Enforcement Administration (DEA) at US $300 million.[12] This is consistent with the estimates reported by Gunst [1995:143]. Another gang, the Gully Posse, was valued at US $100 million [Gunst 1995:220]. These are, however, likely to be overestimates, since very crude measures based on dubious assumptions are used, and US security agencies have self-interestedly tended to overestimate their adversaries as a device for securing increased powers and budgetary allocations. But even if grossly overestimated, the resources at the disposal of these gangs are still vast. Moreover, some of the gangs studied had considerably diversified their sources of income to include protection rackets while retaining fairly lucrative state contracts. In some instances, even state agencies were forced to pay protection money to these gangs in the form of handsome "security contracts".

With these resources and the scope of their operations, the levels of organization of the gangs have become more complex particularly those involved in international drug trafficking. Their success is largely related to their linkages to the formal business sector (particularly in entertainment and other hospitality services), the state and party system, a significant measure of public approval, and the material resources (and social capital) with which to buy immunity from the law.

High levels of organization are not restricted to the drug trade. A huge underground trade in legitimate commodities exists, in some cases involving the operation of "underground" factories. In one case, the labels of a reputable manufacturing company were stolen and used to package an assembled product whose entire components were stolen. This product was then sold through normal commercial outlets as the commodity described on the label.[13] Such activity requires considerable knowledge, a large labour force and wide social linkages to ensure its success.

The endurance of criminal gangs is associated with the political variable. Several gangs have been in existence in the island for over 30 years and are territorially based in politically homogeneous communities where, as noted earlier, the political structures provide schooling in organization. Gang leadership is often either external to, but collaboratively interfaces with or is integrated into, or is identical to the local political leadership. Their organizational development was given further impetus by the quest for drug markets and by having to cope with their international competitors and the more modern police forces of North America and Europe.

As organization is extended over space, it necessarily becomes more complex. Jamaican criminal groups and organizations have moved since the late 1970s from being spatially limited to their immediate communities, located in the urban slums, to being truly international. They now operate, and have formed criminal networks, in Europe, North America, Latin and Central America, and other Caribbean states. The USA, however, is the main foreign province of Jamaican gangs.

The internationalization of the crime networks of Jamaica was driven by the quest for drug markets and was facilitated by the illegal immigration of Jamaican criminals to North American and European cities. The quality of the integration into the global narcotics trade is reflected in the level of local earnings from cannabis exports. This was estimated at US $1 to $2 billion in the 1980s [Griffith 1994:23], with a high of some US $3.5 billion in the early 1980s [de Albuquerque 1996]. By 1990 Jamaican criminals had garnered some 8 percent of the US $8.8 billion American cannabis (retail) market and were a significant player in the US $18 billion cocaine and cocaine derivatives market. All these inconsistent overestimates have as their source the DEA, but they nevertheless indicate a qualitative transformation of the Jamaican underground.

Deportation has become an effective measure for combatting drug gangs; consequently, it is a useful indicator of the extent of internationalization of Jamaican criminal organizations. Deportations began in earnest in 1989. In 1987 and 1988, a total of 11 persons were deported, all from the USA. In 1989, however, total deportations increased to 138 with 72 percent of these coming from the USA. By 1994, deportation increased significantly to 1,434, with 874 or 61 percent from the USA, 28 percent from Canada, 7 percent from England, and 4 percent from other Caribbean and Latin American countries. The exponential increase in deportations after 1988 was associated with a crackdown on Jamaican gangs or posses in the USA, where they had gained notoriety for their use of violent tactics to increase their market share of the drug retail trade. The 1994 deportations indicate a diversification of drug markets and a widening of the geographical scope of posse drug operations.

The structure of offending among deportees centres on drug or drug related violent crimes. The following statistics demonstrate this tendency. In 1978 only 16 percent of all deportees from the USA were connected with drug related offences, 0.4 percent for possession of guns and none for violent crimes. Some 84 percent of deportations were ostensibly occasioned by immigration breaches. In 1993, however, 70 percent of all deportations were drug related, 9 percent for gun possession, 5 percent for violent crimes, and a mere 8 percent for immigration breaches [Table 1.4]. This sharp shift reflects the qualitative change in Jamaican involvement in the drug trade.

Tighter integration in the US drug trade has facilitated the importation of guns, the development of multiclass criminal networks extending upwards into the social hierarchy, corrupt manipulation of the control agents of the state, and the corruption of whole communities and political institutions. The presence of the leader of the Opposition and eminent officers of his party at the funeral of Lester Coke, the alleged leader of the Shower Posse, in 1992 [14] and the attendance of high officials of the governing party at the funeral of Clinton Davy, a prominent figure with a somewhat similar reputation, are not so much statements on the personal integrity of these leaders, but rather manifestations of the social power and political legitimacy, albeit localized, of some of these groups. [15] Jamaica, with its underdeveloped economy but highly materialistic culture, has made it possible for drug derived resources to be easily translated into social and political power.

Table 1.4 Deportations from the USA 1987–94

Year	Possession of Drugs		Possession of Firearm		Violent Crimes		Other Crimes		Immigration Breaches		Total
1994	63%	(545)	10%	(87)	8%	(73)	2%	(14)	9%	(77)	872
1993	70%	(542)	9%	(69)	5%	(37)	8%	(60)	8%	(63)	771
1992	70%	(517)	7%	(54)	2%	(16)	5%	(36)	16%	(120)	743
1991	69%	(401)	4%	(21)	4%	(26)	4%	(25)	18%	(108)	581
1990	68%	(419)	4%	(25)	4%	(23)	8%	(50)	16%	(97)	614
1989	57%	(278)	3%	(16)	5%	(26)	2%	(11)	32%	(153)	484
1988	35%	(190)	2%	(9)	2%	(13)	0		61%	(330)	542
1987	16%	(71)	0	(2)	0		0		84%	(370)	443
Total	59%	(2,963)	6%	(283)	4%	(214)	4%	(196)	25%	(1,268)	5,050

Source: Criminal Intelligence Division, JCF.

The Embeddedness of Criminality

The further development of organized crime and its power in the society rests, to a large measure, on the extent and nature of the connections between the two. The criminal élite is likely to be even more powerful if socially integrated with the economic and political élite. Increasingly, there is an identifiable overlap and interchangeability of persons across these three groups, resulting in more intricate and extensive social relationships that provide protection for criminality. This development is a measure of new structural interdependencies among these groups and changing relations with organized crime. For example, the dons provide a range of services, including various types of security services, the harassment of competitors, customs evasion, and may even involve collaborative illegal economic ventures so forth. The relationship is therefore not strictly parasitic and coercively imposed.

Organized crime is in the process of redefining its relationships with the political élite. As the control of the state via its coercive apparatus and patrol-client relationships weaken, and as the economically marginalized and socially excluded population of the inner city communities appear more threatening, the dons are able to exploit their position as gatekeepers to these communities and their capacity to impose discipline on community members. By regulating access to these communities, and leveraging their capacity to deliver the votes and their powers of control, the dons are able to assert their importance in the two-party competitive system and to continue to extract resources from the state and private business. Their policing services guarantee the preservation of politically homogeneous communities, the protection of the business enterprises within their domains of power and internal order more generally. They have fully exploited the failure of the police and are effectively becoming extrastate (rather then illegal vigilante) policing authorities. These crime networks have become socially embedded.

Criminality is considered embedded when it is formed in interactive networks of social relations. These networks provide moral support and the practical skills needed; in general, they provide what McCarthy and Hagan [1995:65] describe as "criminal capital". The attractiveness of this construct rests on its linking of the economic and the social; more specifically, its connecting the nature of the opportunity structure with the processes of socialization in explaining the development of criminality. In the inner city communities dominated by gangs and crime networks, young males, preferably those with a high school education, are targeted for gang recruitment by involving them in activities such as transporting guns, manning observation posts during times of gang warfare or in support of drug dealing and collecting protection money. They earn occasional income in these ways, and in the process, they fraternize with gang members and listen to glamourous stories of the "heroic deeds" and admired qualities of past and present criminals from the community (including how they are able to outgun and outwit the police), much in the same way that myths that celebrate the qualities admired by a society and holiday jobs would help to socialize the young and facilitate easy integration into the labour force.

In as much as the lack of opportunities in the labour market and the marginalization and even stigmatization of their communities push them in the direction of crime networks, the process of criminal socialization further isolates the young males from social contacts and retards the development of the social skills needed for legitimate work. The possible exception to this is their political relationships, which have traditionally provided direct opportunities for legitimate work. But even this is problematic. For the ordinary members of the community, their party relations yield only sporadic work and return them to the same networks of relationships in which the community dons and gang leaders are principal actors, for in many communities these dons play important roles in the local party machinery and are the ones who get the state contracts. This type of relationship helps to socialize the young into criminality, as it may involve the use of extortion by these dons and the pretence of providing "security" and other forms of manipulation of the threat of violence, and leveraging of the social and political power derived from their accumulated criminal capital, in order to ensure that they are paid by the state for nonwork.

The embeddedness of relations reinforces and protects criminality. The garrison community provides a concentrated expression of the problem of criminal embeddedness. Here the criminal organization is superimposed on the political structures which provide the local narco-political dons with a source of moral authority in these communities. The corrupt aspects of the political processes, such as bogus voting and the intimidation of opponents, in these garrison constituencies lead to the high valorization of the gunman by elevating his status within the parties and homogeneous party communities. In this context, criminal organizations perform both protective and allocative functions [see Harriott 1994]. Their protective function involves not only armed defence against encroachments by political opponents and ordinary criminals but also the function of control agents within these communities, often providing effective guarantees against predatory criminality in a context of ineffective policing. This feature further serves to morally legitimize these criminal groups.

In these communities, violence, even when manipulated in an offensive mode, may be considered legitimate. The "morally legitimating" principle is a communally bounded utilitarianism, the moral boundaries of which co-terminate with the social community boundaries of the moral subjects. To exist beyond this communally established boundary is to fall beyond the pale of morally accountable action.[16] To exist beyond this boundary as an enemy (political, social) is to qualify as a legitimate target.

Despite the above, some gang leaders have become relatively independent patrons or "dads" of their communities. They command considerable reward power. Their drug largesse and other criminally derived benefits may be distributed widely within the communities. Moreover, they are able to assist migration to North America, which is seen as opening up both illegal and legal opportunities. Drug dealing there is often combined with legitimate employment, which their sponsoring dons will encourage as it provides a masking function. However, for some operatives it may be seen as a bridge to full legitimacy. The appeal of the don in this regard therefore extends beyond those narrowly interested in criminal careers. This reward power is combined with even greater coercive power. Direct control over the means of violence in the community and the capability to authoritatively deliver violent punishment via parallel justice systems may be combined with an ability to direct elements in the police force against designated targets. They may be able to get consensus on the punishment of members of the community where accepted codes are violated. Punishment is therefore usually swift and certain. To avoid it, one usually has to sever all of one's social ties and to defect to an "enemy" community, preferably of an opposing political affiliation.

The drug dons often enjoy high status and are seen as models of successful adaptation to today's urban realities. Their social power resides not just in their reward and coercive power but also (on this basis) in their referent power within their communities. These embedded dons are perceived as both criminal and police, victimizer and provider, aggressor and defender, political terrorist and crusading "general". These antinomies simply reflect the realities on different sides of the moral boundaries.

Consequently, in many of these communities of the marginalized urban poor, there is considerable support for these dons and for what they consider to be justifiable criminality. The police are often confronted by this reality when they arrest some of the more powerful dons, only to see a quick mobilization of the citizens in protest of police actions and in support of the dons. Such active support for this type of criminality often resonates within a wider population that may not regard the dons as heroic figures (as is the case in some of these communities) but nevertheless may associate them with some Jamaicanized form of social banditry. This embeddedness and the widening gap between legal and social definitions of crime are important factors conditioning the ineffectiveness of the crime control agents of the state. The fear of social sanctions against criminality is negligible, thus the deterrent value of judicial sanctions has considerably diminished.

While bringing some material benefits to a few, this embeddedness, along with the consequent criminogenic reputation and stigmatization of the communities, out-migration of the upwardly mobile and decapitalization, has led to the further social isolation of the urban poor. In a small society, where life chances are linked to ascriptively based networks, the outcome of this social isolation is exclusion, which in turn often serves as justification for criminality.

Criminal embeddedness therefore has its basis in the fairly high level of integration of the underground, informal and formal economies at the community level. The underground is a supplier and guarantor of cheap goods and services; thus threats to the criminals are seen as threats to these services and consequently to the local economy. These communities therefore tend to develop defensive strategies designed to protect "their" criminal benefactors and to frustrate the criminal justice system.

Thus far the discussion has been focused at the community level (as this was the primary site of the fieldwork), but it is evident from observation, discussions with representatives of some of the gangs identified earlier, as well as personal correspondence with the head of the narcotics division of the JCF, that in the case of organized crime, and the drug trade in particular, these criminal networks extend upwards into sections of the economic and political élite. This may be done via partnerships between the leaders of the traditional street gangs who have been successful in the drug trade and who wish to establish legitimate businesses, on the one hand, and already established legitimate business interests, on the other. Alternatively, these networks are established by the direct organization and direction of these drug trafficking groups by members of this élite.

These developments are the outcome of still underresearched criminogenic processes which have long been germinating in Jamaican society and have become full grown in the last fifteen years. Increased crime rates and the changes in the pattern of offending are primarily adaptations to profound structural changes in the society, compounded by demographic trends and the modalities of political competition.

Conclusion

The exclusion from viable legitimate opportunities and the financial dependence on, and moral acceptance of, drug defined crimes provides the foundations for the structural embeddedness of criminality. Crime is becoming less a direct response to the crisis of the formal economy, and the processes of social disorganization associated with it, than the direct outcome of the dynamics of doing business in a large and growing underground economy that is becoming more clearly articulated and progressively integrated with the national economy. It is more associated with a process of social reorganization than with social disorganization.

Jamaica has become a highly criminogenic society characterized by:
- Pervasive criminality and disregard for law across all social classes

- A developed, well-integrated underground economy
- Majority approval, or at least tolerance, of the types of crimes driving (not those regulating) the underground economy
- Criminality becoming increasingly anchored in institutionalized relations and occupational roles
- Increasing acceptance and prevalence of elements of the criminal normative system and moral neutralization processes (the doctrine of necessity, the shifting of obligation and duty to the victim)
- Criminally acquired resources easily translatable into social power
- Pervasive criminality within the justice system and general authority structures

Yet what identifies Jamaica as a highly criminogenic society is not simply the reality of these elements but their centrality and embeddedness in the different aspects of national life – the accumulation process, market relations, public administration and the political process.

The landscape of criminality has changed qualitatively, becoming more structurally based, institutionalized, rooted in occupational roles and in the informal production and distribution processes, that is, embedded in the processes of social reorganization. These changes in the society have resulted in greater dyscensus in socially defining criminality, in particular some types of income-generating or appropriating (white-collar and street) crimes. For this reason, the control measures of the criminal justice system, including more repressive, rights-depriving legislation and harsher judicial punishments, have become less effective. The effects of these problems on policing will be developed in the next chapter.

2

Police

Organization

In contrast with the qualitative changes in the social organization of crime and criminality already discussed, the mode of police organization has remained largely unchanged and the principles on which these structures were erected unexamined. As part of a more general critique of the traditional political model of policing in Jamaica, this chapter describes the failure to adapt to the changes described in chapter 1 and examines the structural sources of consequent police ineffectiveness. The organizational characteristics and bureaucratic ethos are descriptively analysed. This is also crucial to understanding the internal sources of its ineffectiveness and anticipating the likely difficulties in any attempt at reform.

Police forces are agencies of social control engaged in the reproduction of an established social order. They are all therefore profoundly political institutions. However, they do not all operate on the "political model", that is, being overtly involved in competitive party politics, party dedicated or even regime maintenance security policing, and thus engaged not just in the control of deviants but of whole populations or sections of those populations. The JCF has historically operated on this political model of policing.

On this model of policing, control of the police force is achieved via subjective modes. This involves the permeation of the force by networks of party activists and the determination of appointments (particularly to sensitive posts such as the leadership of the intelligence and special operations units) on the basis of political affiliation and personal empathy. The mode of control allows the political directorate to determine detailed operational matters. This includes, in addition to personnel selection and deployment, the type of operations appropriate in different situations and their timing and targets, the power to have charges proffered or dropped, or both, and to determine rewards and punishment within the force [see Harriott

1994]. In the Jamaican expression of the model, no sphere of police activity is beyond the reach of the minister in charge.

The JCF, like other ex-colonial security police, was designed primarily to preserve order, "keep the lid on" in a hostile environment and to "suppress mass outbreaks against the peace" [see Jefferies 1952:30–32; Danns 1982:13–16]. While during the colonial era the Force was concerned with the preservation of public order in the broader sense of social control (and thus paid much greater attention to offences such as the use of foul language, urination in public spaces and illegal vending than it now does), its focus was decidedly on the preservation of order in a political rather than strictly social sense. This concern with state protection, often leading to a disregard for the rights of citizens, is reflected, for example, in the Riot Act of 1857 [Laws of Jamaica 16], which allows the police to arrest "any persons, to the number of 12 or more, being unlawfully, riotously and tumultuously assembled together to the disturbance of the public peace" on charges carrying life imprisonment. It also indemnifies the police and any citizen who use deadly force against the rioters. This act, which was passed shortly after emancipation, was amended in 1969 after the "Rodney riots" and Black Power activism of that period, to make it more punitive [Laws of Jamaica 16]. Crime control was a secondary function.[1] This is codified in the Constabulary Force Act [Laws of Jamaica 3] and the *Force Standing Orders* [JCF 1992a, 1:9], which requires the JCF "to keep watch by day and night, preserve the Peace, to *detect crime*".[2] This profoundly state-serving rather than society-serving orientation has largely been sustained, not just by the inertia of tradition but also by the sharp class segmentation of the society and by the threat perspective of an upper class more committed to extraction and accumulation than to development.

With the radical changes in the local and international environment (the end of the Cold War and the changes in the social organization of crime described earlier), public concern with crime control has superseded the earlier concern with political control. But the role of the police, its strategies and structures have not been substantially changed, resulting in the JCF being largely unfitted for the crime preventative, problem solving, as accountable and democratically oriented policing are now being required of it, if it is to form part of a wider democratic renewal of the society and state.

The mission statement of the JCF was recently revised to indicate a more service oriented intent, and the near universal (but universally practised in the breach) slogan "to protect and serve" adopted. If this is to be taken as indicative of goal reorientation, and if structures are simply means for attaining goals, then a real change in goals may be expected to signify profound changes in structure. Against this background, the existing structures will now be examined.

Police Ineffectiveness

Rational choice and (formal) control theorists consider criminality as the "natural" or normal predisposition of rational persons as the desired goals of the ordinary citizen may be more easily achieved by such nonconforming behaviour than by normative behaviour [cf. Wilson and Herrnstein 1985; Wilson 1975; Nye 1958]. They therefore tend to view crime rates as being primarily dependent on the effectiveness of the system of institutional social control (the certainty, severity and celerity of punishment). This perspective (in its less sophisticated forms) has had a powerful influence on state policy. However, as it has been increasingly shown to lack empirical support, there has been a developing appreciation of the limitations of the institutions of formal control, particularly policing on crime control. Experimental research on the traditional crime prevention strategies, such as patrol [cf. Kelling et al. 1974], as well as work in the epidemiological tradition [cf. Wolfgang, Figlio and Sellin 1972], suggests that these strategies at best displace rather than reduce crime. Clearance and arrest rates, which are measures of the outcomes of police investigations, were similarly found to have no controlling effect on crime rates [Bayley 1994:7]. Recent research reports tend to confirm these earlier findings. It is argued that policing (as it is now organized) has no effect on crime control [Bayley 1994:3; Gottfredson and Hirschi 1990:270], only a marginal effect [Klockars 1991], or a variable effect – reducing, increasing or having no effect [Sherman 1992].

This limited positive impact of policing on the crime rate may be partially accounted for by factors that lie beyond the traditional scope of police action such as the socioeconomic conditions and, specifically in Jamaica, the centrality of the political variable in violent crime. Despite these limitations, the effectiveness of the JCF (and indeed most police forces) is now judged primarily in relation to its crime control function.

The traditional indicators of crime control are levels of "preventable" crime, cleared-up rates and conviction rates. On the first indicator, using the data presented in chapter 1, the police could be regarded as a historic failure. Similarly, cleared-up rates for both property and violent crimes have been steadily declining. High cleared-up rates were sustained up to the early 1980s (for the period 1977–83, the mean cleared-up rates for property and violent crimes were 50 percent and 70 percent, respectively), but since then they have steadily declined and for the period 1991–94 they were 43 percent and 60 percent, respectively [ESS 1994:23.3]. The cleared-up rate tends to be inversely related to the seriousness of the type of crime. In the case of murder, given the expected priority accorded these investigations, one would expect a high solution rate. Yet the cleared-up rate was 41 percent for 1992–

94, and the mean conviction rate for the same period was 20 percent ($N =$ 1,319).[3] Yet these are overestimates as they exclude those thought to be murdered but who are legally missing. If these cases are included, the true conviction rate would be no more than 18 percent.

The inability to manage violent crime has exposed the increasing ineffectiveness of the JCF and its poor fit for the function of crime control. This is reflected in the inability to establish "legal guilt", which has led to a tendency to treat offenders on the basis of "factual guilt" and to the use of illegitimate methods of investigation and the summary treatment of some offenders. This abuse of power is often tolerated when directed at criminals with established reputations; but when it is more broadly directed, as is frequently the case (when societies become tolerant of this type of abuse), this simply poisons police-citizen collaboration, thereby reducing the effectiveness of the Force. While this has been facilitated by the legal-constitutional framework, which is weak on the protection of individual rights and strong on police powers [see Carnegie 1991; Fraser 1979], the incapacities of investigators have also contributed to this situation. Many constables become detectives simply by securing departmental transfers rather than by specialized training, demonstrated ability and competence.[4] Indeed, recent (1994) internal evaluations suggested that the quality of the personnel in the Criminal Investigations Bureau (CIB) was the worst in the Force.[5] Perhaps this level of incompetence is the outcome of the extensive use of political influence and personal ties to secure detective status, and a permissive legal constitutional framework that has caused their investigative-criminalistic skills to atrophy.

Generally, police structures are configured to effect the reactive principle. This is based on the assumption that rapid responses would lead to swift apprehension and certain conviction of suspects and that such outcomes would serve as a powerful general deterrent to crime. This promised an effective technological-professional policing solution to the crime problem. However, research has shown this to be ineffective even where a mean response time of three minutes is achieved. It is now felt that a response time of less than one minute is required, that is, virtual police omnipresence [Peak and Glensor 1996:38; Bayley 1994:6]. Even if this approach were morally accept-able, conceptually sound and operationally effective, its implementation assumes: (1) The availability of a large number of patrol cars and an effec-tive communications system. In the Jamaican context, it is doubtful whether the resource commitment required to pursue this approach is sustainable. (2) Easy access to telephones by the majority of the population. However, telephone density in Jamaica now stands at only one per ten citizens and is heavily concentrated among the urban middle strata [ESS 1994:13.3]. (3) Sufficient confidence in the police to call them at first impulse. The realities of the Jamaican context would thus present considerable problems for a simple transfer of this approach.

In 1994 the mobility of the JCF was increased considerably, with the size of its fleet of automobiles increasing from 766 to some 1,500, that is, by approximately 100 percent [Knight 1994:32]. Not surprisingly, this has had no apparent effect on the rate of serious crimes. The cardinal problem is not a resource or technical one in the first instance. Rather, it is a social-structural problem with its sources in the internal and external relations of the JCF and the principles of policing on which it operates. Therefore, even with greater and more efficiently managed resources, ineffectiveness persisted.

Internal Sources of Ineffectiveness

The JCF is almost 100 years older than the nation, having been formed in 1866.[6] It is therefore perhaps more profoundly shaped by colonialism than any other state institution. This is reflected in its mode of organization, bureaucratic ethos, dominant political values, style of policing and the nature of its fundamental relationships – that between the officers and the other ranks, between the JCF and citizens, and between the JCF and government (that is, how it controls and is in turn controlled).

The model of security policing imposed in the Commonwealth Caribbean is distinguished by a particular organizational structure and culture, one based on control rather than service delivery and problem solving. Organizational culture refers to beliefs about "how work should be organized (operating norms), the way authority should be exercised (how relationships across rank and with the public are defined), people rewarded, and controlled" [Handy 1985]. Its component features are:

- Operating norms
  - reactive
  - paramilitarism as a mode of organization and tactic
  - avoidance of responsibility
  - avoidance of work
- Exercise of authority
  - centralization
  - command
  - tight subjective political control
  - upward accountability
- Relationships defined
  - excessive police powers (police-citizen relations are framed by poor constitutional protection of individulal rights from police and state abuse)
  - an adversarial relationship to the lower or subordinate social groups

- — treatment of people on the principle of status congruence
- Reward structure
  - — determined by particularistic principles associated with group membership (race under colonialism and later party affiliation)
  - — the empathic principle (individualized affective relationships with a "godfather" being vital for career advance through the lower and middle ranks)
  - — outdated colonial bureaucratic practices that emphasize seniority over performance; military values of bravery (and, in the earlier period, even gallantry as reflected in the cultivation of an image of being amorous, oversexed and civil); and mastery of the delivery of violence over more mundane but socially valued service

These norms have been formed by over a century of practice within the JCF, but in some aspects they extend to other state institutions and the society. The operating norms of the JCF were fashioned to fit its primary function of maintaining order and control rather than service delivery. This focus is reflected in the organization of work, the style in which authority is exercised and its relations internally and externally, and is reinforced by the internal reward system.

The Organization of Work

The security model is sustained by the acceptance of its political control function and, with this, the structures and operating norms which find their justification in this role definition. The prototypical model for these purposes is paramilitarism. As a tactic it entails the use of nonselective or, rather, group suppressive (rather than individually focused) forms, such as raids, curfews and cordon-and-search, which might be appropriate for order maintenance against hostile populations but are of little crime control value and have dubious democratic credentials.[7] As an organizational model paramilitarism has been intellectually reinforced by Taylorist managerial doctrines that emphasize control (via compartmentation, tall hierarchies and upward accountability) and production (number of arrests, miles driven and so forth) rather than service.[8] This has led to a loss of perspective, whereby law enforcement becomes an end in itself rather than a means of crime control and improving the quality of life of the people.

Resources are always directed at treating specific criminal events or neutralizing threatening criminal groups or individuals, not eliminating or managing crime-generating situations. The paramilitary model, in its colonial adaptation, is characterized by closure and a low regenerative capacity. This is reflected in recruitment patterns (entry at the lowest rank only), the use of police personnel for nonpolicing functions (such as car repairs), and the valorization of military type operational skills (acquired within the organization) that are better suited to order maintenance than the need to access specialized fields of knowledge appropriate to crime control (such as criminology, management, computer programming, forensic accounting and so forth). Acquisition of the latter would require a more open institution, as these specializations are normally acquired outside of the police organization.

In the ex-colonial context, paramilitarism emphasizes physical fitness, social malleability and, since the entry point as a general rule is restricted to the lowest rank, submissive-authoritarian qualities rather than leadership potential or the command side of the authoritarian complex (as is the case with military officer cadets, for example). Limiting renewal to insertions from the bottom, plus the seniority principle, ensures that its personnel internalize the cultural rules of the institution long before becoming supervisors or officers. Thus there are entrenched traditions about the conduct of police work. The treatment of people and problems are often reduced to ritualized procedures. For this reason, within the JCF, policing is thus often described as "copy work".[9] Innovation is at best viewed with suspicion, at worst as threatening.

Consistent with its closed and craft-like, rather than professional, character, seniority is valued over performance, and experience over education and training. Police managers and supervisors, most of whom are male (93 percent), thus tend to be old – their mean ages being 50 and 45, respectively. Their level of education tends to be fairly low. In 1994, only 7 percent (13) of police managers had degrees, another 6 percent had certificates or incomplete tertiary education. Although this represents a positive advance, the pool from which it normally selects its officers remains poorly educated. In the JCF as a whole, only 0.4 percent have successfully completed a degree programme,[10] 7 percent have some form of postsecondary education and 40 percent a high school education ($N = 666$) [see Table 2.1].

These officers manage vast resources without any specialized training or even a sound basic education. In no other area of public administration does this obtain. The typical divisional commander has under his direction vast resources, including vehicles and equipment valued at tens of millions of dollars, a staff of some 200 regular constables and another 40 auxiliaries drawn from the Island Special Constabulary Force (ISCF), district constables and civilian personnel. He or she has to contend with a wide range of complex problems and events with potentially grave consequences for the individuals and communities affected. Intelligent performance oriented officers are able to meet the requirements of their commands. But officers who advance on the basis of seniority or the empathic principle (and these are still the majority), or both tend to follow routine procedures or simply ignore the problems for as long as is possible.

The closed system of the JCF is associated with extraordinary security of tenure. This applies to all ranks, but is particularly secure for personnel of and above the rank of inspector. There are only two ways of terminating the services of persons in these positions – if they are convicted on criminal charges or if they are asked to resign in the public interest. The latter requires the approval of the governor general on the recommendation of the Police Services Commission (PSC) and may be subject to the outcome of an appeal to the Privy Council. There are highly protective and tedious procedures to be followed [see JCF1961]. Therefore, it is an option that is not exercised even when serious criminal charges, such as drug trafficking, murder or serious abuse of their powers, are formally levelled against officers by the very police force within which they work but are not upheld by the courts. This is the standard of proof that is invariably required.

Thus, in practice, dismissals have tended to occur only on criminal convictions and, more recently, via administrative dismissals as refusals by the commissioner to renew contracts. Between 1987 and 1992, only 134 police officers (that is, a mean of 22 per year) were dismissed and, of these, 73 (or 54 percent) were after criminal convictions [ESS 1987–92:21.1].[11] Transfers are the most actively used instrument for punishing serious offenders. These conditions of tenure have led to managerial acceptance of poor performance.

Most JCF personnel, given their level of qualification, are unable to pursue alternative career options with similar status, power and levels of remuneration. Any attempt to reduce job security or to open up senior posts to external competition has therefore been met with considerable resistance. As is the case within the civil service in general, security of tenure is based on the idea of insulating the police from political interference, but this near absolute security of tenure has clearly failed to prevent the politicization of the police [see Harriott 1994]. Yet the society remains burdened with its negative consequences of indolence, routine abuse of power and poor performance. Indeed, more open police services with less secure conditions of tenure reputedly tend to be more effective.

In the JCF, education, knowledge and youth are not allowed to operate as change agents. Taken together, these factors suggest that the institution would have a low capacity for self-regeneration. Recent reforms have had the positive effect of incrementally lowering the mean age of the officer corps, improving its educational level and increasing the proportion of females at this level as well as in the JCF as a whole.

A second feature of the operating norms of the JCF is the avoidance of work. This is easily observed in its routine activities: remaining in the stationhouse; discouraging reports and complaints from victims who, depending on the type of report, may be treated as a nuisance or an initiator of unrewarding or potentially troublesome work; and plainly ignoring some

Table 2.1 Sociodemographic Profile of the JCF by Rank (percentage)

| | Rank | | | | | |
	Lower Ranks	**NCOs***	**Officers**	**χ^2**	**df**	**Sig.**
Sex						
Male	81	91	90			
Female	19	9	10	15.3278	2	.00047
Mean Age		45	50			
Education						
Primary	6	39	47			
Secondary	90	55	33			
Tertiary†	4	6	17	16.4912	2	.00026
Place of birth						
Rural	67	82	80			
Urban‡	33	18	20	17.6971	2	.00014
Class origin						
Working class	33	26	30			
Small farmer	23	47	44			
Own account	26	18	25			
Lower middle	18	9	1	42.2775	6	.00000
Colour						
Black	85	86	91			
Brown	12	11	11			
Other	3	3	0			

N ranged from 652 to 660.

* NCOs are corporals, sergeants and inspectors.

† Tertiary education includes nondegree programmes. Only 7 percent have completed degree programmes. As noted earlier, the actual proportion of officers who have completed some programme of training at a tertiary institution was 18 percent.

‡ Urban is defined as the KMA and parish capitals or main towns.

types of offences. This seems to be particularly true of areas with high rates of crime, such as our two research communities. Until recently in Alexanderville, some offences, including violent domestic disputes, did not appear in the records of that station. According to one corporal who was assigned as a community police officer (CPO), "the police would chase people away when they came to make such reports".[12] Even reports of rape were discouraged, particularly when women who were considered by the police to be disreputable came to make such reports. During the period of the research project, constables at the Normanville police station reported seeing a group of gunmen firing their weapons within 100 yards of the station. These gunmen were not pursued as it was felt that this would have been futile.[13] This will be elaborated on in chapter 5.

A further feature is the avoidance of responsibility. This is typical of highly centralized police systems. In organizations in which knowledge is manipulated as a power resource and information tends to flow upward, the authority and basis for accepting responsibility in the lower echelons of a hierarchical structure is undermined. The methodology for developing policy is, as a rule, exclusive. If policy is not explicit and evolves piecemeal in response to events, proximity to the top becomes even more important in order to be able to judge what is acceptable action. In this context, taking responsibility is a high-risk enterprise.

This failure to act responsibly at the lower echelons (conditioned by overcentralization in the first place) further intensifies a progressively more detailed and debilitating control from the centre. For example, shortly after his appointment, Commissioner MacMillan was presented, via the chain of command (up five levels), with a request from a constable in the distant division of Hanover for departmental leave for a single day![14] In an evaluation of the first year of his tenure, the commissioner observed:

Decision-making was found to be a highly centralized function which effectively transferred responsibility for decisions on local matters from Area and Divisional Officers to Headquarters Offices. This affected initiative and creativity on the part of responsible officers leading to under-achievement and a tendency to await instructions from Headquarters before dealing with local problems. [JCF 1993–94:8].

This researcher experienced the problem first-hand in trying to get lower to middle level police officials to release to me data that had already been made public. In one such instance, a request was made to the sergeant directly in charge, who directed me to the assistant superintendent (ASP), who in turn directed me to the senior superintendent (SSP), who required of me written approval from the commissioner. Indeed, the accepted practice in the Force at the time of writing is that every weekday morning divisional commanders are required to report on the operational details of their commands to their area commanders, who in turn report to the responsible deputy commissioner at the High Command, who reports to the commissioner. Because of the pressures associated with such a highly centralized command, informal mechanisms as well as aspects of the formal system are so structured, that as one area commander confessed, "The area knows more about the operational details of the division than the divisional commander."[15] Eventually, fairly senior officers find themselves in positions of authority without responsibility and tend to act like supervisors rather than managers. After critically dissecting the nature of the present system of centralized control with him, an assistant commissioner in charge of an area remarked, "You feel helpless, powerless. You don't feel like an assistant commissioner."[16]

The Exercise of Authority

The exercise of authority is characterized by centralization and command, tight subjective political control and upward accountability. Each is discussed in turn.

Like most public and private institutions in Jamaica (state bureaucracies, political parties, large private corporations, tertiary institutions) the JCF is highly centralized. In 1994, 37.2 percent of its personnel were in specialist, central administrative or support units [JCF1994]. High centralization is accompanied by functional compartmentalization. Relatively large central structures have developed around the main functions of operations, investigation, general function, intelligence gathering and administration. Each of these has developed its own elaborate administrative control systems, and on top of these is an even greater central administrative structure designed to control these control structures. Not surprisingly, a high proportion of JCF personnel is engaged in the administrative function (some 35–40 percent) and it is estimated that, at any given time, only some 19 percent of the Force are usually available for work on the streets [Figure 2.1]. This may represent a modest underestimate of the proportion of the Force engaged in some form of patrol work as the CIB (which accounts for 7 percent of all police personnel) and some of the central operational units, such as the Mobile Reserve, are usually also engaged in this type of activity. Nevertheless, this reality contrasts sharply with some of the more modern police services in the region, such as the Costa Rican police service, which assigns 91 percent of its personnel to patrol duties, another 6 percent for following up cases, leaving only 3 percent engaged in administration [Buendia 1989:422].

This high degree of centralization tends to generate tall hierarchies within each of these functionally specialized departments. Consistent with the military model, this tall hierarchy and the high degree of centralization are designed to ensure effective coordination, tight internal supervision and external political control. It is a command and control model. The rank structure of the JCF is pyramidal, with 13 levels of rank. This is more than twice its 5 levels of command. The colonial model is usually typified by a higher number of ranks (8–13) and levels of command (5–6) than metropolitan forces, which tend to have 6–10 and 2–4, respectively [Bayley 1992:519]. Even by ex-colonial standards, the JCF is extreme, with more ranks and levels of command than India with its relatively vast territory, large police force and tradition of perhaps even more rigid social hierarchies than Jamaica [see Table 2.2].

The high degree of centralization has its roots in the British colonial mode of governance. The concern was primarily with control of the population

Figure 2.1 Proportion of Constables on Patrol Duty

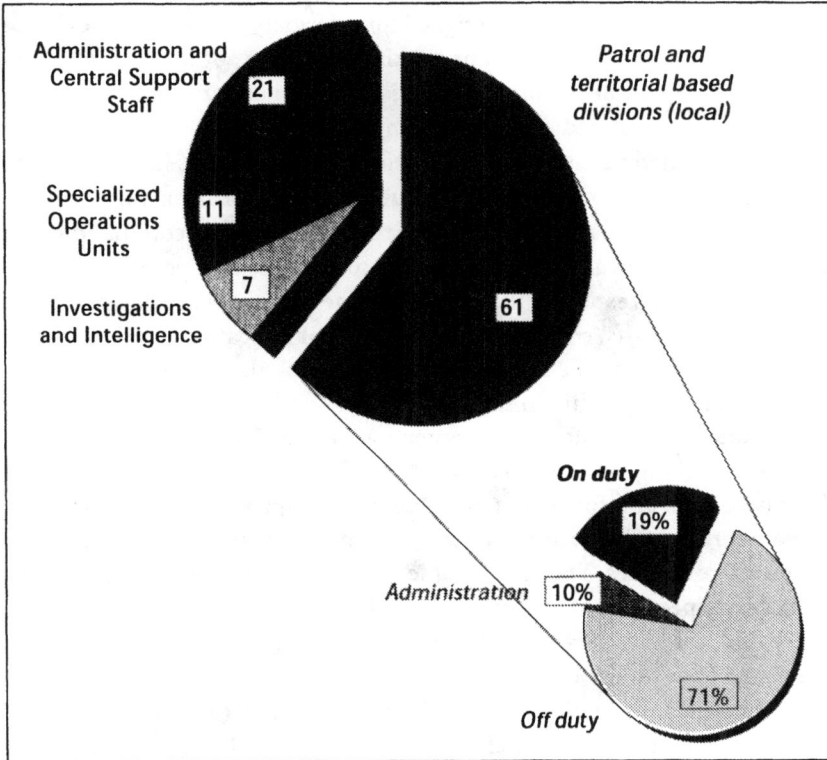

Sources: JCF Computer Centre; and personal communication with appropriate departmental authorities within the JCF.

Note: Civilian administrative support staff is excluded.

by a police force that was itself tightly controlled by a monolithic centralizing colonial power structure. This structure and, indeed, the wider perspective on governance were anchored in the certainty that the black subjects (including most of all the stereotypical brawny police constables) were infantile, unintelligent, irresponsible and politically unreliable. These centralized structures were thus also shaped by this view and were (correctly) seen from a colonial perspective as appropriate for dealing with a politically volatile and potentially hostile environment.

Table 2.2 Proportion of Police in Different Ranks

Rank	Jamaica	Guyana	India	UK	USA
Managers/officers	3.5	4.3	0.8	5.8	13.3
Supervisors/NCOs	21.0	24.0	8.5	15.9	11.7
Operatives/other ranks	75.5	73.7	90.7	78.0	75.0

Sources: Bayley 1992:531; Guyana Police Force 1994; Trinidad and Tobago Police Service 1994.

This legacy of overcentralization in the JCF has meant that the system of information management is designed for information to flow to the source of power and to maximize decision making at the apex of the hierarchy. For example, information required by divisional commanders may first flow to their superiors (the area commander and often even the High Command) before it is routed to them. This distortion, which requires information to take such an indirect route to its effective users (in terms of action not decision), results in decision making appropriate to a lower level of command being taken by higher levels and too great a disjuncture between the power of decision making and the responsibility for implementation. This design of the information circuits, coupled with low levels of education, tends to create miscommunication in the transmission of messages. All focus groups reported that this was a way of life in the JCF.

Moreover, as the information systems are not deliberately organized with the purpose of improving the effectiveness of the operative at the street level, there is no level of information to which there is open access and free lateral movement of useful crime related (not administrative) information to interested constables. Thus a constable in division A might be searching for a murder suspect who may be in the custody of division B on a minor charge, but would not have access to any organized system allowing him to know this at the time points that may be decisive.

This overcentralization also makes coordination between different units difficult and contributes to ineffectiveness. For example, the CIB personnel attached to each territorial division are not primarily accountable to the officer in charge of the division but rather to the CIB. The arrangement reduces divisional officers to supervisors, since it largely relieves them of the planning function and excludes them from much strategic as well as some tactical decision making. This is inappropriate in a setting where there is considerable variation in local problems and needs and where local inputs by police and citizens are vital to problem solving.

Most importantly, the concentration of formal power at the apex of a tall hierarchy, in conditions of weak authority and a legitimacy crisis, is likely to lead, in its internal expressions, to lower supervisory personnel and operatives who are shut out of decision making but who are responsible for the implementation of decisions taken by a leadership in which they have little confidence. The subordinates can then use their negative power to block the translation of these decisions into effective action. In the case of the JCF, this reduces its effectiveness, despite the strong system of upward accountability.

In closed institutions such as the JCF, accountability is usually upwardly directed and focused on outcomes. As noted earlier, these outcomes are usually Taylorist production measures – such as number of arrests, quantity of drugs seized and so forth. Community satisfaction with the service provided was never a major concern. The force thus tends to have poor mechanisms of public accountability.

As noted elsewhere, internally, upward accountability may be easily frustrated by the manipulation of information from below [see Harriott 1994]. The leadership is also able to manipulate the public trust by regulating the outward flow of information. A critical press reduces this ability to manipulate the public when the incompetence, incapacity and deviant practices of the police are revealed to national audiences, thereby intensifying the legitimacy problems of the JCF by weakening this traditional method of legitimation and some of its essential relationships.

There are two basic categories of relationships in which the police are engaged. These are the relationships between the police and government and the police and citizens. As the first has been discussed elsewhere [Harriott 1994] and the second is a central theme throughout the text, the comments here will be introductory.

The organizational environment has tended to be highly politicized. The centralization of power, the use of resources as power tools, the centrality of the empathic principle in organizational life, and the concern with results without regard for means all indicate that the JCF may best be described by what Handy [1985] calls a power culture. Consistent with a power culture, control (including external control), as noted earlier, is exercised subjectively. Loyalty is thus configured on personalistic rather than legal bureaucratic (or task oriented) lines. Each senior officer – once in contention for the post of commissioner – tends to develop his own retinue. These cabals often engage in bitter struggles (invariably mediated by party affiliation) for turf control and power resources.

This presents the problem of overlapping jurisdictions, which is often used as a mechanism of control and is the outcome of a particular configuration of political and bureaucratic power. New (parallel) structures are often set up to circumvent the existing ones in order to ensure politically reliable and personally loyal units. The multiplicity of intelligence and special operations units are the best examples of this. Decisions are based on a balance of power between competing coalitions rather than on procedural or logical grounds. This balance of power usually shifts during every political administration to the extent that the minister and the commissioner may at times be unable to effect their own policing policies.

Police-citizen relations are framed by an essentially state protective legal constitutional setting. This is reflected in both substantive and procedural law. In substantive law (under the constitution) all individual rights are qualified by the proviso that the colonial laws take precedence. Thus there is little scope for judicial protection from abuse.

Substantive law sets the frame for procedural law. The protection of the rights of the citizen in procedural law against police abuse has been steadily eroded by a series of panics in response to crime waves. The Gun Court Act of 1976 removed the guarantee of trial by jury in serious cases where the accused is faced with the prospect of extended incarceration and the Suppression of Crimes Act of 1974 extended the powers of search without warrants (individuals and houses) and of arrest and detention.

Arrest without a warrant is permitted where the police may reasonably suspect that the person has committed or is about to commit a crime. Preventive arrest is also allowed where a breach of the peace is anticipated – even if no crime is about to be committed [Carnegie 1991:15]. The motivation of political control, which inspired the above, effectively removes the safeguards against arbitrary police action. In any event, any check on police powers of arrest is undermined by appointing most of the senior police officers as justices of the peace, thereby making them competent to issue warrants.

The right of access to legal advice at the time of arrest is not constitutionally guaranteed in Jamaica. This contrasts with other Commonwealth Caribbean countries, such as Barbados and Trinidad and Tobago [see Carnegie 1991:11]. The police are required to inform the suspect of the reasons for his arrest "as soon as reasonably practicable" [Jamaica Constitution, ch.3, sec.15(2)] rather than at the time of arrest. In practice, arrest is used as an investigative tool, whereby the bodies of the sources of information, including that of nonsuspects, are held to ransom in order to coerce the transfer of information to the police. In practice, there are usually no time limits on this process.

The use of illegally obtained evidence is left to the discretion of the judge. With the exception of coerced confessions, Jamaican citizens may thus be convicted on illegally obtained evidence [Carnegie 1991:22]. Regardless of this, for all practical purposes, the notion of illegally obtained evidence was effectively erased by the Suppression of Crimes Act.

Generally, censure of the police for false arrests, malicious prosecution and breaches of procedural law are subject only to civil action. Small awards are usually returned by the courts for cases of undue physical harm inflicted by the police. The settlement of such cases out of court or in the civil courts, as is usually the case, has had two unwelcome effects. It does not establish a record of criminal case laws against which the police can be held to account in the event of future abuses of citizens rights; nor does it affect the record of the police officer in question. In the absence of formally established guilt, no documentation is done and the event is therefore never taken into account in considering internal disciplinary action, promotions and the like.

In reality, there is little respect for due process, as evidenced by the treatment of such violations by the state itself. This shows a weak commitment to democracy. As noted earlier, the police operate on the principle of factual rather then legal guilt, and the criminal justice system and state policy tend to be supportive of this, as inferred from their practices.

These practices are structurally reinforced by the system of rewards. In the JCF, reward power is used to advance narrow political ends; therefore, as in any power culture, individuals advance to the extent that they are power conscious and politically oriented. This reward system (and punishment, which is based on the same principle) tends to encourage deviant rather than socially valued behaviour. For example, promotions and even symbolic rewards (national honours) tend to reinforce crime fighting by any means.

This is congruent with the JCF subculture (which is action oriented and rights disregarding). Service oriented work is not usually rewarded, neither is it associated with high status. Behaviour is thus consistent with a reward structure that reinforces the traditional style of police work. Stagnancy, indolence and ineffectiveness are outcomes associated with security of tenure coupled with this nonmeritocratic reward system. As any worthwhile programme of reform of the JCF must entail fundamental changes in its structures, some examination of the attitudes of the members of the Force to the organizational principles of the JCF is therefore warranted.

Attitudes to the Organizational Principles of the Traditional Model of Policing

These attitudes are explored in relation to the following aspects: the paramilitary application of the principles of hierarchy and centralization, internal participation in decision making, exclusivity (that is, female and civilian inclusion) and openness.

The survey data suggest that most police personnel are critical of the organizational principles on which the existing paramilitary model of policing is based. Generally, these attitudes are conditioned by rank. It is to be expected that the more assimilated one is into the system and the more power one wields in it, the less critical one is likely to be of it. The data confirm this. This is especially so with regard to the principles governing the internal relations of control, that is, hierarchy, centralization and participation in decision making.

As expected, a monotonic pattern was observed in the data, with the lower ranks being most critical of these principles and the officers being least critical. Interestingly, supervisors tended to be almost as critical of these principles as were the lower ranks. Thus, while only 28 percent of the officers felt that the Force was too hierarchical, 77 percent of noncommissioned officers (NCOs) and 76 percent of those in the lowest rank were of this view ($p < .0013$). Similarly, while 35 percent of the officers felt that the JCF was too central- ized, 58 percent of the NCOs and 59 percent of constables were of like view ($p < .0000$), and logically associated with this, majorities among all ranks but increasing as rank decreases were for greater participation in the decision-making process. Fifty percent of the officers, 61 percent of NCOs and 89 percent of the constables were supportive of a more participatory process ($p < .0000$).

Although critical of the principles on which the model of policing is based, they tend to be very conservative on the correctives to these principles. Support for change is not consistent with the degree of criticism of existing structures. For example, whereas 79 percent felt that the JCF was too hierarchical, only 20 percent agreed that the hierarchy should be further flattened. This inconsistency was most evident among the lower ranks. The exception to this contradictory attitude set was that opposition to the level of centralization was accompanied by support for decentralization. Consistent with this, the majority across all ranks were supportive of a more participatory organization of their work, and more collegial team type structures rather than military command type relations. This seemed to have been based on a fear of their supervisors becoming oppressive, seemingly omnipotent demigods. During the tenure of Colonel MacMillan, many warmed to the idea of their supervisors being held accountable rather than passing the buck downward and scapegoating the lower ranks.

These attitudinal inconsistencies are strongly shaped by self-regarding concerns. For instance, it was expected that (being historically disadvantaged) there would have been greater support for change among the women than among the men, yet they tended to be more conservative. They were supportive of changes narrowly related to women, but not for the associated universal principles. For example, they were for greater inclusion of women but against greater openness of the Force in general; for more promotions of women but not for the consistent application of the principle of merit. These self-regarding attitudes suggest complications for any reform process, and will be discussed in chapter 9.

It is apparent that, although most of the members of the JCF are critical of the existing organizational principles, their response is mediated by narrow self-interest. Further analysis, examining the sociopolitical assumptions on which these principles were based, is warranted. This analysis will attempt to extend the critique of the colonial paramilitary model of policing beyond issues of its ineffectiveness, as already discussed, to a more explicit philosophical scrutiny of its principles.

Principles on which the Security Model of Policing is Based

The discussion will centre not on the principles as they were received but as they are nuanced today – principles of authoritarianism; differential policing against the poor; a statal view of offending, policing and punishment; and a nonparticipatory approach to governance, especially on issues of security and policing.

The overriding principle is one of profound authoritarianism, which governs all of the relationships of the JCF. This authoritarianism is nurtured by a bifurcated view of the society – rulers and ruled, knowledgeable and ignorant, respectable and disreputable, good and bad. These differences are ascribed to groups due to the nature of the class-race structure of society, that colours all social relationships, and which is based on notions of "place" as a social position carrying role expectations. Thus it is believed that order could be easily maintained if only these roles were embraced.

This belief rests on a peculiar view of the nature of the urban poor – that they are not rational, that they are incapable of deferring self-gratification in order to achieve more lasting goals, and that therefore they cannot be trusted to act in their own interests. Thus they need to be ruled by force if any constructive developmental project is to succeed. The police are responsive to the locus of social and political power and therefore tend to practice differential policing against the poor. This is further reinforced by a statal view of offending, policing and punishment. From the standpoint of the offender, most forms of criminality are only offences against the state, not the society. Thus policing is, first and foremost, state interested. And as law giving has no roots in our indigenous customs or commonly accepted authority, law enforcement is not based on authentic and consensual processes.

This paternalistic view of the people as being incapable of taking responsibility for their own security has partially contributed to a nonparticipatory approach to governance, especially on issues of security and policing. Furthermore, as the people are not treated as a source of authority and legitimation, the police are not regarded as being accountable to them.

Conclusion

A profoundly Hobbesian view of man and society informs the model of policing in this society. The necessity for control is evident and generally accepted, but a state-police monopoly, or even primacy, as agents of control is more associated with an authoritarian control model than a democratic one. This approach is unworkable for problem solving, which requires community engagement and partnership with the police. Even more importantly, this authoritarian model of police style and administration may degenerate into a new (undemocratic) mode of political administration.

The structural changes within the JCF have not kept pace with the changes in the society and crime – criminality. Little regenerative capacity is possible as it is presently structured. At the level of internal relations, this state precludes initiative and team work – both vital to modern policing. An alternative model of policing, based on a democratic ethos, is needed (which is therefore more resistant to the degeneration of democracy). Problems associated with the model will be explored in more detail in the following chapter.

Section II

The Problems

3

Rank and

Money in the Bank:

Corruption in the JCF

High levels of police corruption are usually associated with low levels of police responsiveness to the public, a negative service orientation and ineffectiveness in detecting crime [cf. Danns 1982:92–96; Goldstein 1977:187]. In the ex-colonial context, these features are not necessarily caused by corruption but are certainly intensified by it. Police deviance tends to subvert internal and external accountability, as well as public confidence in, and cooperation with, the police. Indeed, institutionalized corruption may signify a breakdown in law, with the security forces becoming predators rather than protectors. The extent and character of corruption in the police institution may not simply affect its effectiveness but, more important, it may, in very profound ways alter its symbolic representation in the consciousness of the population it is supposed to serve, thus contributing handsomely to the legitimacy crisis. Also of importance from the viewpoint of this study, it props internal resistance to reform by providing additional motivation and the social bonding that facilitates the sociopolitical networking for the reinforcement of a conservative coalition, and the material resources that enable aspects of the resistance to change.[1] Thus the prospects for any reform project cannot be properly understood without reference to police corruption. Here police corruption is studied as both a target of reform and a source of resistance to it.

The aim of the chapter is to uncover the logic of corruption in the JCF and to explore the aspects of its effects associated with the legitimacy crisis. The prevalence of police corruption, its nature and the various forms of its expression, the process of its institutionalization (including the socialization process by which corrupt practices are transmitted), the levels of tolerance of corruption within the JCF and its justificatory rationalizations are analysed. The attempts at censuring it and the resistance to this are discussed later in chapter 7.

The attitude survey is used as but one data source on police corruption. Anticipating the limits placed on this instrument by the sensitivities and subcultural codes of the police, and the high threat level at the time of the survey (corruption was then a central target of the JCF High Command), this probe was limited to rough measures of the institutionalization of corruption, with indicators of its prevalence, perceptions of its sources and attitudes to its treatment (which are taken as indicative of the degree of permissiveness within the Force). The data are most useful as measures of permissiveness.[2] Police records, interviews with senior officers and citizens' complaints provided useful additional sources.

Police *corruption* is defined here as the misuse by police personnel of their office or authority for personal or other particularistic ends [Goldstein 1977:188]. These ends are not restricted to pecuniary or material values; symbolic values, such as power and status, are also included. Nor is the beneficiary restricted to the constable involved; it may also be an institution such as a political party or the police force itself. This definition, as its author notes [Goldstein 1977:88], avoids being either too inclusive (for example, including the acceptance of hospitable gestures from citizens with no intent to secure preferential treatment or the waiving of sanctions in the future [cf. Lundman 1985:158]) or too exclusive (for example excluding transactions involving symbolic values [cf. Danns 1982:92]). The definition of corruption adopted by the JCF is similarly broad [see JCF 1992a, 1:8].

Corruption must be distinguished from criminality. The former need not entail a violation of the law, and the latter need not entail the exploitation of the authority of the police. However, in forces where corruption is institutionalized, both corruption and criminality tend to be strongly associated, and for this reason, while police criminality is treated as conceptually distinct, it is included in this discussion.

Typology of Corruption

Having defined corruption, the next analytically useful step would be to categorize its forms. Typologies commonly use as their organizing principles the forms of corruption [see Alpert and Dunham 1988:100–104], the degree of corruption of the subject (conceptualized as a continuum from "grass eaters", through to "meat eaters" and rogues) and the intensity of the activity (habitual meat eaters, occasional meat eaters and so forth) [Goldstein 1977:193]. An understanding of the internal and external stimuli inducing corrupt behaviour is essential for developing enduring solutions to this problem. An analytically useful typology, it is argued, should therefore illuminate both the motives of the subjects and the opportunity structures [Alpert and Dunham 1988:94–97]. Attempted below is a typology consistent with these principles and the above definition. The types isolated are: entrepreneurial corruption, administrative corruption, police brutality and political corruption.

Entrepreneurial corruption involves the use of the authority of the office of constable and the power resources derived from it as assets and sources of opportunities to be aggressively and systematically exploited for personal material gain, not simply to acquire additional income or wealth but for the accumulation of capital. The forms of this type of activity vary across units and are closely related to the functions of the units and the associated opportunity structure. Thus, the Mobile Reserve, which has primarily a public order riot control function, corruptly provides security services for major sports and entertainment events. The Canine Division facilitates drug smuggling. The members of the Narcotics Division exploit professionally acquired information to shakedown drug traffickers and even directly participate in drug trading for the export and local retail markets. The Transport and Repairs Division is involved in the illicit sale of car parts that are provided for the maintenance of the police fleet; members of the Traffic Division participate in the minibus protection rackets; and the CIB operatives engage in the establishment of tributary relations with criminals in exchange for protection, and so forth. The popular Jamaican adage, which Bayat reminds us is of Cameroonian origin, states, "The goat eats where it is tethered"; the saying fully applies here [Bayat 1993].

The most extreme cases of entrepreneurial corruption involve total immersion in the underground economy. Some constables have become major players in large international drug trafficking and local distribution networks. Others operate at lower levels, for example regularly spending their vacations engaging in street level drug trading in the USA, where some have been convicted of these crimes.[3] Entrepreneurial corruption tends to lead to the development of stable relations between police and criminals and an interchangeability or blurring of the distinction between the two. With successful accumulation and the establishment of regular businesses, they tend to remain in the force simply to better protect their illegal projects.

The main areas of legitimate investment (using this illegitimately acquired wealth) are in transport, entertainment and the security services. In these areas they are best able to exploit their skills, the authority of their office, and contacts within the state bureaucracy and the government for the approval of licences, contracts and so forth.

Because of the highly visible models of success in this form of corruption, many of whom are celebrated inside and outside the JCF, policing has increasingly come to be seen as a relatively low-risk (not just in relation to criminal sanctions but also career costs) window of opportunity for rapid accumulation in the underground economy, thereby attracting those in search of such opportunities. These opportunities are to be found not only in the operational field, where contact can be made with drug trafficking networks and other lucrative criminal enterprises, but also in the mundane administrative functions of the force.

Administrative corruption has external and internal dimensions. Externally, interface with the public in the execution of one's duties is used to maximize personal financial returns from these transactions, and internally, it is associated with the management of personnel functions. The first involves predation, that is, the extortion of "taxes" for the provision of normal services such as the issuing and renewing of firearm licences, and the processing of passports and police records. This exploits the bureaucratic inefficiencies and poor internal systems of accountability. Opportunities for this type of corruption exist at all levels of the hierarchy, but they tend to be concentrated at the managerial ranks. Internally, the manipulation of promotions (allowing previews of the papers for promotional examinations, politically inspired performance evaluations) and postings, as rewards for corrupt services, are some expressions of administrative corruption. The activities involve transactions within the security establishment and are usually associated with organizational positioning, as well as power and status acquisition and preservation as ends in themselves or in the service of party political ends. These forms of corruption lead to internal dysfunctions. They corrode discipline and distort the internal reward system, consequently discouraging performance. Administrative corruption also protects those engaged in other forms of deviance such as brutality.

Police brutality involves the unwarranted, unjustifiable, often illegal use of violence as a policing tool. These boundaries are practically impossible to establish. Nevertheless, as a tool, brutality may be applied investigatively, punitively, as a summary judgement in the delivery of street justice, and generally, as a means of social control by the state.

Like the other forms of corruption, police brutality is motivated by the drive for socially valued goods – in this case, the affirmation of authority or at least power over the citizen, and status within the organization. As his authority has tended to be problematic (historically, authority was associated with class and colour identities other than his own), the constable, like other lower level state officials in the Caribbean, seems to regard the assertion of power and particularly its negative use, including the withholding of services, as validation of his self-importance. In the Jamaican, and perhaps wider Caribbean context, police brutality is thus largely authority-seeking violence. The more problematic their moral and legal authority become, the higher the levels of violence. In the face of "disrespect from young males" or displays of any disregard for police authority, police brutality often becomes an exhibition designed to demonstrate the total power, including the power of life and death, over the victim, and its corollary, the powerlessness of the victim. Thus this power must appear to be demonstrably absolute, unmediated by law, unaccountable to and disregarding of public protests. This is the police expression of the more general tyranny of the petty official that pervades most state institutions and beyond. Here, the self-importance of the petty official is affirmed by having people unnecessarily wait on them or misapplying rules and in some fashion demonstrating arbitrariness in their treatment of people, as a way of communicating their power. It is perhaps an invitation to those of higher social status to show respect and those of lower status to show deference.

The struggle for respect and status is bound up with the quest for power. Status deprivation has led to a prevalence of power oriented personalities, perhaps as the modal personality type in Jamaican society. This power is, for the constable, largely limited in its expressions to physical aggressiveness. Physical power is perhaps the most widely distributed, easily commanded and readily amplified (by accessible implements of violence) power resource. The constable is even more greatly advantaged in this regard, enjoying a legal monopoly on its use, often with little real constraints. Disregard for police authority, a defiant attitude, or, simply, inadequate demonstrations of deference therefore easily precipitate police violence.

This negative power orientation is universal, but the diffused authoritarianism and tyranny of the petty official associated with it have some specific Caribbean expressions and sources, which have been analysed in some of its political expressions as authoritarian leader-led relations by Singham [1968] and Stone [1980:91–110], with Beckford [1972] laying bare its socioeconomic roots in plantation work relations. In the JCF, this abuse of power reveals and reinforces, via its arbitrariness in treating with routine events, the existing powerlessness of the citizen and apparent omnipotence of the state. As it is socially controlling, this type of behaviour is institutionally rewarded, and consequently pursued by individual constables as instrumental in securing other goods, establishing visibility and reputation, and enhancing one's status and authority within the Force.

Its prevalence is guaranteed by a rather good fit between ex-colonial structures of power (exclusive and controlling) and the power oriented personality types which are attracted to the Force. It is also indicative of the increasing difficulties in controlling large sections of the urban poor, and the extension of the use of coercive force beyond protection to repression (this is discussed below). The police, of course, engage in other forms of abuse, but this discussion will focus on the physical forms, as they are perhaps the most injurious and measurable.

In 1994, 40 percent of all complaints by the public against the police were related to cases of brutality and the unjustifiable use of violence [JCF 1994:Appendix B]. Police brutality is highly institutionalized, especially within the action oriented "front line" units, and finds wide approval within the Force. In 1991, 52 percent of the officer corps approved of the then relatively high levels of police violence, and 54 percent specifically supported the extrajudicial killing of gun criminals as a means of crime control [Harriott 1994:324]. At the time of the 1994 survey on which this study is based, the level of police violence had decreased but still remained problematic. Some 66 percent approved of the level of violence at that time and 12 percent felt that the Force was becoming ineffective as a result of the restraints on the use of violence imposed by the new commissioner.

Police brutality in the Jamaican context is not simply violence imposed on the innocent and the unsuspecting by the police [cf. Americas Watch 1986]. In its protective mode, that is, when directed at known violent criminals, it is usually supported and often encouraged by at least a large minority of the population and quite publicly in very explicit language by some opinion leaders [cf. Stone 1995:169; Cargill 1986 cited in Chevigny 1995:215] and often members of the political administration [see Harriott 1994]. This is why, at the level of the JCF as an institution, police vigilantism is understandably but somewhat contradictorily inspired by a quest for legitimacy; a legitimacy of ends. By police vigilantism is meant the organized, systematic and usually state approved efforts by individual members and groups within the police force to summarily execute criminal suspects. It profoundly reflects the crisis of policing in that it is a measure of the extent to which the state is forced to violate its own rules and to step beyond the boundaries of democratic governance in order to maintain order.

The primary justificatory argument for police vigilantism that presents it as being essentially benign runs as follows: if crime is controlled and order achieved then, on this logic, the legitimacy stocks of the Force would have been enhanced, regardless of the means used. Such an approach treats the instrumental-utilitarian principle as the fundamental legitimating canon. Thus rights, including the right to life, are not seen as inalienable. Rights are attached to a particular concept of personhood whereby they may be acquired to different degrees based on ascribed or achieved status, and may similarly be lost by degrees, as changes in the community lead to a re-evaluation of the roles of the subject or as these subjects lose their capacity to contribute to the social good. It may certainly be lost if one becomes a serious threat to one's *own* community (thus the regaled "community protector" of today may become a parasite and pariah tomorrow). One consequence of this is social excoriation of such "nonpersons" who may then be seen as morally acceptable targets for vigilantes, including police vigilantes. Support for vigilantism has tended to be somewhat lower in the general population than among police personnel but nevertheless has remained fairly high since the mid 1980s (a minimum of 42 percent), at times reflecting majority opinion [Stone

1991a:30]. This licence for brutality *in the protective mode* is, however, often misdirected, at times becoming repressive and politically engaging.

Political corruption entails the use of police power by the political parties in furtherance of party objectives, including the securing and maintenance of political power. Police interventionism in support of police interests similarly corrupts the political process, but this is discussed elsewhere [see Harriott 1994]. The expressions of political corruption include participation in election rigging, intelligence gathering on police operations for the parties enabling them to better protect party strongholds from police actions, supplying ammunition, political terrorism, and murder. There are few limits. The JCF has contributed handsomely to the corruption of the electoral process and to the reproduction of the antidemocratic texture of local urban politics.

The JCF has been a major player in elections since 1980. Its activities have been characterized by politically biased law enforcement, especially during election campaigns. This includes the unjustifiable arrest, detention and general harassment of activists of the opposing party; collusion in ballot rigging; and permitting and aiding the violent intimidation and even, in some cases, elimination of the more violent competitors of the opposing party [Kaufman 1985; Duffus 1989:9–12; Jamaica Labour Party (JLP) 1993:18].

The impact of politically biased police activity is great and the effect systematic, as police tend to vote *en bloc* [Harriott 1994:452–55]. The minority party will thus tend to face the full weight of this police activism. The Maverley incident of 1993 is an example of this. The leader of the Opposition JLP was barricaded in a polling station on election day by a group of progovernment People's National Party (PNP) supporters who accused him and his party of ballot rigging. This led to a confrontation between rival police operatives affiliated to both parties, which was eventually nonviolently resolved by the intervention of the army and prudent party leadership.[4] It is this aggressive activism that led to the labelling of police personnel as PNP and JLP police, and the blurring of the distinction between the police and political thugs. If policing is seen as policing for either political party, then it become increasingly regarded as politically repressive. The consequent delegitimization of the Force led to a proposal that the army displace the police in the more problematic urban areas during elections [Duffus 1989].

Political corruption in the JCF is not limited to election rigging. The day-to-day operations of the Force are manipulated, and selective law enforcement encouraged, in order to preserve the hold of the party in power. In 1991, 36 percent of the JCF officer corps reported that the political directorate had intervened to restrain police operations and protect party strongholds, and only 28 percent denied this was a reality (the remaining 36 percent refused to confirm or deny as they claimed not to have had any direct encounters with this). Some 20 percent reported having experienced interventions by politicians to have charges against suspects dropped, and another 40 percent refused to confirm or deny this [Harriott 1994:462]. Impressionistic evidence, based on interviews with police of all ranks, suggests that this interventionism has decreased considerably over the last two years, but the problem remains acute in some police divisions. Political patronage and immunity from sanctions are some of the levers used to effect political corruption. The intensity of party activism, the extent of political interference in the routine operations of the Force via both formal and informal channels, the ability to influence, indeed direct, punishment (transfers) and rewards (promotions, postings, perks) all serve to widen the scope for political corruption.

Corruption in its various types and forms affects every aspect of police work, with implications for the entire criminal justice system. The *corruption of the judicial process* may be contrived to ensure either acquittals or convictions. Efforts to ensure acquittals typically involve tampering with evidence (which seems to occur most frequently in drug cases), suborning or intimidating witnesses, or both, and in a few cases even physically eliminating them (usually where police personnel with a violent history are on trial for capital offences). This latter practice has severely damaged the reputation of the Force and contributed to difficulties in its, and indeed Jamaica's, relationship with the USA. Distrust of the police has led to increasing demands by the USA for its drug enforcement agents to operate independently of the Jamaican police within the jurisdiction of Jamaica.[5]

Corrupt practices may also be used to secure convictions. This may be done by "connecting" contrived or real evidence to a suspect. This has occurred in failed extortion bids but is more commonly used to convict elusive criminals who may be innocent of the particular charge levelled against them, but who are at least reputationally known to the police as criminals, and who flaunt their criminality and are able to escape justice or effectively negotiate immunity from the justice system. It also involves the violent extraction of confessions and less direct self- (and other) incrimination [Focus Group 1994; Americas Watch 1986:38–44].

Jamaica's procedural laws are relatively weak with regard to the powers of investigation and arrest by the police [see Carnegie 1991]. They compare unfavourably with the UK's Police and Criminal Evidence Act 1984 (PACE) [see Sanders and Young 1995] and the US system [see Potts 1983; Incardi 1993:229–66]. For example, there is no right of access to a lawyer; corruptly acquired evidence may be permitted in the courts; and there is little real protection against searches without warrants and against false arrest. Even if convictions are not secured, the police may punish with impunity, as suspects may be forced to spend lengthy periods in jail without recourse. These practices have been protected against constitutional challenges by a clause that establishes the priority of colonial laws which predate the Independence constitution.

These types of corruption are expressed at the individual and institutionalized levels. The latter is more far reaching in its effects on the state system, its consequences for governance, and the difficulties for control. The analysis thus focuses on this aspect. Alpert and Dunham [1988:98] and Lundman [1985] distinguish the former from the latter by the following: peer support for corruption; support for corrupt behaviour by the dominant administrative coalition; collective approval of law breaking as a means of achieving legitimate and/or illegitimate institutional goals; and compliance with the internal operating norms supportive of corruption ensured through recruitment and socialization.

Deviant socialization and peer group support are not features peculiar to institutionalized corruption; they are also features of individual corruption. However, they are the structures that corrupt individuals. Thus, while the attributes listed above are all necessary, they are not all distinguishing features of institutionalized corruption. However, taken together they sharply distinguish corrupt police forces from police forces with corrupt individuals.

Institutionalized Corruption

Corruption in the JCF has been highly institutionalized, and despite the recent disruptions, remains fairly well organized, with some variation across units. Motivated by the misplaced desire to safeguard the authority of the police, to evade public scrutiny and deflect demands for greater accountability of their organizations, and plain self-preservation, the JCF High Command, like most police administrators elsewhere, has tended to accept only the existence of individual corruption. This is the "bad egg" thesis. It personalizes the problem, obscures its quality (that corruption has become an attribute of the Force itself) and oversimplifies the solutions (reform, neutralize or remove the bad eggs) by focusing on the need for individual rather than institutional changes. Image management is seen as fundamental for masking the nature of the problem, protecting the institution and constructing its legitimacy.

The institutionalization of corruption as a process is seen as having two general features: first, a bottom-up process permeating the organization; and second, a top-down process of increasing permissiveness that progresses from endurance to tolerance to acceptance of corrupt behaviour [Alpert and Dunham 1988]. As individual corruption endures, negative sanctions tend to be waived. Corruption consequently becomes more prevalent, permeates the organization, including the top echelons, and gains acceptance as a perquisite and, in some instances, as an entitlement and customary right. Thereafter it is routinized and done overtly with impunity. Finally, it is defended and justified. Such outcomes, as is widely recognized in the literature, are largely but not solely due to the inducement of structures; they are the result of an interactive process (between structural inducements and individual behaviour) which include the impact of individual behaviour on the institution.

This general pattern of corruption largely holds true for the JCF. But the process was accelerated by the early postindependence approval of the use of illegal means in crime fighting, and politically corrupt conduct. The political élite and police High Command were thus largely responsible for the growth of corrupt activity. It was largely a top-down process. In this setting, the bad eggs provide a highly visible model of successful achievement by illegitimate means. They symbolically affirm that corruption is a viable strategy for quick, easy and relatively safe accumulation of wealth, status and power within the JCF. They are usually aggressive and open purveyors of deviant values, who constantly test and seek to extend or redefine the boundaries of subculturally acceptable corrupt practices. They are products, as well as reproducers and reshapers, of their institutional milieu.

Central to the passage of that phase in the process of institutionalization, from endurance to acceptance, has been the waiving of sanctions. Official encouragement of rule breaking by approving the use of illegal means in crime control confronted the police High Command with the obligation to protect the individuals and units involved in such actions. This official protection was exploited for other more self-aggrandizing and materially rewarding forms of corrupt behaviour.

The complicity of the officer corps, and the consequent moral difficulties in treating with corruption, led to a generalized waiving of sanctions with regard to all disciplinary matters. Some 30 percent of the respondents did report having to face disciplinary charges (including orderly room charges) at some point in their careers. That 41 percent of these were within the two years prior to the study (that is, during the tenure of Commissioner MacMillan) indicates the recency of the use of negative sanctions. Even then, these were in the main for minor infractions, more related to disciplinary breaches than corruption and usually involved the imposition of small fines. This is often meaningless to the offender, particularly the police entrepreneur. Disciplinary charges are usually imposed in cases of flagrant rule violation and repeat offending. Yet only 51 percent of all offenders were found guilty for the last offence with which they were charged.

Sanctions against corruption are skewed to the bottom of the rank structure, while, as will be shown, corruption has been skewed to the top. This in turn led to reduced internal surveillance and willingness to impose sanctions. This generally permissive attitude to corruption and managerial indifference to disciplinary matters are further evidenced by the reluctance to investigate citizens' complaints and to treat with internal disciplinary matters. Of the 1,406 cases reported for the period 1990–93, only 22 percent were investigated and settled. Moreover, according to the records of the Police Complaints Division, JCF, in only 20 percent of these cases was internal disciplinary action taken.

Corrupt behaviour is able to evade censure as, in addition to the poor record of treating the reported cases, much of it goes largely unreported. This applies most fully to the entrepreneurial and administrative types of corruption which are largely consensual and involve the complicity of the public. But even for the other victim-generating types, such as police brutality, complainants are, in some instances, dissuaded by the constables taking the reports, and the investigative process may be frustrated or corrupted. Serious censure is usually associated mainly with criminal convictions. As the officers became more tolerant, internal reluctance to report corrupt behaviour and even breaches of discipline grew. To many, it made no sense to report one's peers "if officers are tolerant and unlikely to act".[6] Corruption thus endured, became omnipresent and increasingly overt, yet unseen. It had become accepted.

The institutionalization of corruption, as reflected in its pervasiveness and range of forms, is evidenced by more objective measures. Complaints from the public (either directly to the Police Complaints Division or to the Police Public Complaints Authority) and internally initiated action, confirm that corruption, misconduct and criminality are extensive and affect most units and divisions with the exception of innocuous zero-opportunity units such as the band.

In 1994 there were 787 complaints from the public against police personnel, representing an increase of 53 percent over 1993, and in 1995 there were 962 complaints, representing an additional increase of 22 percent [JCF *Annual Report* 1994:Appendix B; 1995:10].[7] At the end of 1996, the commissioner of police reported that some 1,000 cases of corruption were being investigated by Internal Affairs, that is, one for every six constables in the Force.[8] This increase was consistent with the historical trend. But its magnitude suggests that it was perhaps stimulated by greater responsiveness and willingness on the part of the High Command under the new reformist leadership to act on the complaints of citizens. (This is indicated by the shift from reporting to the ombudsman and the Police Public Complaints Authority to complaining directly to the police.) As the justification for these units was public distrust of the willingness and capacity of the police to take self-correcting measures, increased direct reporting to the police may reasonably be taken as reflecting renewed confidence in the self-regulatory efforts of the leadership of the Force, although most complaints against police violence are reported to the Police Public Complaints Authority [see Table 3.1].

Our immediate interest, however, is in the structure of the complaints, as it may assist in sharply defining the problem from the perspective of the subpopulations who are usually targets of policing. In 1994, 40 percent of the complaints to the Police Public Complaints Authority were related to acts of violence, 9 percent to harassment and intimidation, and 33 percent to entrepreneurial type corruption [Table 3.2]. The pattern of police criminality and corruption shows a predominance of violent offending. This excessive use of violence is not restricted to the special units but is mostly associated with them. In 1995 complaints regarding the use of violence and intimidation had increased to 56 percent of all complaints [JCF *Annual Report* 1995:Appendix D].

If police violence is such a central concern of the public, then not just outcomes but the means used to achieve those outcomes are perhaps more important to the process of delegitimation than is thought. Such lawless violence may reinforce its symbolic representation as "Babylon" or a repressive force whose political values are not consistent with a democratic ethos. This kind of symbolic representation is perhaps more profoundly delegitimating than the reality of ineffectiveness in managing or controlling crime. An ineffective force may simply be regarded as being in need of improvement and reform; a repressive force may be viewed as something to be defeated and abolished.

Table 3.1 Police Criminality, Corruption and Misconduct 1994 (percentage)

Offence	Reported Complaints by Data Sources		
	Police Complaints Division	Police Public Complaints Authority	Internally Initiated
Brutality/violent crimes	22	43	13
Incivility/misconduct	28	25	22 *
Harassment/political	3	6	5
Violations of due process	5	–	14
Administrative corruption and property crimes	4	7 *	31
Maladministration	–	–	10
Negligence/indolence	9	30	5
N	472	318	143

Source: Internally initiated disciplinary actions – JCF Register of the Court of Inquiry

Note: The sum of the columns is less than 100 percent as only the categories of interest are presented. In the case of the Police Public Complaints Authority, missing data is great as these data were not reworked into the categories used by the author.

* Year ending March 1994.

Some of these complaints (and investigations) result in criminal charges being laid against offending police officers. In 1993–94 the rate of offending among police officers was 2,500 per 100,000. This was considerably higher than the crime rate for the society as a whole which was 2,110 per 100,000. Even more alarming, but not surprising, the rate of violent crime among police officers was 2,033 per 100,000. This was more than twice the rate of violent criminality among the general population which was 897 per 100,000.[9] This trend has persisted since the mid 1980s. For the period 1987–94, the mean rate of violent offending in the JCF was 2,793 per 100,000, while for the society it was 733 per 100,000. There is no sharper commentary on the pervasiveness of deviant and criminal behaviour within the Force than this.

Increasingly, police violence is not just directed at citizens but also at colleagues internally. In 1993, 13 percent of all internally initiated disciplinary charges were based on violence of this sort [Charge Book JCF; Table 3.1]. This pattern of police offending is an intensification of the pattern for the society as a whole. The society is caught in a contradictory situation in which its most violent offenders are charged with "keeping the peace".

Entrepreneurial corruption is less visible in the official statistics. Arrests for drug offences have tended mainly to result from externally initiated sting operations, and only more recently, from internal investigations. In 1994, there were three cases of charges related to assisting in the export of drugs [see Charge Book JCF]. As with other Caribbean countries that have become integrated into the international drug trade, the Jamaican police force has become deeply involved. In 1994 there were some 60 confirmed cases of the involvement of police personnel in drug trafficking, with another 20 cases then under investigation.[10]

Table 3.2 Frequency of Police Corruption and Criminality 1988–94 (percentage)

Type	1994	1992	1990	1988*
Administrative	–	–	–	–
Brutality	40	52	48	..(49%)
Case tampering/false arrests	–	7	3	..(5%)
Entrepreneurial	33	4	2	..(1%)
Harassment and intimidation	9	10	12	..(12%)
Political	1	–	–	–

Sources: Police Complaints Unit; Police Public Complaints Authority

* Here misconduct is included. The sum of each column is thus less than 100%.

The popular perception within the Force is that the prevalence of corruption is directly related to rank, with the managerial ranks being regarded as the most corrupt. Returning to the survey data, while 12 percent of the

Force felt the majority of their JCF colleagues and members of their unit were corrupt, 30 percent felt that most officers, and 32 percent that most senior officers were corrupt ($p < .0001$) [Table 3.4]. When cross-tabulating for rank, this pattern was enhanced. Those in the lowest rank (constables) were highly critical of their supervisors and officers, with 38 percent being of the view that most of their senior officers were corrupt ($p < .0000$).

These data should be interpreted in the light of our knowledge of police subcultures – their sense of group loyalty and code of protective silence, especially with respect to unit members. The data suggest that peer bonding is stronger at the bottom than at the top of the hierarchy. The top tends to be more competitive. Most senior personnel have a record of participation in the intensely competitive politico-bureaucratic game that is played within the JCF, and at times, the figurative blood of losers and other casualties has been left on the court. All personnel tend to have vivid memories of the various battles. They are thus less cohesive.

The attitude of the rank and file to the integrity of the officers and the belief that corruption is greater at the top have grave implications for the officers' authority and ability to maintain discipline. This difficulty is captured in the euphemistically labelled category "incivility" in Table 3.1, which accounts for 22 percent of all internally initiated charges. These are usually cases of extreme insubordination, including verbal and even physical abuse of supervisory personnel. Indeed, officers were seen as agents of the deviant socialization, and thus the prime source of corruption in their commands. Some 43 percent of the Force and 49 percent of constables and junior NCOs reported that pressure from supervisors was a major source of the growth of corruption within the JCF.

Peer support for corrupt behaviour is intense and pervasive. Some 43 percent of JCF personnel reported strong peer support for corrupt behaviour, and 49 percent cited this as a major source of pressure for corrupt involvement. With this level of institutionalization, the associated negative reputation of the JCF in the society, and the consequent anticipated socialization of new recruits, successive cohorts of police recruits are increasingly likely to attract persons in search of corrupt opportunities.[11]

The force of the justification for corrupt practices is reflected in the feeling of social isolation of those constables who seemed most concerned with its corrosive effects. They reported that to eschew corruption and to "walk the straight and narrow" is to risk being labelled as an "idiot" or an oddity. However, while "idiots" may be tolerated in some sections of the JCF, in others, where corruption is institutionalized, they may find it impossible to successfully fulfil their duties. They may be placed under close surveillance, victimized by their superiors with respect to promotions, and eventually hounded out of the unit.[12]

A good illustration of the degree of peer support for corruption was demonstrated in a case reported at the police station in one of the research communities during the period of this study. The complainant claimed he had paid a detective for providing him with a clean criminal record, and demanded that his money be returned as the detective had failed to honour the arrangement. The duty officer responded by attempting to broker a settlement of the dispute, but the loud demonstration by the complainant unavoidably brought the matter to the attention of the senior supervisor who simply verbally reprimanded the offending policeman, following which the money was returned to the presumed criminal and the matter considered settled.[13] This degree of open peer support and supervisory tolerance makes for the easy organization of corrupt networks.

Organization

Corruption in the JCF thus rapidly progressed (after 1977) and became not just institutionalized but "highly organized" [Focus Group 30 April 1994]. Institutionally organized corruption involves the conflation of the structures of the organized networks with the formal police hierarchy and departmental structures.

Unorganized corruption tends to be most pervasive in intelligence and investigation units. The activities of intelligence operatives and detectives are highly individualized. They are subjected to relatively low levels of internal surveillance and supervision, and as their visibility is lower than that of the uniformed constable, their behaviour also more readily escapes public scrutiny. They enjoy greater autonomy than their uniformed colleagues, and are able to individually initiate investigations and carefully manage the information flow (to their supervisors) on these investigations. They are therefore able to individually exploit their control of information to tap the wealth of their targets.

The worst cases of organized corruption were and are to be found in the (now disbanded) Operations Squad, the Canine Division, Immigration and the Central Records Office. The scope of corrupt activity in the case of the Operations Squad was perhaps the widest. This unit enjoyed extraordinarily wide functions, including political intelligence, counternarcotics operations, homicide investigations and so forth. It was a sort of force within the Force, with its own intelligence, investigative and operational capacity, and with direct streams of resources channelled to it.

Corrupt activity became a team effort here, always with the passive support and often the active engagement of the chain of command within the unit. Accountability to police administrators was routinely breached (with their compliance) in order to facilitate direct reporting to and politically confidential operational direction of this unit by the political directorate.[14] After the removal of the JLP administration in 1989, various criminal charges were laid against a number of the members of the unit, including the operational head of the unit, who was charged with three drug related murders.[15]

At the Canine Division, corruption was coordinated through the established hierarchy. The division relies on the use of sniffer dogs to inspect outgoing cargo at the island's ports. The effectiveness of the dogs hinges on a systematic programme of retraining – otherwise, after six months they lose their capability to detect narcotics. The dogs were neutralized by not retraining them and were used in a manner designed to deceive inspectors from outside the division (JCF and non-JCF). The deliberate use of ineffective dogs could hardly have been achieved without the collusion of the supervisors and officers in the division.[16] This degree of organization was perhaps the outcome of failed attempts at individual efforts. As early as 1990, this practice was detected. A constable was then charged for "not properly utilizing police sniffer dog 'Wolf' to sniff an Air Jamaica baggage or properly checking the luggage for drugs for flight 017 between the hours of 10:00 am and 1:00 pm on 13 April 1987 at the Donald Sangster Airport".[17] Moving large volumes of illegal drugs through customs requires organization and collaboration with the different persons and units involved at the different stages of the security process. Organization within the division was therefore likely to have extended externally into other security units.

The units in which organized corruption tends to be most entrenched are characterized by the following:

- Functionally structured high-reward opportunities for corruption. An example would be the units most involved in antinarcotics operations or access to the ports of entry, or both, such as the Canine Division. The provision of services to assist the export of drugs is priced as a percentage of the value of the cargo, rank of the assisting police person and the risk associated with the particular service. With Jamaica being a major exporter of cannabis and a developing transit country for cocaine, the opportunities are many and the rewards great.

- High levels of coherence. This is generally true of the Force as a whole but tends to be even greater in the small specialized units. The Canine Division, which is a small unit with similar training and physically isolated from the rest of the Force, is a case in point. Similarly, political homogeneity enhances trust and strong interpersonal loyalties, as was the case in the Operations Squad and its precursor as well as subsequent successor units.

- Low visibility within the Force as well as to the public. This is a common feature of most of the units within which corruption is institutionalized.

- High levels of autonomy and low levels of accountability. In the case of the Operations Squad, it operated outside the normal hierarchy and reported directly to the political directorate. The low levels of accountability provide convenient insulation and distance for the High Command and senior officers, as some of these units may be expected to routinely use perverse and illegal means.

- Engagement in officially approved violations of both procedural and substantive law. This is probably the most significant factor. It leads to low levels of formal accountability, to efforts to break the normal channels of internal control, and to setting up of special reporting mechanisms based on politically "reliable" officers. Professional officers tend to put distance between themselves and these operations on ethical grounds as well as for fear of scapegoating.

This process of self-exclusion by those who would resist such activity and the reputational self-selection of those who would engage in these types of operations (where legitimate ends are pursued by illegitimate means) ensure that the leadership of these units tends to fall completely into the hands of the most corrupt individuals. Similarly, at the lower levels of the Force, constables are faced with conformity or exclusion.

Despite the differences in opportunities, with the exception of the General Service personnel, there were no significant discrepancies in perspective across the various units with regard to the pervasiveness of corruption either within their unit or within the Force as a whole [Table 3.3]. Similarly, with the exception of the Intelligence functionaries, there was little variation in proportion of persons engaged in the different functions who felt that the attitude to corruption within the Force was a permissive one [Table 3.3]. There are various possible interpretations of this. One is that most constables are equally protective of their unit, with the exception of the general purpose function where there is weaker unit identity and loyalty. The other more cynical interpretation is that corruption is so endemic that the expected differences have been erased.

Table 3.3 Pervasiveness and Permissiveness of Police Corruption by Function (percentage agreeing)

Item	Intelligence/ Investigation	Traffic Control	General Service	Ops	Admin
Pervasive in unit	10	10	24	12	14
Pervasive in force	29	38	37	37	21
Pervasive among officers	32	33	37	35	21
Permissive unit	41	18	40	41	36
Permissive force	58	30	36	30	33

N = 620–61

Level of Tolerance and Justificatory Arguments

The JCF, like the society, has become highly tolerant of most forms of corruption. This is associated with a process of justification and guilt displacement and diffusion. There are different justifications for the different types of corruption, but they all rest on a common doctrine of necessity.

Entrepreneurial and other materially self-rewarding forms of corruption are tolerated as "survival" or economic necessity. Political corruption is similarly tolerated as career survival, an adjustment to reality, with nonpartisanship being cast as untenable in the context of the JCF, and perhaps an ideological illusion. The corruption of the judicial process in order to secure convictions is regarded as a necessary corrective to an ineffective criminal justice system, with long delays before trials, which make it easy for criminals to corrupt witnesses, jurors and even complainants. It is seen as a self-correcting mechanism that cancels the unjust effects of similarly corrupt activities among defence lawyers. From their perspective, corruption simply balances the tilted scales of Jamaican justice. Just outcomes are perversely delinked from just procedures. Guilt is presumed and procedural law seen as an obstacle to establishing it.

The application of the doctrine of necessity as justification for police vigilantism and the more general use of illegal means in the attempt to control violent crime are grounded in both situational or social-environmental factors and in the attributes of the criminal. The frightening threat of crime to society is coupled with the dehumanization of the criminal as part of a special dangerous class of nonpersons habituated in the use of violence, who may be pursued without regard for the law. As they are presumed to be creatures of a culture of violence who understand only the language of violence, this (it is argued) is the only effective form of discourse [cf. Stone 1995:170]. A sort of "social cleansing" is seen as necessary for the survival of the society.

This has led to the valorization, even celebration, of those constables most adept at using illegal means. As noted earlier, informal mechanisms traditionally associated with political control have been crucial in regulating order in some inner city areas. (Here the gangs effectively constitute an informal local police force. Despite the decline of these mechanisms, they are usually more effective than the formal criminal justice system.) Using their ties to the party machineries as the point of contact, these policemen are able to tap into and to manipulate the informal control systems. They are able to get the gang leaders and dons to surrender or discipline criminals found to be in violation of the informal codes. This is the key factor in their "success" as crime fighters.

This includes not just remote manipulation of these informal community based mechanisms, but the direct use of these methods themselves. Internally, it is largely accepted that the JCF needs both its "Peters" and "Johns". The

"Peters" or "good" police are seen as being useful for public relations purposes while the "Johns" are essential to its core function of crime control. "If you have a problem in the garrison [read inner city] areas you need John" [Focus Group 1995]. Both are seen as complementary and necessary. (This partly explains the protective attitude to the bad eggs.)

The changes in the social organization of crime and criminals (described earlier), and the attendant difficulties for the police, have made resort to these tactics and the general indifference to means more acceptable to the police and the public. But there are problematic aspects to this. For example, police complicity with criminals may yield valuable information, but this information is invariably regulated by the criminals and is usually designed to harass their enemies and competitors. The difficulty, then, is that the police may be treated by the target group as an extension of the collaborating group and as active players in intergang rivalry. This is similar to the delegitimization associated with being regarded as PNP and JLP police.

The use of corrupt means to attain institutional goals (rather than personal ends) is an old dilemma associated with policing [Klockars 1985]. These practices of law enforcement by illegal means, and justice by unjust means, are not occasional or special instances, are not "Dirty Harry" type dilemmas (where reluctance to use illegitimate means against offenders ensures serious negative outcomes for the intended victims of these offenders), but rather routine practices. Thus an intuitive sense of paradox and the view that violations (of the law) that seem to have some social utility are justifiable account for the high levels of tolerance of this type of deviance and explain the difference in the attitude to police cover-ups from cover-ups in other occupations and professions. This crude utilitarian resolution of this problem facilitates guilt diffusion. However, guilt diffusion with regard to the more self-aggrandizing forms of corruption is associated with attributing corruption to structural-situational factors – the structure of human nature, societal pressures and coercion from peers, superiors and external agencies, and so forth.

Within the JCF, it is widely held that corrupt conduct, in its self-regarding and acquisitive forms, is rooted in the innate structure of human motivation. Some 57 percent shared this natural deterministic view that humans are inherently corruptible. High levels of materially self-rewarding corruption are thus easily accounted for by low levels of remuneration. Some 79 percent supported this view. This transfers blame to the government-employer who awards the poor salaries.

By grounding the justification for corrupt activity on a doctrine of necessity, the activity is thereby placed beyond the scope of morality. And even if accepted as within the province of moral discourse, it may even be given a positive moral value. For example, with regard to entrepreneurial forms, this may be taken beyond survival to its celebration as a form of social struggle. Brutality, including extrajudicial killings, is similarly treated by some of those most actively engaged in it, as a morally desirable form of social cleansing.

While the entrepreneurial forms are regarded as within the experience of an empathetic public, brutality and other police specific forms are considered to be truly comprehensible only to fellow police officers. Even if conceded to be within the realm of morality, competence to pass moral judgement only resides within the Force or, even more narrowly, among officers with similar "front line" experiences. This judgement is passed every day in the form of reinforcement. It is at worst dirty work, to which an ungrateful public at times acquiesces, even supports, and at other times opposes, but most of all needs to have done as a necessary condition for the quality of life it enjoys.

Consistent with the view of corruption as necessity is its pervasiveness. This pervasiveness is in turn taken as evidence of its necessity. Police officers tend to cynically associate material success, especially in the field of business, with the use of illegitimate means. Jamaica is seen, with justification, as a corrupt society. As success is based on illegitimate means, to be honest is to suffer a relative disadvantage, without any compensatory benefits to the society. In this context, corrupt behaviour is not viewed as socially corrosive but, rather, as a corrective distributive mechanism.

Two internally popular explanations of corruption within the JCF are associated with this view of the society: a bad society infiltrating the Force; and a bad public tempting the humanly frail police. In the first, police corruption is explained as the outcome of this "rotten public" infiltrating the Force. This was presented initially as a problem of poor recruits. The second variety of the bad public hypothesis blames the public for corrupting the police through bribes. Some 69 percent cited this as a major factor in police corruption [Table 3.4]. It falsely depicts police corruption as passive rather than active and opportunity seeking.

In the lower ranks, guilt diffusion may take the form of presenting themselves as victims who were coerced into corrupt activity by their superiors. They argue that noncompliance might have ruined their careers, as failure to become involved makes one a threat. This extends beyond initiation efforts within the Force to similar efforts on the part of drug dealers who "may report you to the senior officer". Not being corrupt is not simply to forego the rewards offered but to suffer internal sanctions.

The constables who resist deviant socialization risk isolation from the group. The police subculture is not simply a source of tolerance of corruption; rather, it is an expression of this tolerance. Similar codes and even greater coherence in the military do not provide a general protective device for all forms of corruption. The tolerance of corruption is prior to the protection of it.

These factors in their generality are universally encountered in police forces [Niederhoffer 1969]. From a dissection of the justificatory arguments, the analysis may proceed to an examination of its sources.

Table 3.4 Attitudes to Corruption by Rank (percentage agreeing)

	Rank			χ^2	df	p
	Cons	NCO	Officer			
Pervasiveness of corruption						
Pervasive in unit	9	4	6	12.6730	4	.0129
Pervasive in Force	19	18	6	18.6932	4	.0129
Pervasive in officers corps	22	19	8	44.9245	4	.0000
Among senior officers	41	12	4	44.9245	4	.0000
Permissiveness						
Permissive unit	17	15	6	22.3093	4	.0001
Permissive force	37	36	17	14.0004	4	.0172
Sources of corruption						
Poor salaries	89	77	57	61.5140	8	.0000
The public	67	71	82	40.2090	8	.0000
Frustrations with the justice system	51	31	28	30.2430	8	.0000
Peer pressure	48	31	21	26.6100	8	.0000
Pressure from seniors	49	23	21	45.8470	8	.0000
Human nature	61	49	32	20.7490	8	.0000

Sources of Corruption

The intensification and institutionalization of corruption in the JCF has its sources in both external environmental and internal factors. Corruption is a function of the sociopolitical environment. Sherman, for example, highlights community anomie and the outlook of elected officials as perhaps the most important external factors [Sherman 1978, cited in Lundman 1985:162].

The high level of public acceptance of corruption, its presence in routine day-to-day transactions, and the expectations people have in their encounters with them constitute part of the environment in which the police force operates and shapes its notions of what is acceptable. In this sense, and this sense only, there is some substance to the police blaming the public for police corruption.

The protracted economic crisis, the years of hyperinflation and the steady decline in real wages have altered the psychology of the labour force. The unstable and crisis-prone character of the economy and steady social decay have resulted in a shortening of people's time horizons. Long-term planning to achieve life goals, even modest ones such as owning a house, is regarded as pointless. This leads to a "get rich quick" mentality, which pervades the society and the Force. As one constable explained,

My parents could plan for the future. They knew that if they worked hard they could earn a house in their later years. Not so today. Things keep getting out of your reach, the prices keep moving. I couldn't save to buy a car. The only hope is quick accumulation. This is only possible via corruption.[18]

Life goals are not adjusted to the available means; rather innovative means are sought. Given the expansion of opportunities in the underground economy, such an approach is regarded as realistic. This appears to be a classic case of anomie in the Mertonian sense of a means-ends disjuncture, which in the Jamaican setting is the outcome of blocked opportunity and a warped and unjust social structure. (This is why moral neutralization occurs with such facility.) In this context, the distinction between legitimate and illegitimate means becomes blurred. Success is increasingly associated with the latter, while failed social adaptation is associated with conformity to the traditional means of social mobility. The new justificatory arguments and responses to the structural changes in the socioeconomic environment described earlier are associated with a generational shift that was captured by one officer who reported being told by a young constable that, "You are interested in rank, but I am interested in how much I have in the bank."[19]

Expansion of the opportunities for rapid material accumulation and freedom from particularistic discriminations are associated with the underground economy. As crime "industries" and informal and illegal activity grow (and as the police set up specialized units to deal with these problems), so too the opportunities for police corruption have grown. In this context, internal controls and fear of social stigmatization are hardly sufficient constraints. Greater emphasis has to be placed on systems of accountability. In the case of the JCF, this must include accountability to the political leadership.

The outlook of the political leadership sets the tone of public life. In recent years, it has been enveloped in a self-regarding ethos, characterized by a privatization of the political mission and integration into networks protective of narrow special interests, which, as noted earlier, contribute to a corrupt criminogenic market structure.

Politics was the most important initiating factor in the case of the JCF. Use of patronage (for example, arranging privileged access to government housing), the manipulation of promotions and other rewards, and sanctions (transfers) are some of the ways of corrupting the Force. Approval of rule breaking and law breaking undermined the internal systems of accountability.

The operating norms of the Force allowed the exploitation of the new opportunities associated with the expansion of the underground economy. These norms are:

- Poor accountability and control. Centralized systems of upward accountability are easily frustrated by the subculture and the manipulation of information from below. Indeed, centralization has, in the past, been exploited to concentrate the opportunities for administrative corruption at the top. For example, contrary to the established rules of the Force, firearm licences had to be approved by the commissioner of police. This simply concentrated the rewards from this in the form of predation.

- The closed nature of the bureaucracy. Appointments and firing are the purview of the Services Commission. It is difficult to fire police personnel, short of criminal convictions. The rationale for this regime was to protect the Force and its personnel from political manipulation and victimization. The regime failed. The society remains saddled with both a highly politicized Force and the negative consequences of security of tenure (corruption and unresponsiveness).

- Informal networking and bonding on personalistic criteria, which provides protection for deviants. As an institution, the JCF offers unqualified protection of some of these elements and units because, having encouraged the use of corruption as a means for crime control and for narrow party political ends, and having created these deviants, it is in turn obliged to protect deviance.

Corruption in the JCF is thus the product of a concatenation of powerful factors and is highly institutionalized. A multifaceted approach is therefore required if corruption is to be successfully tackled. The institutionalized character of corruption in the JCF meant that prior to the reforms of 1993, investigations and sanctions were rarely initiated internally, but rather derived their impetus from external pressures on the Force.

Difficulties in Treating Corruption

Corruption is generally regarded as too pervasive within the Force and the society (particularly among the economic, administrative and political élite), too structurally rooted with a developed justificatory ideology, for it to be effectively controlled within the Force. Moreover, the entrepreneurial character of corruption provides the social and financial resources to stoutly resist sanctions, while the managerial instruments with which to fight it are ineffective. With this view, campaigns against corruption are at best futile; at worst, they are efforts to offer up a few scapegoats for sacrifice and exercises in victimization and revenge.

This high level of cynicism and tolerance presents difficulties for controlling corruption. There have been three approaches: acquiescence, selective treatment and counterdemocratic repression. Until recently, little attention was paid to corruption control within the Force; the leadership had largely acquiesced. The "bad egg" thesis was widely accepted within the Force and among policy makers. Episodically, symbolic action might be taken as a result of public pressures, which are usually galvanized around incidents of brutality. This is usually the focus of the press and demonstrative actions by the public. Venality, that is, victimless and victim-compliant corruption, is less visible and is left to internal police self-control.

This approach rests on a benign view of corruption and may well have been the result of the mutually beneficial outcomes of police corruption for both the police and the political élite, as well as the latter's fear of police power. Anticorruption drives, initiated by the political leadership, are usually translated into politically selective treatment.

Within the security establishment, the impetus for anticorruption efforts was largely derived from politically corrupt motives and designed to further partisan objectives – a subterfuge for political control and reorientation of sensitive and strategic units. With a change of administration, activists (affiliated to the losing party) who were in strategic units or posts, and who were vulnerable to charges of corruption, were investigated with a view to exacting revenge and smoothing a change of personnel in order to effect tighter control over these units by the incoming administration. This was facilitated by the use of the Special Branch – the most politicized and tightly controlled unit – to conduct these internal investigations. These selective investigations are thus usually quite thorough, and have from time to time led to criminal charges being laid and even convictions secured. This is the source of the view within the JCF [Focus Group 1994] that police self-investigation is effective. This thoroughness, however, was usually absent when the investigations were not self-initiated, but, rather, stemmed from the complaints by citizens or the demands by the ombudsman [see Harriott 1994]. A spin-off effect of the realization of these politically selective anticorruption efforts was the manipulation of public trust in the police and government, as an appearance of effective self-correction is given.

Efforts to break with the above two traditions of treatment (acquiescence and selective treatment) resulted in a strong disciplinary approach during the period under review. But the intractable nature of the corruption in the JCF and the inadequacy of the legal and bureaucratic instruments may propel reformers in a counterdemocratic direction – for example, the Barbados model of informal spies within the Force personally selected by, and loyal to, the commissioner.

For the disciplinary approach to gain acceptance and to work, it must be democratic in orientation and consistent with a wider programme of reforms. These cannot be democratic in some aspects and yet authoritarian, counterdemocratic, in their treatment of corruption. Reform would require new and better instruments of accountability and greater openness to external scrutiny at the local and national levels.

Conclusion

The cost of police corruption in human lives and in its economic and social consequences is great. There are direct costs associated with payments to its victims, indirect economic costs associated with aiding criminality, fines imposed on air and shipping lines for drug cargoes smuggled in collusion with corrupt constables, and so forth. Importantly, there is the damage inflicted on the reputation and authority of the JCF, the popular distrust of it, its poor responsiveness, and its resistance to a service orientation. Furthermore, drug trafficking and US drug policy responses to this have made what were hitherto purely internal security and policing issues more central national security concerns with serious international implications. International economic relations are now more directly tied to Jamaica's effectiveness on domestic security issues. Ineffectiveness born of drug related corruption may therefore have a great impact on these outcomes.

This work has tried to show that the institutionalized nature of police corruption is deeply rooted in the operating norms, organizational principles, processes of accountability and power imbalances between the people and the state. Its effective control requires structural change.

The entrepreneurial character of much of the corruption in the JCF, the direction of the more violent and victimizing forms of corrupt behaviour at ordinary criminals, and the celebrated status of prominent police officers who have been successful in both fields account for the great referent power of these corrupt constables within the JCF. This power accounts for the resilience of corruption and, as shall be discussed later, is a prime source of resistance and threat to any reform movement.

4

The Somnolent yet
Aggressive Watchman:
The JCF's Style of Work

The sources and state of the legitimacy of police forces as agencies of social and political control, and consequently their effectiveness in crime control and the maintenance of public order, are acutely portrayed in the style of policing. Style is expressive of the political values and power relations that inform and condition collective police behaviour. It is thus a cardinal issue and a necessary target of reform.

In this chapter, the nature of the style of the JCF, its structural underpinning, its impact on relations with the people, and its effectiveness are analysed. It is argued that the style of the JCF is both an adaptation to and source of its legitimacy deficit, and is cultivated by structures of power, originating in the colonial period, that treat the policed like subjects rather than citizens. More effective crime control requires redefining police-citizen relations, a prerequisite of which is a more service oriented style of police work.

Wilson identified three styles of policing – the legalistic, service and watchman – each being associated with the three types of police-citizen encounters, that is, law enforcement, service situations and order maintenance respectively [Wilson 1968]. Elements of each style may coexist in particular police forces but the defining style can be identified by the predominant type of encounter. The *legalistic style* adopts a narrow law enforcement perspective on the varied problems of crime control and public order. While this approach is clearly inadequate for treating today's socially embedded criminality, ideally it equalizes the treatment of all.[1] The *service style* purports to treat all citizens and types of demands seriously, if not equally. It is more given to problem solving, and thus tends to encourage the exploration of wider options (beyond reactive law enforcement) and the adoption of more inclusionary problem-solving methodologies (involving nonpolice agencies and local stakeholders). The service style best facilitates the fashioning of community and offence-specific solutions. With the *watchman style,* order maintenance is central and prior to crime management. Watchman type police forces tend to be highly politicized, sensitive to the locus of social power, biased against the least powerful social groups (both in the treatment of their demands for police services and in the character of police-citizen interaction), and closed and evasive of public accountability. Their operating norms are characterized by ritualized unresponsiveness to the public, work avoidance and the tolerance of many types of legal infractions. This is usually coupled with a high degree of aggressiveness or "hard policing", which forms part of the police routine designed to demonstrate control and may be intensified in the form of campaigns whenever this control appears to be weakening.

Individual and institutional styles tend to be highly congruent. The individual officer enjoys considerable discretion [see Sykes, Fox and Clarke 1985; Goldstein 1977], but is constrained by the institutional and social structures within which he or she operates and is forced to adapt to these structures of control. The modal individual style thus tends to reflect the institutional style.

There are multiple determinants of style: organizational variables (degree of bureaucracy, size); environmental variables (class structure, crime rates); individual officer characteristics (age, attitudes); and situational variables (visibility of the encounter, characteristics of the suspect) [see Brook 1993:121; Erickson 1982; Wilson 1968]. Generally, institutional style is largely determined by the nature of the social structure and of the power relations between state and citizen. It is the pattern of police behaviour associated with how the police respond to the articulation of social power in the society.

In many of the former colonies, the police still tend to be very sensitive and responsive to political and social power. And as law may be seen as a foil to the arbitrariness of power, these police forces do not as a general rule enjoy a legalistic tradition. By a similar logic, a consequence of the grossly uneven distribution of power in these societies (where civil society is usually weak and there is a small and relatively powerful élite) is that the police do not have a tradition of treating people equally. State protectiveness, disregard for the law, and socially discriminating treatment of suspects and citizens who make claims for police services are therefore typical features of policing in many former colonial countries. The predominant mode of policing in the ex-colonial countries is thus watchmanlike [cf. Cain 1996; Ahire 1991; Danns 1982]. In the Caribbean context, this mode of policing is characterized by work avoidance, paramilitarism, poor accountability to the citizenry and class differential policing. As the latter two features are discussed in chapter 5, only the first two are discussed in what immediately follows.

Work Avoidance

The priority accorded public order management over crime control is reflected in the structures that shape the behaviour of the police. Among these are the nature of government control of the Force and the judicial-constitutional framework. As Brogden [1987] notes, where the primary function of the police is public order management, the level of police autonomy of the government tends to be low, since much of their activity is explicitly political, thus falling within the field of competence of the political administration. A corollary to this point is that where law enforcement or crime management is primary, the justification for an independent professional space is more evident and greater police autonomy is more likely. The watchman style is consistent with the historical role of the JCF, the consequent tradition of politicization and low levels of autonomy.

The primacy of public order is similarly reflected in the laws, most of all the constitution, which virtually nullifies all individual rights by subjecting them to vague public order concerns [see Fraser 1979].[2] Invested in the police are considerable powers to control political action, subject to executive rather than judicial review. Without special measures, the national security pretext may thus be easily used to suppress opposition political movements.

Consistent with this primacy of the state protective function, these forces tend to be unresponsive to the priorities of the ordinary citizens, profoundly reactive, and given to work avoidance and plain indolence. The scope of action by the "watchman" is always constrained by the imbalances in the social power of the different groups in the society, the politicization of crime and his limited autonomy. For example, attempts to impartially enforce the traffic laws and to confront socially influential offenders have led to career disasters for many police officers.[3] This is also true of more serious infractions, as in the not too distant past, the prosecution of politically influential street criminals has, on occasion, produced similar results. Thus the western district of Kingston, which records the highest rates of violent crime in the country, has a reputation within the Force as the "easiest" or sleepiest posting. Avoidance (at the level of the individual officer) is to a large measure experientially rooted. It is not simply indolence (although it may be associated with it); it is more deliberate and politically calculating.

Avoidance is evident even in the priority function of the Force. Many politically nonthreatening public order laws are not normally enforced, such as urination in public places and the occupation of the streets by higglers. Not surprisingly, some 52 percent of the Force held the view that "some laws cannot be enforced".

Only the more political aspects of their public order function are approached (pro)actively. For example, systematic intelligence on political and trade union movements is done in anticipation of, and with a view to, preventing or containing strikes, demonstrations and other mass manifestations. These types of operations long preceded, and were historically accorded greater priority than, criminal intelligence. While systematic political intelligence and infiltration of groups hostile to the political order (such as the Marcus Garvey–led Universal Negro Improvement Association, or UNIA) occurred as early as the 1920s, similar treatment of criminal organizations did not begin until the late 1970s, although fairly organized criminal networks were active a decade earlier [see Harriott 1994]. Even then, criminal intelligence was largely stimulated by the opportunities to incriminate the politically affiliated gangs.

At the level of the individual constable, there is a reluctance to prosecute "normal" crimes, particularly if they do not have a high visibility or excitement quotient. For example, on a visit to the High Command, the author observed the handling of a complaint from a lady who, on informing her local station that she had been robbed of the fairly large sum of J$200,000, was told by the local police that her report could not then be considered as they had to attend a cinematic production nearby – presumably as formal duty. This was not an isolated event as during the course of this study a number of similar but less dramatic events were observed in the guard rooms of different police stations.[4] Only a small proportion of police personnel are involved in active "crime fighting". In western Kingston, of the 197 constables assigned to the division in 1994, 10 percent (or 20 constables) accounted for 95 percent of all arrests in that year [Statistics Unit JCF]. These were mainly detectives keen on establishing their reputations as "crime fighters".[5] This trend predates Independence. As early as 1910–11, 1 percent of *detectives* (that is, some 0.1 percent of the Force) accounted for 40 percent of all arrests [Harriott 1994:146].

These data reflect the happy coexistence of somnolence and accommodation to criminality among the majority, with an aggressive anticriminal crusading by a minority of constables. Both tendencies represent deviant work norms. The data counterintuitively suggest an intensification rather than a weakening of this historical trend. Perhaps the sources of this problem lie in the tendency of the "avoiders" in the uniformed sections of the Force (particularly in these volatile areas with high rates of violent crime) to direct most reported incidents to the CIB for investigation. This has had the unhappy consequence of burdening detectives with impossible caseloads and thereby reducing their effectiveness, while many uniformed constables are by this design left with rather light duties and few tasks. If major offences are neglected, minor violations tend to be completely ignored and the priorities of complainant citizens disregarded.

The JCF, like most state institutions, has no tradition of service. This is evident from even a perfunctory analysis of the complaints from citizens.

In 1994 some 8 percent (65) of all formal complaints to the JCF were against police misconduct [Police Complaints Division, JCF] and 35 percent of the reports to the Police Public Complaints Authority were occasioned by police negligence or other service related failures [Police Public Complaints Authority 1995]. This is very conservative since most of this type of complaint is not usually recorded but, rather, is informally directed to officers known to the complainant.

Preventing avoidance has been problematic. Throughout the history of the JCF, there have been very few cases of constables being convicted for criminal negligence.[6] Both a strong legal framework and an effective mechanism for investigating the police are needed. Although in the USA a strong legal framework exists [see Potts 1983], the problem persists as there has been little enforcement [Brook 1993:178]. In Jamaica both have been missing, but there has been a recent attempt to provide a better investigative machinery. Two investigative units, one within and the other external to the JCF, are now operative. They have thus far had a mixed record in coping with police resistance.

The Force has neither a tradition of service nor of crime preventive problem solving. Reorientation along these lines would be revolutionary, and it could hardly be accomplished by simply improving the "quality" of personnel, that is, recruiting persons with the desired individual attributes in the hope of altering individual styles. Such dramatic behaviour modification is impossible within the old structure, which fails to reward and, indeed, assigns a low status to service and community-level problem solving.

The watchman style of policing relies on the informal mechanisms of social control as the first line of social defence [Wilson 1968:180]. With each dramatic crime event and "crime wave", the perception of a progressively deeper failing of these informal mechanisms is confirmed, resulting in an aggressive response of crackdowns, indiscriminate arrests, liberal use of violence and disregard for due process. This is a disastrous spiral whereby neglect of the problem is followed by public panics and an extreme response of crackdowns and special operations involving the army. With each spiral, each phase seems to gain intensity with the cycle becoming shorter.[7] This approach of avoidance and aggression is consistent with the paramilitary design of the Force.

Paramilitarism

In the ex-colonial variant of the watchman style, order maintenance is prior to crime fighting, which is in turn prior to the service functions of the police force. Paramilitarism is thus an appropriate form, given these priorities and the relative freedom of the police from the normal legal constraints on the means available for their accomplishment that tend to accompany this perspective. For example, the colonial authorities provided the police force with various instruments, such as the Riot Act, which, when invoked, effectively suspends the rule of law, allowing the unconstrained use of state violence.

Paramilitarism may be defined as a mode of organization [Auten 1985], a tactic [Emsley 1983; Waddington 1987] or a relation (of the police to the military) [Hill 1995]. It is a complex of relationships: a mode of organization and control of its members typified by a high degree of centralization; a mode of interface with and control of the mass public typified by the targeting of threatening subpopulations (usually those at the bottom of the social hierarchy), and relatively indiscriminate (legally dubious and morally unjust) subjection of individuals within these groups to interrogation at will and generally aggressive techniques. Paramilitarism is based on political values that favour the primacy of order over freedom and justice, and as Auten [1985:125] notes, it assumes that (as is the case with citizens who are subject to its authority), people in the internal police work environment must also be coerced, controlled and directed in order to achieve the goals of the organization. As a set of controlling relationships, it is directed both outward and inward.

As an organizational model, paramilitarism was adopted by modern police forces because, according to Auten, it was the most attractive of the few available models of complex organization in the nineteenth century, when most of these forces were formed [Auten 1985:122]. However, in the English case, even though influenced by the military model, their home police services evolved out of a strong tradition of local and civil policing. These services must therefore be distinguished from the constabularies that are associated with a hard paramilitarism, and which became the model of policing that was exported to the colonies [see Harriott 1994]. Indeed, Peel and the founders of the modern English police were involved in the development of both models – the more civil English model and the constabulary that was developed in Irish conditions for the colonized and other subject populations. Auten records the organizational characteristics of the paramilitary model, the features it exhibits and elicits. He lists 17 such characteristics, most of which are grouped and presented below:

- A centralized command structure, with a rigidly adhered to chain of command, and rigid superior-subordinate relationship as defined by prerogative of rank.

- Control ensured through the issuance of commands, directives or general orders. The communication process is thus primarily vertical from top to bottom.

- An authoritarian style of leadership, with employees encouraged to work primarily through threats and coercion. Initiative at the supervisory and operational levels is not sought, encouraged or expected.

- Emphasis on the maintenance of the status quo and a highly structured system of sanctions and disciplinary procedures to deal with nonconformists within the organization.

- Excessive formalism – with strict adherence to organizational guidelines in the form of commands, directives, general orders or policy and procedure. Consequently, there is a lack of flexibility when confronted with problems and situations not covered by existing directives, general orders, or policy and procedure.

- Feelings of demoralization and powerlessness at the lower levels of the organization, and the concept of the administration and top command as arbitrary [Auten 1985:123–24].

Not all of these characteristics are necessary features of paramilitarism. The JCF, however, displays them all. Influenced by changes in their societies and advances in organization theory, in Europe and North America, fairly fundamental changes have been made away from this model, or at least significant adaptations to the model have occurred. In the developing world, however, few planned adaptations have occurred.

Within the JCF, paramilitarism is valued for its capacity to ensure internal discipline and control [Harriott 1994:373]. Danns reported a similar view in the Guyana Police Service [Danns 1982:44]. As late as the end of the first decade after Independence, the level of control exercised over police personnel remained similar to that in the military. Internal control rested on leveraging physical, material and symbolic normative means. It was a carcelized institution with constant surveillance of and great control over its operatives. The recruit was subjected to intensive institutional resocialization designed to produce, primarily, a disciplined, obedient and loyal constable. This, of course, resulted in a lack of initiative and overdependence on the superior ranks.

The marked decline in discipline within the JCF may be reasonably attributed in part to the collapse of the coercive instruments of control associated with the paramilitary model (as is the view of some officers), as well as the weakening of the authority of many police managers. The scope for physical coercive control has progressively narrowed with the decline in the proportion of constables domiciled in police barracks. Promotions are now the major lever of control as they bridge the material and the symbolic. But political control of the promotions process and its manipulation as patronage have made it an instrument for reinforcing the informal mechanisms and deviant norms. It is therefore doubtful whether paramilitarism offers much prospect for restoring discipline, and even then, the desirability of building discipline on this basis is questionable.

There is a growing recognition of the dysfunctions associated with the paramilitary model. The basic organizational principles of the model are hierarchy and centralization. Constabularies thus tend to have a large number of centralized units. This reduces the capacity of the territorially based divisions since they are consequently starved of already scarce resources and made heavily dependent on the central structures. Centralism discourages lateral coordination and tends to make the divisions (especially those that are responsible for policing the hot spots) highly dependent on the support of central operational units for any significant action. The divisions must then endure the communications confusion, the feeling of powerlessness and demoralization associated with the high degree of interdependence between specialized units. For example, there is no structural arrangement to ensure that information relevant to the divisions is utilized by the divisional managers in developing area specific crime control strategies. These data may be treated as the property of the CIB or other specialized agencies with independent channels of reporting. This level of centralization hardly facilitates local initiatives.

Information is often treated as a political resource to be manipulated in the competition for departmental and personal glory and power. Even with the best of intentions, communications tend to be distorted as they are relayed downward, and in turn may be manipulated from below in order to frustrate the decisions of the upper echelons. This manipulation is notorious in the state bureaucracies, but is most extreme in the police force as it is such a highly politicized centre of power, fractured into competing groupings and implanted in protective networks that help to make distortions seem credible and the truth seem false. The manipulation of information may be used to obstruct internal accountability and to resist reforms by discrediting internal change agents.

A consequence of the high degree of centralization typical of paramilitary organizations is the evasion of responsibility. It ensures that little is accomplished. This evasion of responsibility is particularly comprehensible in the context of a politicized force, where the informal rules are primary but unclear and the basis of decision making appears arbitrary. In this setting, to take responsibility and initiative without being connected to the sources of power is to put one's career at risk. Furthermore, overcentralization is unnecessarily exclusionary. It impedes creative problem solving based on police-citizen cooperation since key decision making is removed from the point of contact with the community (which is the locus of the problem and best site for the elaboration of control and preventative measures).

As has been argued above, the principles of paramilitarism (as they structure internal relations) fail to ensure effectiveness and even internal control; this is even more true of paramilitarism as a tactic. Its most salient tactical features are aggressiveness and the use of indiscriminate methods of control and law enforcement.

Jamaica has a history of episodic political violence, but an even longer history of paramilitarism. The JCF developed in the context of the harsh postemancipation period, the popular rebellion of 1865 and a retrogression to Crown Colony government. It thus carries the historical baggage of being originally fashioned as an instrument of domination and continues to be associated with the excessive use of violence.

A distinction must be made between police violence as a necessary means for accomplishing a duty (as in making an arrest) and its use as punishment, often based on "factual" or intuitively established guilt. Procedural notions of democracy find a ready parallel in procedural law (just outcomes being linked to rights-protecting and power-checking procedures). From this perspective, police interventions, especially in their reactive mode, ought to be essentially procedural. Yet the JCF has had an abiding indifference to procedural law and due process. Police interventions have become less procedural and more substantively concerned with punishment. Police forces with this kind of punitive tradition tend to exhibit high levels of violence.

Punishment is often summarily meted out to suspects who may spend long periods in police jails, suffer loss of income and even loss of life. A survey of prisoners in the jails conducted by the author in March 1995 confirmed the prevalent use of arrest as an investigative tool and as punishment.[8] Police "excesses" and punishment take both violent and nonviolent forms – harassment, degrading treatment and the excessive use of violence.

Harassment involves overt intensive surveillance and the use of nonviolent punishment and control techniques, and may be targeted at groups or individuals. It usually takes the form of repeated dispersal of seemingly threatening groups or individuals, usually occupying public spaces in their communities, and repeated detention of targeted individuals on unjustified charges. The colonial laws provided the police with instruments (such as the recently repealed Vagrancy Act) that encouraged these methods. Harassment may have different sources and motivations, such as social control of deviant groups, political control in assisting one of the competing political parties, corrupt intent (it may be a particularly persistent way of soliciting a payoff) and personal vendettas. It is usually associated with overpolicing, an exceeding of the scope of the legal authority of the police in efforts to control suspect and deviant groups. For this reason, it usually encounters resistance from its targets.

This resistance to harassment often results in the police resorting to the use of degradation ceremonies designed to keep these target populations in their "place". *Degrading treatment* involves the use of verbal and physical abuse to humiliate and to dramatize the low status of the subjects in the universe of the police and their subjection to the will and power of the police. It overtly demonstrates a disregard for their entitlements as citizens and the absolute power of the state control agencies over their lives. These practices are intended to induce greater conforming behaviour among those sections of the population presumed to be less law abiding and generally lacking in commitment to the norms of the society. In reality, it generally results in the opposite, as such treatment is seen as being reserved for the poor.

Such unequal treatment may not present similar problems of resistance to the police authorities everywhere it exists, and it did not always have this effect to a similar degree in Jamaica. But this is not difficult to explain. Unequal treatment tends to be less problematic where caste, class and other systems of social segmentation have a long tradition and are more or less accepted by lower status groups. In these settings, policing styles characterized by such practices simply fit the pattern of expected and accepted behaviour. The difficulty arises most sharply when unequal treatment is contrary to the proclaimed principles of the institution. The lived experience of inequality before the law thus contrasts with the legitimation rhetoric and thus undermines respect for police authority and state authority more generally.

Degrading treatment may take soft forms similar to the induction rituals of boarding schools, such as coercion into self-ridiculing performances for police audiences and being forced to act on every whim of police interlocutors on pain of being detained. The power of the police is dramatized by demonstrating the facility with which they can punish and hold the bodies of their subjects to ransom at the behest of the arresting officer. In 1994 some 11 percent of prisoners in police jails (in the KMA) had served more than one year prior to the completion of trial.[9] This amply demonstrates the impotence of the legal structures to effectively protect them.

Unjustifiable police violence has a special dynamic to it. It is used for asserting police power in a quest for greater authority and compliance, punishing its subjects, and as an interrogative-investigative tool. With this style of policing, brutality is not simply aberrant and deviant behaviour but a work norm. It is an acceptable means of attaining police goals and a valued part of their tactical repertoire. This is evident from the pervasiveness of these practices and the taken for granted ways in which the transmission of these techniques to new police initiates occur. From the above mentioned survey of prisoners in police jails, a significant minority (35 percent, $N = 141$) reported being subjected to violent interrogations and a few others to violent punishment.

The most acute expression of brutality is, of course, unjustifiable homicide. Few are unintended outcomes of brutality; most are acts of social cleansing targeted at violent criminals. Unjustifiable extrajudicial killings are the extreme end of a continuum of brutality based on an indifference to means and a loss of perspective due to pressures for quick low-cost solutions to the increasingly complicated problem of violent crime. This approach is partially rooted in the notion of the criminal as a dehumanized enemy and a military approach to problem solving that focuses on neutralizing "the enemy" rather than the problem.

This has been a major issue since the late 1960s [see Chevigny 1991; Lacey 1977] and the practice has since become more widely accepted. The high frequency of homicides committed by the police is not a chance outcome. It is the product of the institutionalization of this practice within the JCF with special structures erected for this purpose. However, recent reforms and deliberate efforts by the High Command to discourage brutality have contributed to a decline in police killings. These have decreased from some 200 per year during the 1980s, to 132 per year during the 1990s, and from a high of 37 percent of all homicides in 1982 to a low of 13 percent in 1994 [Table 4.1]. Of these killings, for the period 1990–94, only 2 percent to 3 percent were ruled unjustifiable by the Office of the Director of Public Prosecutions and the offenders charged with murder.[10]

Table 4.1 Police Killings 1976–96

Year	No. of Police Killings	Rate	As % of All Homicides	No. of Police Killed	Ratio*
1996	148	5.9	16	10	1:15
1995	132	5.3	17	4	1:33
1994	100	4.0	13	6	1:16
1993	123	5.0	16	10	1:12
1992	145	5.9	19	–	–
1991	156	6.4	22	13	1:12
1990	135	5.6	20	11	1:12
1988	181	7.7	30	6	1:45
1986	179	7.7	29	10	1:26
1984	355	15.6	42	19	1:20
1982	236	10.9	37	10	1:24
1980	234	10.9	21	28	1:10
1978	167	8.0	30	18	1:09

Source: Police Statistics Unit, JCF

* Ratio of police killed to the number of people killed by the police.

The excessive use of deadly force and police vigilantism finds considerable support within the Force. Police brutality is often presented, especially in the popular press, as being imposed on the society by an authoritarian police (often with the tacit consent of particular governments) in contrast with, and alien to, the democratic ethos of the society [cf. Americas Watch 1986:3; Lindo 1990]. This is a misconception. For reasons similar to those offered within the Force, police brutality, including extrajudicial killings, finds considerable support within all classes in Jamaican society. In surveys conducted in 1991, Stone reported 56 percent support for vigilantism among the adult population [Stone 1991a:30], and the author found 54 percent support for police vigilantism among JCF officers [Harriott 1994:324].

These data suggest that on the issue of brutality, the attitudes of the police are no different from those of the rest of the population. They are simply better empowered to act on their beliefs. This level of support within the society, including its élite, provides a powerful basis for resistance within the JCF to any efforts to curb its activity.

Selectivity

The excessive use of violence is made even more problematic as it is often seen as too loosely directed. The JCF is often criticized for arbitrary arrests and the disruption of life in whole communities by its adoption of stop-and-search tactics, raids on public places, in which patrons are subject to detention and processing, curfews, cordons and search, and the use of similar "net fishing" techniques in search of guns and criminals.

Police attention is not just fixed on the criminally suspect behaviour of individuals but to attributes, places and events. These attributes and the routines that lead to encounters with the police are often shared by whole groups and even the majority of some subpopulations, such as young, inner city males who tend to dress in distinctively norm-violating styles from which their rejection of authority and exclusion from the labour market is often inferred by the police.

The selection of police (to be distinguished from policing) targets on the "group" rather than "individual" principle is applied not just with regard to the public order function (for example, demonstrators who are in breach of the law, or even the pacification of communities where intense gang warfare keeps recurring) but also to routine crime control, and it occurs at every stage of the process – contact, apprehension, detention and investigation. Much police contact with "suspects" is initiated as stop-and-search. This is a generally ineffective, legally dubious and socially harmful method [Harriott 1994].

The practice of detaining and processing people *en masse* is at times used in the hope of apprehending specific individuals, or some unspecified wanted person or persons; but most of all, this practice provides opportunities for the processing and accumulation of information on large numbers of persons usually from specially targeted communities, many of whom may not have had prior contact with the police. For example, during political gang warfare between two western Kingston communities of Tivoli Gardens and Wilton Gardens, the latter was raided "in search of wanted men, guns and ammunition". Forty-three men were detained, following which the commander, Detective Superintendent Pusey, reported to the press that "if their records are clean they will be released".[11] Residency in a "trouble spot", or a record of contact with the criminal justice system, is unquestioningly accepted as sufficient grounds on which to make an investigative detention. In some cases, these investigations are completed without grounds for charges but the suspect is left in jail – sometimes simply forgotten![12] This easily happens when the arresting and investigating officer are separate persons and when the prisoner is socially isolated with no support system, as is the case with many.

The practice of investigative detention is usually justified as a protective measure aimed at safeguarding victims and informants from intimidation by suspects. It seeks to deflect attention away from its primary purpose, which is to hold the body of the suspect or source of information to ransom in exchange for his or her collaboration. The target is not restricted to suspects; the practice is applied to any vulnerable but reluctant source of information, including friends and associates of the suspect. This is thus a blunt tool. Broadly applied it breeds resentment. In small communities, when crimes are committed, the police usually correctly assume that the offender is known. They then subject the assumed sources of knowledge to this process. But precisely because the perpetrator or perpetrators and motives of the offence are widely known, when the police err in their judgements, condemnation of the police for unjust and seemingly arbitrary treatment of those subjected to this process tends to be intense.

This indiscriminate mode of crime control is also applied to routine law enforcement. It involves the use of roadblocks, cordon and search, and curfews – methods that disrupt normal life and treat the general populace as suspects. The reliance on stop-and-search and arrest "on suspicion" techniques, as opposed to "on warrant" and "on information" techniques, may be taken as further expressions of this approach. In 1986–87, 35 percent of all arrests were made on an "on suspicion" or stop-and-search basis, but this has since declined to 20 percent in 1991 [see JCF *Annual Report* 1986; 1991]. Ninety percent of arrests "on suspicion" are done by mobile patrols and are really on the intuition of members of the police party in the hope that on processing the suspect after arrest, their judgements (often based on stereotypes) will be confirmed. This activity is therefore often correctly perceived as police harassment.

These methods of targeting communities are ineffective and alienating and are seen as such by many of its practitioners. According to the members of the Mobile Reserve who rely heavily on these tactics, while the approaches usually yield large finds of knives, they rarely result in the apprehension of criminals.[13] They are considered (within the military and police) as most useful for pacifying or "quieting" an area or as psychological operations to assuage the fears of the middle strata. This reflects the primacy of order over law and justice.

In summary, among the features of paramilitarism as a tactic, we may list the following:

- A heavy reliance on indiscriminate "net fishing" tactical forms such as roadblocks and raids
- Indifference to means
- The use of guns as the main tactical weapon
- Excessive use of violence – paramilitarism feeds and facilitates the pursuit of action, excitement and glory via violence as valued ends in themselves
- Use of huge personnel resources
- The group as the basic operational unit – often a coordinated network of groupings
- Military approaches to problem solving – this focuses on the physical neutralization of the "enemy", not the social aspects of the problem (in this approach the main factors to be manipulated are space and time, not social variables)
- The people are treated as passive onlookers rather than active participants with some responsibility for their own security

Illustrations of Style

The style of the JCF has been explained largely in terms of its colonial heritage, the configuration of social power in the society and the expression of this power in state-citizen relations.

In this section, the style of the JCF and the associated problems are illustrated by examining two aspects of police work: special operations and public order management. These problems are also reflected in investigations, which is the third major aspect of police work, but for reasons of space a discussion of this aspect is excluded.

Special Operations: The Case of Ardent

Special operations are paradigm cases of paramilitary policing. Usually, these involve intensive policing activity targeted at a small urban area, with the invocation of special legal instruments that extend police powers and approve the involvement of the military.

Unlike the earlier postindependence period of the 1960s into the 1970s, when they were more associated with public order problems involving violent political competition and rioting, current special operations are usually policing responses to ordinary crime when it is perceived that the threshold of acceptable violence has been exceeded. Operation QuickDraw, which was designed to pacify western Kingston and which culminated in the state of emergency of 1967, is an example of this type of operation in the earlier period [see O'Gilvie 1984:44], while Operation Ardent typifies the special operations of the current period.

The more recent "crime waves" are usually triggered by incidents that transgress the boundaries of "acceptable" criminal behaviour and depict a loss of control by the police. These boundaries are defined less by the frequency of violent crimes than by the type of victim-offender relation. Violent interclass and interrace victimization violates this boundary. In a setting where there is a steady accretion of anxiety and fear, one such event may occur that dramatizes the transgressions. The sharp class segmentation, the consequent social distance between groups and negative stereotyping of the "threatening" urban poor, and the attendant social insecurities of the upper classes and racial minorities, tend to result in an amplification of these fears. Moreover, the press vigilantly patrols these boundaries, orchestrates these panics and demands exemplary punitive action by the criminal justice system.

Operation Ardent was precipitated by three boundary-breaching events, all of which occurred in quick succession and in the context of an already developing crime wave. These were the shooting of the 80-year-old mother of a prominent businessman on 6 October 1992,[14] the killing of a German tourist in the quiet resort town of Oracabessa on 16 October 1992,[15] and the murder of a highly visible businessman engaged in the promotion of tourism and international golfing tournaments, on 17 October 1992.[16] All of these victims enjoyed high status in the society and were white persons, members of the business élite or were associated with the delicate tourist sector.

All of these tripwire events may be interpreted as demonstrating a disregard for the established boundaries. They thus set in motion the various anticrime lobbies, particularly the powerful tourism lobby. Powerful voices from among the economic élite, led by Gordon Stewart, owner of the Sandals chain of hotels, called on the government to seek international help to police the country,[17] and Dennis Lalor, an important player in the financial sector, urged "an all out attack on crime".[18] The threat level was amplified by characterizing the violence as "motiveless", thus implying that the victims were being randomly chosen and, hence, the entire population was equally threatened; and by targeting the criminals deported from the USA as the source of this new, alien and bewildering threat.[19] Against the background of a press campaign and growing panic, the government was put under great pressure to act in a disciplinary manner designed to demonstrate control.

The response, Operation Ardent, a joint police-military operation, was initiated in late October 1992 and was concluded in February 1993. As officially stated, its aims were: to restore confidence in the ability of the security forces to control crime, to pacify the communities engaged in violent group conflicts either between gangs or political parties, to apprehend criminals, to seize illegal firearms, and to reduce the fear of crime. This was captured in the slogan "attrition, deterrence and reassurance" [JCF 1992b]. Generally, its aims were short term and restorative, to deconstruct the crime wave and to restore the status quo ante.

The operation began at the planning stage with an "appreciation" or military approach to analysing the problem-situation involving "mission analysis, factors and plan". The important factors are usually viewed from a military perspective, and include the enemy, physical features of the area in question, time, space and options open to "the enemy" and self [JCF 1992d]. The enemy and self are the only actors in a profoundly dyadic construction of the agencies involved. The citizens are excluded and treated in a manner similar to that of noncombatants in conditions of warfare. Yet they, their associations and their leaders must become key actors if viable solutions to the problems are to be found. At best they are treated as a support force for the security forces (although there is no evidence of this in the plan and other available documentation on Ardent) rather than as independent actors in their own right with useful analyses of the problem and their own solutions.

These types of operations require considerable resources. For this reason they are difficult to sustain. In the case of Operation Ardent, the personnel requirements were: five task forces consisting of seven rifle companies of the Jamaica Defence Force (JDF); a small group of female soldiers; and the JDF coastguard – in all, a total of 850–900 soldiers (one-third of the regular army). The police commitment involved the Mobile Reserve, most of its regular personnel in the KMA, and full mobilization of all reserves. Vehicles of all types, including military and police armoured vehicles and helicopters, were engaged. It was thus estimated that this level of commitment was not sustainable for more than six to eight months [JCF 1992b].

Operational activity was intense. Some 955 motorized and foot patrols, 35 flag marches, 398 roadblocks, 108 cordon and searches and 90 raids were conducted. These activities resulted in 13 guns, 114 rounds of ammunition, 32 cocaine pipes, 17 motor vehicles and an aircraft seized, and 572 persons being detained. Most of these persons were simply detained for processing, as only 15 "were found" to be wanted men and only 281 were charged [JCF 1992c].

These outcomes may be taken as measures of the extent to which the goal of attrition was achieved. Understandably, no mention was made of the number of suspects killed. But the neutralization (elimination) of "hard core criminals" (the enemy) was a clear aim of the operation. Special structures were proposed and were in fact erected for this purpose. In the coded language of the operational planners "personnel will be dedicated to specific criminal and law enforcement situations which require swift decisive response actions using the principles of high mobility, flexibility, deception and surprise" [JCF 1992d]. This has been a lasting feature of these special operations, not just Operation Ardent [see JCF 1992d].

Consistent with its aims, "a quieting" of the target area was achieved and the population given some psychological reassurance. As with most special operations, the target area was the Kingston inner city, particularly western Kingston, which is correctly regarded as the locus of the problem of political and ordinary criminal violence. This success was, as always, only temporary and quickly faded, as within months after the conclusion of Operation Ardent the area was plunged into a major political war between two of its garrison communities.[20]

A cyclical process – from one operation to the next – may now be observed, with the periods between these special operations steadily decreasing, and the criminals learning to adapt to the modus operandi of the security forces (by becoming more mobile, suspending and shifting their operations in local and international space until after these special operations). The fact that these operations have to be repeated so frequently and are usually focused on the same areas is an indicator that they at best only provide some short-term relief for the society but are certainly not able to solve or manage the source problems.

This approach may even be counterproductive. By making the crime problem seem more intractable than it really is, these operations highlight the ineffectiveness of the criminal justice system, the limits of the coercive power of the state and the social embeddedness of the criminals. For example, "Natty Morgan", the leader of a large Kingston based gang, was made to seem invincible when hundreds of soldiers and police were unable to apprehend him, despite their best efforts over a period of almost one year.[21]

Even these short-term successes are often at a great cost to police-citizen relations, particularly among the urban poor. This is best depicted in the Constant Spring case. During Operation Ardent, on 22 October 1992, in a routine raid, 47 young men from the poor Kingston community of Grants Pen were detained by the police. Two days later, three of the detainees (Agana

Barrett, Ian Forbes and Vassell Brown) died in police custody at the Constant Spring jail. They had been put in a cell with 19 others and had expired from asphyxiation after being beaten by fellow prisoners and/or the police.[22] It seems that they had been detained for processing as part of an intelligence gathering procedure which was one of the aims of the operation. Their deaths were then not chance outcomes but consistent with the aims of the exercise, which were to make them maximally uncomfortable and thus willing to cooperate in return for their freedom. They were deliberately interrogated under harsh conditions. According to the evidence of some of the prisoners, on Friday morning they were given five minutes outside the cell, fed at 7:00 P.M., and then were left locked in the cell behind closed steel doors (not bars) until Sunday. Consistent with police objectives, their cries for attention were ignored.

Having lost the weekend, suffered the heat, hunger and overcrowding, powerless (as all efforts to have them released would have so far failed), and fearful of losing their jobs (if they had one) for failing to turn up for work on the Monday, the men would have been more cooperative and ready for processing. This was only complicated by police miscalculation of the endurable physical limits of some of the prisoners.

All five police persons charged were acquitted, despite an earlier finding by a coroner's inquest that the police were responsible for the deaths of the men.[23] The following day (23 March 1996) demonstrations were mounted against the verdict. The police were now enveloped in a partisan political controversy as it was claimed (with some credibility regardless of its truth-worthiness) that the men were detained because of their political affiliation.[24] The events thus served to aggravate social and political tensions and hostility towards the police and courts, which were (correctly) seen as unjustly favouring the police and biased against the poor.

The Constant Spring case was extreme only in its outcomes. It is, however, typical of the police techniques adopted and the expressions of the power relationship between police and citizen – group treatment and the absence of any specific crime as the trigger for police action. This is a style that emphasizes order over justice.

Operation Ardent may have been a turning point in the thinking of some senior officers and for the society. Some elements of learning and change have been evident since then. This is reflected in aspects of the design of Operation Crest, the special operation that began in February 1995 under the new commissioner, to confront the old problems of political and ordinary criminal violence. These changes included:

a.   An effort to make police operations more targeted (at the level of the individual suspect) and less disruptive of normal life in the target areas.

Operation Ardent, in contrast, was a major dramatic production that made life difficult in the target communities and was disruptive of normal life in the entire city with road blocks and so forth on main roads – in an effort to reassure the public.

b. Community relations as part of the operation.

c. Nonpolicing aspects of situational crime prevention (clearing of "open lands" and derelict buildings, removal of garbage, opening the streets) were introduced.

d. Interagency coordination on the delivery of situational crime preventive services, such as the demolition of derelict buildings.

e. A recognition of the need to pursue more long-term aims "preparing for the next generation" by tackling the social and political problems at the source of much of the violent criminality in the area [JCF circa 1994].

The elements (b) to (d) are, however, secondary. Much of the old remains.

Public Order

In Jamaica, four types of public order problems or issues are usually encountered. These are conflicts associated with political mobilizations (including intermittent localized shooting wars), industrial action, land seizures and squatting, and "hustling" or aggressive high visibility haggling in the main commercial centres. These problems are associated with the basic divisions and conflict points in the society – class and politics.

Political conflicts remain important, but the ideological and policy convergence of the 1980s and 1990s has reduced the level of violent competitiveness. These are treated elsewhere [see Harriott 1994]. Here, the discussion is focused on cases of police handling of the eviction of squatters, which is more typical of the main problems currently encountered.

On 11 March 1994, a special police squad, supported by privately contracted "toughs", proceeded to demolish the buildings and other property of a community of squatters in an attempt to evict them from their long established settlement at Flankers in the tourist resort town of Montego Bay. In response, the residents "rioted"; the police were stoned and the leader of the police party, Inspector Steadman Roache, "pelted and knocked flat"; five citizens were shot (but not killed); and the office of the landowner (Joe Witter) burnt.[25]

The police action had inflamed the squatters as the special squad appeared to have been acting at the behest of the landowner, as evidenced by the accompaniment of the toughs, the unnecessary destruction of property and disregard for the (procedural) law.

This case is instructive in a number of ways. First, the police have generally been reluctant to enforce the emerging attempts to suppress squatting and criminalize hustling in the resort towns. In a more recent instance of this, contrary to the wishes of the minister of national security and justice, the commissioner of police expressed his reluctance to have the police remove vendors from the main streets of Montego Bay until alternative facilities were prepared for them [MacMillan 1995].[26] This problem is being resolved in two ways. In the first, as occurred at Flankers, individual police officers and the units led by them are simply bribed to resolve these cases by the use of force. At Flankers, these corrupt influences led to a loss of judgement and an aggravation of the situation on the part of the police. The second solution, which is a more formal institutionalized response, involves the formation of new single-issue police forces for policing both squatting and illegal vending. These forces are directed by the Ministry of Housing and the Environment and Ministry of Tourism, respectively. These forces are less competent and their members enjoy less secure conditions of tenure than the members of the constabulary, and they must justify themselves on the basis of performance on a single issue. They are thus likely to more zealously pursue their functions. These problems cannot be solved by criminalization and police methods only, and by being less than enthusiastic in using force to resolve them, the police have in effect, forced a more conciliatory approach.

Second, such evictions before a national and international audience in the era of the communications revolution have far-reaching implications for police-society relations. There were few real internal controls on the unit led by Inspector Roache. After the fact, the unit was found to have violated the law, was publicly reprimanded by the commissioner and disbanded and its commander transferred.[27] Such police public order actions might eventually produce a movement for greater police accountability. Alternatively, poor handling of similar cases may lead to further loss of autonomy to the political directorate, which may arguably feel that it is more competent to manage public order issues.

These cases reveal a ritualized police disregard for procedural law, excessive use of force and a differential responsiveness in favour of the rich. These features are evident in the investigative process and public order management. Moreover, as a specific event, the Flankers case gives insight into the general problem of the low level of institutional legitimacy of the JCF. Resistance on this specific issue quickly led to a general condemnation of the institution and created a mini-crisis that was only diffused by the commissioner speedily and publicly punishing the offending constables.

Just as strong diffused support or institutional legitimacy may cushion the negative effects of specific policing events that may incur public disapproval, so too, if diffused support is weak and institutional legitimacy low, will mass disapproval of and resistance to specific policing events tap into this diffused dissatisfaction and continue to create these kinds of crises.

Conclusion

The watchman-paramilitary style is the outcome of colonial security policing. It is a nonintegrative rather than consensual style of policing and thus has continued to be a source of socially destructive conflicts. This style of policing is sustained by the exclusionary nature of the social structure and the perceived threats and insecurities generated by it (which are best comforted by security policing). It is propelled by the cultural structures of the society, in which individual rights tend to be undervalued, and by the subculture of the police, which may be characterized at its core by masculine values, an action orientation, love of guns, bonds of secrecy and a strong attachment to the group, and indifference to the means used to achieve their objectives. High status and respect is acquired by developing a reputation for violence. When police come into contact with young people who share similar values, a zero-sum game results, in which face and respect are either lost or gained. This is a formula pregnant with conflict. Changing the style must therefore involve changing the formal and informal reward structure within the JCF.

The attitude data suggest some scope for change, but within the existing style of police work. Any attempt to go beyond this to changes in the style would in all likelihood be very problematic and require considerable preparation of the Force. Such a rejection of paramilitarism would reduce the capacity of the state to enforce compliance and would force it to rely more on the consent of the governed.

Persistence with the watchman-paramilitary style of policing has resulted in a growing tension between the new relations of social power in postindependence Jamaica and the institution of policing. This is most sharply expressed in the problems of police-citizen relations. It is to this that we now turn.

5

Police and Community:

Policing the

Inner City

In this chapter the relationship between the police force and the community is examined. The nature of this relationship as a source of police ineffectiveness and impetus toward routine violations of democratic norms is analysed. In so doing, it explores the interplay between police strategies and the defensive mechanisms of the communities and how and why in this process these strategies are nullified. Finally, the attempts at correcting the problems in police-citizen relations, particularly the current innovations in inner city policing, are analysed.

The construct "police-community relations" originated in the late 1950s in the USA but was popularized after the conflicts with the civil rights movement of the 1960s as an instrument for treating racial relations [Maynall, Baker and Hunter 1995:41]. In the context of the developing negative reputation of the police for their liberal use of violence, and in the postcolonial spirit of imitation, the construct was imported in 1972 and an administrative unit set up in search of a mission. It became and remains a public relations concept. The purpose of the unit is "to foster improved communication and mutual understanding between the police and the community" [JCF *Annual Report* 1994:68]. This approach is founded on the notion that trust and confidence in the institution can rest on information and image manipulation. Decline in public confidence is thus often diagnosed as a failing of image management rather than a substantive quality of justice problem. This is a manipulative, unidirectional interpretation of the concept.

Here the concept of police-community relations is used descriptively, to map the power relations and modes of interaction between the police and citizens, and prescriptively, as a process of mobilizing the communities for crime related problem solving. It entails an examination of behaviour and their attitudinal sources rather than the police public relations processes.

Good police-community relations that are infused with a democratic spirit are participatory and inclusive rather than manipulative, reciprocal rather than unidirectional; police priorities are operationally integrated with the felt needs of the communities rather than centrally imposed, ongoing rather than intermittent, and substantive rather than a public relations device [Maynall, Baker and Hunter 1995:41–46]. This type of police-citizen relation is instrumental to crime control and political stability, but it is also a measure of the realization of political values (of justice, participation, people's self-management). The issues of police legitimacy, effectiveness and rectitude are encapsulated in police-community relations. Getting this relationship right must therefore be at the centre of any meaningful police reform.

These issues (of legitimacy, effectiveness and so forth) are structurally most problematic in the inner city communities. There poverty, long-term exclusion from the labour force, a highly developed (perhaps dominant) informal and underground economy, ordinary criminal and political violence, police brutality, systematic violation of citizens' rights (dubious formal and few substantive rights, to borrow Bottomore's distinction), injustice, and constant encounters with varied social prejudices are features of everyday life. The inner city provides an ideal laboratory for the study of police-citizen relations and their impact on crime control. It throws these processes into sharp relief, representing an intensive depiction of the problems of crime control, the maintenance of order and police-citizen relations. As these areas remain the locus of the problem, and as events in these areas tend to shape the national image of and the policy responses to violent crime, these are the spaces in which any worthwhile solutions should be considered.

If the problem of violent crime is to be solved and if new models of effective policing on democratic principles are to be developed, they are best developed and tested in the inner city. Moreover, Jamaica is becoming increasingly urban. According to the 1991 census, 50.1 percent of the population was then urban [*ESS* 1994:17.3], an increase from 41 percent in 1970 [*Statistical Abstract* 1976:8]. The problems of crime, disorder and police maladministration associated with the inner city are likely to be (are already being) replicated in other towns, including the more vulnerable tourist towns. For these reasons, two Kingston inner city communities were chosen as the research sites.

The Research Communities

Community connotes spatial boundedness and a shared way of life. But it may be argued that community in this *Gemeinschaft* sense has been largely destroyed by the sociological concomitants of the market, thereby replacing the principle of territoriality with that of interest. Nevertheless, the significance of place continues to be recognized in general [Day and Murdoch 1993; Matthews and Danns 1980] and in urban Jamaica in particular [Seymour and Wint 1993]. In the Jamaican context, class, and in the Kingston inner city, political identity, tend to be conflated with place, thereby giving place significance as an intensifier of social and political conflicts. The indicators of community are: citizens' identification with the area, level of social inter-action (distinctive patterns such as school used and police station served) and the extent of political cohesiveness.

Urban communities vary in their social structure, political traditions, and relationship to the law (formal versus informal tenure, garrison versus nongarrison), that is, in the social experiences of their citizens and in the character of their relations with the police. The communities of Normanville and Alexanderville were chosen. Both are communities with high and increasing levels of informal housing tenure, which exhibit political homo-geneity and sociodemographic profiles typical of the inner city. Normanville is located in western Kingston (where the problems are intensively expressed). It is not a garrison, and thus not an extreme case, but lives in the shadow of the principal garrison, or rather, to use a depiction that better captures the colonial type relations of dominance, the "mother garrison" of one party. Alexanderville shows garrison features of the "subject garrison" type and lives in the shadow of the "mother garrison" of the other major party. This community is the site of an experimental project in community based policing (CBP). The experiences here could decisively shape the attitudes of both the public and the police to the direction of police reform and crime control.

Normanville is bounded by Arnold Meadows (a pro-PNP garrison community) to the west; "no man's land", a vacated area created by the displacements from the political "war" of 1980, which separates Normanville from Green Villa (a pro-JLP enclave) and Clementville (a former pro-JLP satellite garrison and now contested by the newly formed National Democratic Movement [NDM]) to the south; Trinity Park (a pro-PNP community) to the north; and a declining commercial area to the east. Its identity is in many ways defined by this political geography.

It is a small, densely populated community with a population of 11,000. It has been fairly cohesive, is politically homogeneous and enjoys a strong sense of self-identity [see Seymour and Wint 1993]. This cohesiveness has been largely forged by political conflict with adjoining communities, the police and other "outside" institutions. However, in recent times, as there has been greater convergence and fewer violent conflicts in national politics, the community has become more divided, or rather, Balkanized, with the assertion of new area identities, leadership formation within these locales and new, often violent, conflicts between these areas. Many lament the passing of a not too distant past when Normanville was more cohesive, more orderly and more integrated with the rest of the society, however. Older residents constantly refer to Normanville's middle class past, when the homes were well kept and utility services were legally installed. They are quick to argue that it still has a "respectable" working class and is being erroneously stigmatized as an inner city ghetto.

The population of Normanville suffers multiple deprivations. Some 42 percent of its labour force are unemployed and 40 percent are squatters who occupy the homes of those displaced by the violence. Government services, such as garbage disposal, are irregular. In practice, they are also deprived of various political rights, including freedom of association and the right to vote.

Local power, as is the case in most politically homogeneous communities, is channelized and vertically integrated into the party structures. Being co-opted in this way provides access to scarce state resources (mainly housing) but on a patron-client basis. Such a political methodology is somewhat disempowering for the clients. Consequently, their efforts have had little effect on outcomes for the quality of life in the community, despite the efforts of a council that coordinates the work of the civic organizations in the area. In not entirely fair elections, the community has voted homogeneously for the PNP, returning between 91 percent and 100.3 percent for the PNP since 1976 [*Report of the Director of Elections* 1976, 1980, 1989, 1993]. Politics has long been a prime source of upward mobility and access to various socially valued goods. These benefits, Figueroa [1994] convincingly argues, are derived from being members of these homogeneous communities (not as individuals). Sections of the population therefore have a stake in its closed, controlled-cum-protected, and conflict-ridden state.

Exploiting the closed character of the community is a thriving underground economy organized around drug trading, robbery, gambling and protection. At the time of the fieldwork, three crack bases were operating within the area alongside a larger number of cannabis outlets. The illegal survival strategies of the males have led to their popular classification as "modellers", who live on remittances from relatives and friends or support from their female consorts, or both; "rude boys" or delinquents and petty criminals; or "dons" who are usually drug entrepreneurs and organizers of major income-generating crimes and who may also be able to acquire state contracts. Most males express little hope of viable jobs as their skill levels are low, and community stigmatization further reduces their chances of acceptance by prospective employers (with the exception of some state agencies where their political connections provide the necessary entrée).

Such exclusion from viable legitimate opportunities in the private sector and reduced access to state resources provide justification for the most predatory forms of illegality. According to one typically aggressive young man, "Yu have fi just look your own . . . take it from a man."[1] While this predatory behaviour is primarily directed outward, in Normanville the members of the community are increasingly being preyed upon by their own. All types of work, including illegal work, and all types of community businesses, without exceptions such as small sidewalk stalls, are now "taxed" by the gangs. Their activity puts a premium on turf control, which provides sovereign territory and a "taxable" population, secures drug bases and markets, and allows greater leveraging of politicians and state agencies. This premium stimulates expansionist tendencies and consequently foments conflicts.

The underground economy is becoming increasingly integrated. The larger gangs provide protection (in some instances, more effectively than the police) and supply a variety of goods and services. Warehouse burglars are able to regularly supply cheap, stolen goods to a local shop and to vendors. One of the local gangs engages in auto theft and supplies scarce car parts cheaply to a local garage and individual taxi operators.

Accumulation via the underground economy and the entertainment services has accelerated the process of social differentiation in the community. The more visibly affluent, upwardly mobile and physically secure are to be found at the intersection of the underground and the formal economy. They provide the young males with models of successful social adaptation and tend to become the leaders and new patrons of the community. They are asked and, on the accepted principle of reciprocity, are able to in turn ask for favours, thereby extending their linkages and networks.

Three territorially based gangs operate in the area. The dominant gang is international in the scope of its operations and has strong historical ties to the dominant party in the area. These gangs have erected clearly defined internal territorial boundaries, marked by wall murals, are fairly organized. with clear hierarchies, and meet the diverse needs of their members for physical security, economic welfare, entertainment and status. They are more than just criminal enterprises. This explains their longevity and social entrenchment.

Historically, these gangs, and indeed the community, have been subordinate to the neighbouring garrison community of Arnold Meadows. This is reflected in the location of their respective leaders in the party hierarchy, their dependence on Arnold Meadows as a source of arms, the payment of tribute from robberies and other illegal activities, and their subjection to the informal system of criminal justice administered by the gang leaders from Arnold Meadows.[2] Their subordination has been broken and the structures of party political control weakened by the changes in the local political economy, namely, the decline of state patronage, access to more independent, albeit illegitimate, sources of income, and migration of the leadership. The party administration (the centralizing authoritative force) of the informal control mechanisms has been largely, but not completely, dismantled. The present, more decentralized, power arrangement and the more widespread access to the means of violence have resulted in a multiplicity of conflicts among and within communities and the more frequent resort to the use of violence to settle these conflicts.

Normanville has a long and continuing history of political violence. The sociodemographic (51 percent are under 20 years, and the mean age is 22.9 years), political and economic profiles are highly criminogenic and facilitative of violence. In 1993 its rate of violent crimes, such as murder (128 per 100,00) and robbery (516 per 100,000), was, with the exception of rape (168 per 100,000), above the national and city (Kingston) levels [Table 5.1]. Property crimes, which are externally directed, were, not surprisingly, well below the national level. This type of community tends to display patterns that are consistent with, but acutely expressive of, the national trends. This community, like many others in the inner city, has been stigmatized, thereby locking its young males out of the labour market, depriving it of social services and targeting it for "hard" policing. It is caught in a catch-22 that leads to fatalism and provides many with self-justification for criminality.

The other research site, Alexanderville, is a small community with a population of approximately 7,000. Its physical-cum-political boundaries are discretely circumscribed, giving it a clear identity. It is a pro-JLP community bounded by the harbour to the south, and the pro-PNP communities of Ralph Town to the north, Alan Town to the east, and Lebanon to the west, and is within close proximity to the main commercial area in the centre of the city.

Legitimate economic activity in Alexanderville centres on small-scale craft, artisan, commercial and other self-employed projects. The northerly shift of the centre of commercial activity away from the city centre has decapitalized the area. The physical expressions of this, and the general inner city blight, are evident in the large number of destroyed and abandoned buildings in the "no man's land" or border area between Alexanderville and Lebanon, the Chinese shops vacated by owners who have fled to safer territory, and, just across the border with Lebanon, a lodge building (evidence of a socially active working class in the not too distant past) that now houses a large number of squatters. These buildings (with the exception of those captured by squatters) now serve as receptacles for garbage, billboards for entertainment events and political graffiti, and sites for rape and other forms of criminal activity.

The progressive physical decay of the area is paralleled by growing social disorganization. In 1993 the level of unemployment in the community was estimated at 60 percent. The dependency ratio was 5:1, with 50 percent of households being headed by females, many of whom held low-paying jobs in free zone garment manufacturing and domestic service, were self-employed or dependent on insecure sources of income. Some 47 percent were squatters living in captured dwellings, and 72 percent of all households occupied a single room. As in Normanville, these squatters derive some benefits from the garrisoning of the area, because owners are unable to access their homes or enforce the payment of rent, and 80 percent of the houses have a free and reliable, albeit illegal, supply of electricity.

This migration of physical and human capital and consequent social disorganization were hastened by the episodic gang-political violence and the vulnerability to criminal victimization. The community is politically homogeneous and, like other urban party strongholds, tends to be expansionist, thus fomenting political conflicts with the neighbouring pro-PNP communities (of Lebanon and Alan Town), particularly during periods of electoral competition. Its history is thus marked by high levels of political violence and major gang wars.

In this community, there has been an unbroken line of continuity between political violence and ordinary criminal violence. Two decades of "warring" between the community and its neighbours, between the political parties, and between gangs and families who have lost relatives and friends, have led to the accumulation of a great blood debt. Between 1986 and 1993, murder rose 80 percent; shooting, 300 percent; rape, 100 percent; and robbery, 100 percent. Thus in 1993, the murder rate for the community was 112 per 100,000; shooting was 308 per 100,000; and rape was 112 per 100,000. The national patterns are highly accentuated – with the rate of violent crime being 1,248 per 100,000, while that of property crimes was 406 per 100,000 [Table 5.1].

This persistent violence has skewed the age distribution of the population in favour of the young, with approximately 47 percent of the community being under 20 years, and 65 percent under 30 years. While this age structure is not radically different from that of the nation as a whole, a distinctive feature of these communities is the seeming invisibility of the middle aged section of their populations and their withdrawal from the central public spaces in which interaction with the young is usually facilitated. This demographic pattern in turn increases the potential for violence, as the moderating influence and authority of the older generation is weakened.

The density of gangs and crews is very high. There are nine of these terri-torially based youth gangs and organized crime networks in Alexanderville, with colourful names that mark their territorial domains (for example, the Alexander Street Posse), or that connote male sexual prowess (Superstud, Okro-Slime), symbolize a normative inversion (Renkers),[3] or competence in the use of violence (Snipers, Raiders). This high degree of fragmentation has led to greater intracommunity violence and greater difficulty in imposing order and compliance with community codes. However, this may still be coordinated by the local party leadership during periods of political contest.

As in Normanville, these processes have given rise to a thriving under-ground sector. Earlier, this was based on prostitution, but it is now organized around drug distribution, protection rackets, robbery and gambling. Proximity to the harbour and to the commercial district in the city centre gives the community a comparative advantage in these areas. While females are more integrated into the lower end of the labour market and numerically dominate the own-account occupations, males predominate in the underground. In contrast with Normanville, where the petty hustlers and small community groceries are exploited by the gangs, in Alexanderville, this is directed outward against the commercial enterprises in the city centre.

Table 5.1 Crime Rates for Research Communities 1993 (per 100,000 citizens)

Violent Crimes	Alexanderville	Normanville	Jamaica
Murder	112	128	26.5
Shooting	308	360	45.6
Rape	112 *	84 *	52.5 *
Robbery	406	516	220.1
Total violent	1,248	NA	857.2
Total property	406	NA	622.4

Source: The Normanville and Alexanderville Police.

* Rates for rape are per 100,000 females.

The Doctrine of Survivalism

The inner city conditions are highly criminogenic. Social scientists are well advised to draw the concepts that are used to describe and explain human behaviour from the social lives that are being studied. In these communities, the notion of survival takes on a very literal meaning. People individually, and indeed their communities, are engaged in a constant and intense struggle (against the social, political and natural forces) for their very existence:

- The level of poverty and the absence of any reliable social support networks (with the exception of the gangs) direct a consuming struggle for physical (food, security) and psychological (the preservation of one's dignity and humanity) survival.

- Dependence on illegal sources of income, particularly street crime, and the constant risk taking involved, or simply having to live in an embattled community, adds another dimension to the struggle for physical survival.

- The intermittent "wars" often put the territorial and political integrity of the community at stake. Geocidal mapping indicates that the incidents of violent crimes are concentrated on the outer perimeter of the communities, and now (perhaps) the internal boundaries as well.

- The high vulnerability to natural and man-made disasters (given the state of the housing stocks and their density), such as fire, flooding (in the case of Normanville) and hurricanes, could easily erase large sections of these communities. Poor solid and liquid waste management, and outright state neglect, have created ecological hazards and an ever present danger of epidemics.

The concept survivalism implies rules and beliefs about social life and what constitutes appropriate behaviour. Here, the people are confronted with stark evidence of the precariousness of their existence in the highly visible cases of social failure – the friend who met a violent death at the hand of a rival gang or the police, mentally ill persons who have been abandoned by family and society, the hopeless crack addict, and the destitute street people of all ages who were once members of the community. In these conditions, criminality is increasingly seen as a form of social struggle. And as unvarnished market relations permeate most aspects of social interaction, giving greater impetus to competitive individualism, the society is perceived as operating on the principles of social Darwinism – whereby all are fair game, and one may resort to any means in the pursuit of one's goals.

Social transactions in the wider society are characterized by an instrumental attitude to people. People are rarely treated as "good in themselves" with intrinsic value to their lives, but rather as tools to be "used". Indeed, in Southside, a poster advertising a community dance with the theme "Gal fi mind wi, right behind the winery",[4] was prominently displayed. Dance themes usually reveal aspects of the current thinking of young urban males. This theme may prefigure a redefinition of gender roles (based on the greater integration of females in the labour force), but essentially, it sought to extend the idea of the instrumentality of the female beyond that of sex provider (the winery) to that of a general material provider, in the service of her demanding and dependent male partner.

This crass *cosification* of people reduces societal resistance to victimizing behaviours.[5] It is solidly anchored in our history of chattel slavery, which was perhaps the most acute expression of this objectification. In this Hobbesian world, the nominal normative order and the law are seen together as an ideological façade that, if taken seriously, dulls one's survival skills and increases the vulnerability to victimization and social failure. These illegal and corrupt means are, after all, seen by the urban poor (especially the youth) as the main means adopted by the élite and the contemporary local models of successful social adaptation.

Survivalism and the pervasive criminality associated with it offer a radical practical critique of the old normative structure. Acceptance of this normative system rested on the old compact of high rates of social mobility (via training and education), high social wage (public health, free education), state protection of the poor and the powerless, and commitment to change. Its rejection is linked to the reality that the normative structure has failed to "work" for the majority. In these communities, the faces of the working poor are all too familiar. Order is thus increasingly based on coercion, which cannot, in the long run, successfully substitute for internalized controls.

However, while generating greater distrust, this individualism is mediated by notions of moral obligation to the members of one's community. The boundaries of moral obligation tend to coterminate with the group, whose boundaries may be social, political or spatial [see Collins 1995]. In the inner city all three overlap perfectly. These shared characteristics tend to foster strong internal solidarities. This partially explains the strong sense of territoriality in the research communities and the inner city generally. Beyond this is a zone of amorality where violent and predatory activity is tolerated and even encouraged. This perspective is nurtured by the highly segmented character of the society, with its discrete social and political boundaries, which makes it easier to negatively stereotype other groups and to suspend the capacity for empathy with their members. This peculiar process of moral neutralization, coupled with survivalism (the Jamaican variant of social Darwinism), makes outwardly directed criminality, predatory behaviour and political violence more acceptable to the offender and his community, and makes the dons valued community assets because they erect the structures and provide the means to enforce these informal codes inside the community and direct predatory behaviour outward. For example, rape victims are preferably selected from the members of another community, or passers-by. Thus, despite the high rates of violent crimes in these areas (three times the national mean), impressionistic evidence, and, indeed, data from a recently concluded survey conducted by the author,[6] suggest that the rate of violent *victimizing* crimes tends to be lower than that of the country as a whole.[7]

This presents great difficulties for police-community relations. In what follows, the public image of the police in the inner city is described. Finally, in contrast to the traditional mode of policing the communities, the experiences at CBP (a police reform pilot project) in one of the research communities is analysed.

Policing the Community

By all the standard measures described earlier (cleared-up rates, complaints from citizens), the police are even less effective in managing crime in the two research communities and the Kingston inner city than generally. The cleared-up rate for murder in western Kingston (which in 1995 had the highest murder rate of all the police divisions, accounting for 20 percent of all murders islandwide) was approximately one-third (14 percent) that of the national average (41 percent) [Statistics Unit JCF]. In Alexanderville, the cleared-up rate for murder was 11 percent.[8] The conviction rates are thus likely to be negligible (certainly in single digits). The key players in the underground operate with near immunity from the law. In both communities, crack houses operated openly in close proximity to the respective police stations. Indeed, both cooperation and some competition between the criminals and corrupt police are evident in Alexanderville, where both parties are involved in the drug trade and the protection business in the city centre.

The research communities, and others like them located in different sections of the city, remain beyond the effective reach of the control agents of the state. The police have in effect accommodated to the norms of illegality that prevail in these communities. Thus in Alexanderville, despite the high density of crack houses, for the three-year period 1992 to 1994, there were only two arrests for dealing in illicit drugs.[9] Police interventions are usually triggered by threats to social order, such as major gang "wars". Beyond the capacity to enforce the laws, state agencies have instead had "taxes" levied on them in the form of protection money or "security contracts" as a condition for simply being able to deliver much-needed services, such as solid waste disposal, to some parts of the capital city. This accommodation with the gang leaders is based on both their social influence and coercive power.

Enforcement of community norms has been more related to the assertion of power by a dominant party, whose representative enforcers administer the informal justice system, rather than the police. The success of the high profile police "crime fighters" has been largely based on the exploitation of their position as political insiders to enforce the community norms rather than the laws (in many instances of violent crimes there is a happy coincidence of the two). As insiders they have easy access to information related to these violations, but they are obliged to ignore other violations of the law that are compatible with community norms. In these ways, the style of policing in effect legitimizes the existing norms of illegality.

The weakening of the system of party control, which is one of the consequences of the weakening and discrediting of the state in the 1980s, and the subsequent assault on the old politically affiliated dons who were at the centre of this system of control, has resulted in internal fragmentation and disorder, and in more intensive paramilitary type police interventions in the communities. This intervention has contributed to the poor state of police-citizen relations, which is reflected in the perceptions of the police. Generally, the police are seen as uncivil, disrespectful, disregarding of procedural laws, brutal to citizens, corrupt, behaviourally conditioned by negative stereotyping of the urban poor, often politically partisan in their actions, indolent and unresponsive to the security needs of inner city residents, and unjust and oppressive when they actually intervene [see Stone 1991a].

The local police (in Normanville) are discredited for their alleged collusion with criminals. This is sharply expressed in the following, which also captures the personalized nature and record of acceptance of the community codes that characterizes acceptable policing: "The police are informers. When you make a report, they carry your name back to the gunmen especially those [policemen] that drink [rum]. When I want to make a report I go to Central [a distant station] or tell Bigga."[10] And as another respondent chided, "When you go to the police with a problem, they always have an excuse [not to act]. They never have vehicle. They do nothing. And as someone dead, they run come. So I say they are with the gunmen."[11]

As noted earlier, since 1991 public opinion on the police has been fairly uniform across the different social classes [Stone 1991a]; the views of inner city residents are not particularly extreme; they are simply more experientially grounded and thus more emotionally charged. Discontentment with an institution, its leaders, and specific actions or failures must be distinguished from alienation from the institution, or what Easton calls diffused legitimacy [Easton 1965]. With regard to the JCF, people tend to circumvent the structures in order to deal with selected individuals who, either from personal experiences or their reputations, enjoy their trust. This happens at all levels of the Force and was a regular occurrence at the police stations that serve the two research communities. This indicates not just a preference for personalized service, or a working of the informal circuits of political power, but also a profound alienation from the institution.

These perceptions and the conflicts in police-citizen relations are rooted in the logic of reproducing an unjust social structure, the definition of the police function and the style of policing that attends this. The colonial definition of the police function led to the construction of structures and practices that have since framed police-citizen relations. This highly centralized configuration of power affords little protection from abuses of power by the state.

The experiences in the research communities, particularly in Alexanderville where there has been an attempt at community policing, seem to suggest that the people favour a more service oriented police engaged in problem solving and conflict resolution (such as helping drug addicts, controlling the trade in hard drugs, managing violent domestic conflicts and mediating in gang wars). The people tend to prefer informal settlements of disputes, because they cohabit the same community with the families and friends of the offender. This is better facilitated by preventive interventions rather than arrests after the fact. This kind of redefinition of the police function requires reshaping the style and structures of policing and a new attitude to the people.

Indeed, the CPOs are already doing many of these things, but without the institutional support required to do them effectively. This apparent lack of institutional support and the evident differences in style between the CPOs and the units of other sections of the JCF that interact with the people, and even the other officers in the local station, give the correct impression that community policing is an isolated operation rather than a new policy initiative that may prefigure a profound change in policing style. The relationships of the CPOs with the community therefore tend to become personalized and viewed as exceptions that do not belie the rules and traditional dynamic of general police conduct. Consequently, the benefits of their work tend to have very little positive impact on police-citizens relations and the general perceptions of the police.

The negative attitudes of the people toward the police are matched by equally negative views of the people among the police. Three readily identifiable attitudinal predispositions toward the urban poor permeate the JCF. First, there are notions of the inner city poor being in a state of dependency (much like children). This leads to a paternalistic disciplinary approach to policing. Second, they are seen as dangerous, resulting in the belief among the police that their job entails primarily political control. And third, the people are viewed as somewhat less than full citizens who are totally responsible for generating the problems and conflicts that consume their lives. This leads to the notion that the police function ought to entail some social cleansing. These attitudes are grounded in a Nietzschean view of the world as marked by an ethic of power in which the right to absolute power over the poor is presumed, as well as a dualistic view of people as either good or evil, engaged in struggle. This latter idea is linked to class related notions of the virtues and value of people. Such a perspective effuses a profound disdain for the marginalized poor and is hardly democratic.

In the tradition of policing that has generated these negative stereotypes of the urban poor and mutually reinforcing negative attributional biases in citizen-police relations, police at times foment gang-political warfare by the practice of detaining youths and releasing them in politically hostile territory. This practice has on occasion led to the death of the detainees. It is born of the idea (which is represented in the JCF) that the police should simply allow inner city males to kill each other. It is indirect social cleansing – with the unintended consequence of waiving the negative sanctions for the commission of murder and failing to consider the implications of this for the general problem of violence.

The population of inner city areas suffers overcriminalization, over-policing, class bias and stereotyping in law enforcement, and unresponsiveness to their policing needs. Overpolicing is evident in the use of paramilitary tactics.[12] This is most apparent in the inner city research communities. Here young males are invariably treated as suspect and dangerous.

The concept of dangerousness has its genealogical source in the profoundly political idea of "the dangerous classes", which was initially a referent for the "riotous masses" who were confronted with the harsh conditions of urban England during the Industrial Revolution. In Jamaica, the idea was applied to the jobless urban poor during a similarly turbulent transition period after emancipation. It was then (as now) related to being black, poor and urban, that is, to otherness from the perspective of the élite. As blacks moved from the plantations into the towns, in closer proximity to the white élite, and became more densely domiciled and resentful of the social and political oppression they were forced to endure, they were perceived as more threatening. This notion tends to be central to discourses on crime control and public order in highly segmented and unjust societies with large socially disadvantaged populations, and a vulnerable and insecure élite. Control innovations, styles and the boundaries of acceptable control practices by state agencies are, after all, but responses to perceived threats.

The extent of dangerousness is usually determined by five indicators [see Morris 1994]:

- Place of residence. This is taken by the police as a proxy variable for class, status, proneness to criminality and to attracting or committing violent acts. Inner city communities are considered "hot spots" and their residents most dangerous.

- Relation to the labour market. The less integrated one is into the formal labour market, and the lower one's status is in it, the more dangerous one is taken to be. Most young males in the inner city communities are unemployed, underemployed or engaged in informal economic activity. These "locations" are taken to imply laziness, criminality or potential criminality.

- Record of contact with the criminal justice system (CJS). This serves to condemn and exclude.

- A defiant disposition. This is usually (correctly) interpreted by police interrogators as rebelliousness and resentment of police authority.

- Physical features. These include gladiator marks such as scars from knife or bullet wounds.

When inner city residence is combined with unemployment or low status occupations, the individual is correctly seen as socially disadvantaged, which is in turn incorrectly equated with dangerousness. The perceived dangerousness is amplified by an assumed socialization into a ghetto culture of violence, of irrationality, of a different value system and of otherness generally. This otherness attracts intense surveillance and harsh treatment by the police. The criminalizing treatment of these persons then leads to a record of contact with the police. Such unjust treatment in turn leads to resentment and hostility to the police (and the society), and solace is then found in gangs or crews. Involvement in gangs tends to invite violence, which results in gladiator marks. All the identifiers are now present, making for more frequent and difficult contact with the police in the future.

The social construction of dangerousness serves to legitimate security policing. Both are inextricably associated concepts. The concept of dangerousness serves to justify the treatment of crime as primarily a political rather than a social phenomenon. This notion thus incites indiscriminate group treatment of inner city residents by subjecting them to paramilitary policing tactics and providing justification for the suspension of individual freedoms.

Defensive Strategies Adopted against the Police

The alienation from the police has led to the development of elaborate defensive strategies against the police. The present mode of security policing assumes the existence of effective informal controls that support the legal codes; but both internalized controls and the traditional community-cum-party organized controls have been weakened. The normative codes and informal mechanisms instead reinforce consensual approval of some types of crimes and discourage cooperation with the criminal justice system. The gang often tries to get the approval of their "corner" on potentially divisive crimes. The "base" where collective cannabis smoking regularly occurs is often used as a forum for collective decision making on these issues. In working for a consensus, focused lobbying is at times done in order to neutralize any opposition to the proposed action.

Those outside the decision making (the older folk) are powerless to resist, although on some "corners", older males with a record of past involvement in illegality and who are part of the "base" are included in the decision-making process. In one such case, a female member of one of the research communities decided to give evidence in court against someone who had committed a group approved murder. The murder of this witness was negotiated over a period of weeks. The difficulty was in evaluating whether she would actually cooperate with the court or was simply threatening to do so. As part of the process of confirming this, the witness was provoked, and in response she openly threatened to "go to (Commissioner) MacMillan". This was later cited as conclusive evidence of a serious commitment to attend court and her disrespect for community codes of conduct. Thereafter, a mountain of evidence was cited to show that she had a history of socially undesirable behaviour and had become a general threat to all. She was, of course, murdered.[13]

The normative reorientation, the communal benefits derived from illegality and the embeddedness of criminals have given impetus to the development of community based defence strategies aimed at neutralizing the police. These are aimed at nullifying intelligence, patrol and investigation. Each is discussed in turn.

The police force is highly dependent on specially cultivated, and often paid, informers as its primary source of information. Police intelligence is nullified by stigmatizing, socially isolating and punishing these individuals, and labelling those who collaborate with the police as "informers". The social power of the criminal and the isolation of the police find concentrated expression in the attitude to the informer. In the community setting, the informer is labelled an instrument of the most threatening out-group (the police). In this dualistic world inhabited by insiders and outsiders, friends and enemies, members of Party A and Party B, poor and "rich", the informer/informant is an anomaly, a violation of this order. He or she is both insider and enemy – the worst expression of bad faith. The essence of bad faith is the attempt to escape the self – in this case, the identity as a member of the community and the duties and responsibilities associated with this identity, including the duty to protect one's own. The informer is, according to this logic, pretending to be what he is not and refusing to choose himself (as member of the community). In becoming an informer he dons an identity mask. From this perspective, it is not sufficient to simply unmask the informer; he or she must be punished by death. The stigmatization of informants, as a defensive tactic that cuts the sources of information to the police, is thus usually very successful.

In some communities there are elaborate early warning systems designed to detect the entry of police patrols. These were developed during intercommunity political and gang warfare, and later perfected against the utility companies. The early warning system against prosecution for using illegal utility connections involves a wide cross-section of the community, including children.[14] This is even regarded as somewhat of a duty. They operate in both research communities, but are most developed in Alexanderville, which has more entry points. There the drug dealers have furnished the system with cellular phones and erected permanent observation posts.[15] Beyond this, physical barriers, such as the narrow, poorly maintained roads, and even sleeping policemen erected by citizens to protect against drive-by shootings, also serve to check the movement of the police. Finally, if all this fails, police patrols may be persuaded to abort their missions by the rifle fire directed at them. Patrols are particularly at risk at night when full territorial control of the communities is asserted by the gangs. And during periods of intense conflicts, the local police stations are usually closed and operate as forts under siege until morning.

Investigation is nullified by obstructing police contact with suspects and prospective informants, misinformation, and by independently negotiating informal settlements with the aggrieved party. The outsider is never allowed free access and is always an object of suspicion and surveillance. A protective code whereby information is never freely given to outsiders or the control agents of the state, and networks that may actively misinform such agents, exist in the two research communities. Counter-reporting is used to divert and often redirect the police away from offenders within the community and towards the members of a hostile group. The response of the police to these obstructions usually to physically hold to ransom (in jail) the suspected sources of information until the needed information is released. As with every other problem rooted in poor relations with the people, the police are forced to use illegal solutions that deprive citizens of their rights.

Informal agreements between victim and offender are perhaps most frequently used where victim and offender are from the same community. It is most easily done in cases of property crimes but is also negotiated in violent victimizing crimes such as rape. Informal settlements usually involve the return of stolen items or payment of restitution to "compromise" the case. Incidents involving persons from different communities, arising from violent group conflicts, may even involve the trading of cases, whereby each community agrees to withdraw its witnesses in the cases already brought before the courts (that is, a mutual dropping of charges), thereby completely disregarding and frustrating the criminal justice system.

Settlements of the latter type are assisted by the code that in some types of disputes (where relations are nonvictimizing, as is usually the case with young males or gang warfare) the police are to be avoided. Thus, where disputes cannot be properly mediated and where there is little trust between the parties, the result is usually protracted gang wars.

Where these methods fail, witnesses may be suborned or eliminated. Given the overreliance of the police on witnesses, to the neglect of physical evidence, the investigation usually collapses. In highly politicized communities with high crime rates, as in the two research communities, the local police station is often completely neutralized. Traditionally, this is accomplished by political permeation. Where this is effectively accomplished, as has been the case in Normanville, the local police may even be co-opted, thereby forcing not just a waiving of law enforcement but even assistance on local illegal projects. Reflecting the power and primacy of community and party identity in relation to their occupational identity, the constables with social ties to the community are expected and, indeed, tend to form part of its protective network. These elements in the local police station then assist in neutralizing all police action within the locale.

Recent events in Normanville – during the life of the research project – may illustrate this. There one of the major gangs was able to (unwittingly) use the police as a reserve in its war with another gang. During a firefight between the two gangs, the leaders of one set of combatants was able to direct the police against the opposing gang. This was made possible by contacts (usually political) within the local police force who received the report and gave credibility to it, as though it were a legitimate distress call by a concerned informant. Recognizing the apparent partiality in the police response, the opposing gang then came to regard the police as an extension of their opponents, for in effect, the local police force was manipulated to act as the tactical reserve of one of the gangs. Earlier, overt manipulation of this sort was a feature of political conflicts; now it is done in less direct and more covert ways.

The local police having been nullified, special units of police simply make incursions from time to time. Night (foot) patrols are rare and must function as coordinated teams operating on guidelines that state the maximum distance one from the other and minimum number of units by area. Such tactical deployments suggest that these areas are treated as enemy territory in a war zone.[16]

This resistance to the police in the communities has its local bases in:

- People rightly attributing most of the crime to the social environment. Policing is thus seen as repression of their responses to these structural arrangements, that is, what is regarded as survivalism.
- Whole communities living beyond legality. Community benefits are derived from illegality and state corruption.
- The need for protection from outside predators (for example, rapists) and political competitors. Police are unable to fulfil this function, so community gunmen are accepted.

This process of resistance is perhaps most developed in western Kingston. An embryonic warlordism is evident, whereby communities are dependent on the power of local dons, who lead politically affiliated networks that are usually engaged in organized crime, to preserve order and to protect them. These communities exist, to a large measure, outside the jurisdiction of the state, beyond the reach of its fundamental institutions, such as tax paying, and have neutralized institutions such as the local police. While the state structures have not been completely supplanted, these communities have proceeded to develop their own alternative institutions, such as the payment of tribute and protection tax, and an alternative justice system. In one of the research communities this alternative system was fairly developed – and it would be a grave mistake to regard it as simple vigilantism. In many respects, it is an attempt to replicate the state system, but it operates on the inquisitorial principle whereby a judge or panel of judges is responsible for the investigation of reported incidents. It is fairly intrusive and deals with cases from child neglect and abuse to theft and murder. It is reportedly very swift and effective – operating primarily, but not exclusively, on the principle of retribution. Many readily report incidents to this institution rather than the police because there is a much reduced danger of reprisal from the offender and because the outcomes are speedier and the service less costly. It is seen by many as being more effective than the police. Thus, following a spate of killings in Alexanderville during the course of this research project, one party representative and prospective member of Parliament for the area publicly appealed to the local don to retake "control" of the area.[17]

This alternative system of justice first made its appearance in the urban areas in the 1970s with the maturity of the garrison communities.[18] Using the "model" that was developed in one of these garrisons as the prototype, it has spread fairly rapidly across the city in the 1990s.

Any informal system administered by underworld figures is likely to be highly problematic. The abuses meted out to these control authorities led to a revolt by citizens of the (subject and thus relatively deprived) garrison community Clementville against this system and the political leadership, which was viewed as approving it. But generally, as an alternative police, they tend to be more effective than the JCF as they employ a wider range and, in some instances, a more sophisticated combination of sociopolitical control mechanisms and resources – welfare and coercion, mediation and social ostracism, psychological manipulation and naked terror, among others.

This development is not just a response to the ineffectiveness of the state system; it is also a response to the experiences of injustice. Specifically, overcriminalization leads to disrespect for formal procedures, and the criminal justice system. According to Stone, "a disrespect for formal legal procedures" is fairly general in the society [Stone 1992].

The crisis has highlighted the failure of the traditional approach to policing the inner city, and its contribution to and envelopment in a cycle of criminal impunity. As the formal economy continues to decline relative to the informal, and the state remains feeble and incapacitated in opening viable legitimate income-generating opportunities for young people, the underground and the institutions and skills associated with it may be expected to continue to flourish. This will result in deeper criminal embeddedness in the communities and, consequently, a greater disjuncture between informal internal community controls and formal external police controls. In response, paramilitary modes of policing are reinforced, which in turn leads to poor police-citizen relations and poor information flow from citizens to the police, reluctant witnesses and low conviction rates. This in turn leads to police vigilantism, which further corrupts and delegitimizes the police force, thereby reinforcing the paramilitary mode of policing. These largely nonrecursive processes reflect the general crisis in policing. A schema of this process is presented in Figure 5.1. Although the broad process depicted in Figure 5.1 is presented as a sequential chain of interdependent developments, the process it attempts to describe should not be taken as a simple linear one. Some feedback and interactive effects are described, and the strongest of these are indicated in the figure by reverse arrows. The main positive feedback loops are indicated by the plus signs. It is a simple description of the process and it is not claimed that the factors described in the schema are all causally necessary for the outcomes that have been identified. As aspects of the processes in the schema have been elaborated in some of the earlier chapters, particularly in chapter 1, to avoid repetition, the discussion here is limited to the more direct aspects of police-citizen encounters.

This cycle of impunity cannot be broken by the mix of hard paramilitary policing and community relations. The strategic approach of the police has been one of containment, which in effect attempts simply to maintain the status quo. This reactive approach may be appropriate where criminality is not embedded and the status quo is tolerable, but where drug dons dominate aspects of the life of the communities, this approach is unable to restore the rule of law to these communities. Providing the conditions for a turn, or return, to the rule of law would seem to involve altering the local power relations by removing the sources of the power of the dons (their drug wealth, guns) while simultaneously empowering the citizens so that they may feel free and justified in collaborating with the criminal justice system and ultimately to take greater responsibility for their own security. Such an approach would suggest a change in the style of policing.

Community Policing: The Case of Alexanderville

In an effort to develop a new approach, community policing was attempted in Alexanderville in 1994 as part of a pilot project initially involving four communities in the KMA staffed by 18 constables. CBP has its intellectual origins in the Kansas City preventive patrol experiments of 1972 conducted by Kelling et al. [1974] and its practical birth in "team policing", which was introduced in North America in the 1970s. However, it matured as CBP during the early 1980s [Trojanowicz and Bucqueroux 1990:67–68; Leighton 1991:488–89]. As with other innovations in policing, the transfer of CBP to Jamaica was effected long after its development and without adaptation.

The essence of the construct is the idea that the police are most effective as partners with the citizens in the prevention and control of crime, and in ensuring an improved quality of life. This implies new power relations between the police and the public, their direct accountability to the communities, and a redefinition of the very goals of policing [Trojanowicz and Bucqueroux 1990:5; Skolnick and Bayley 1986:21–22].

CBP is based on a recognition of the limits of the police and the necessity and benefits of popular participation in policing. It represents a more civil model of police work and is more contractarian than power oriented. This intimates a profound philosophical shift from the notion of security as the sole responsibility of the state, which has been a feature of Caribbean polities.

Having redefined the role of the citizen in the formal system of social control in this way, community policing has exhibited considerable potential for breaking the mutually reinforcing negative attributional biases of the

Figure 5.1 Schema of Police-Citizen Relations

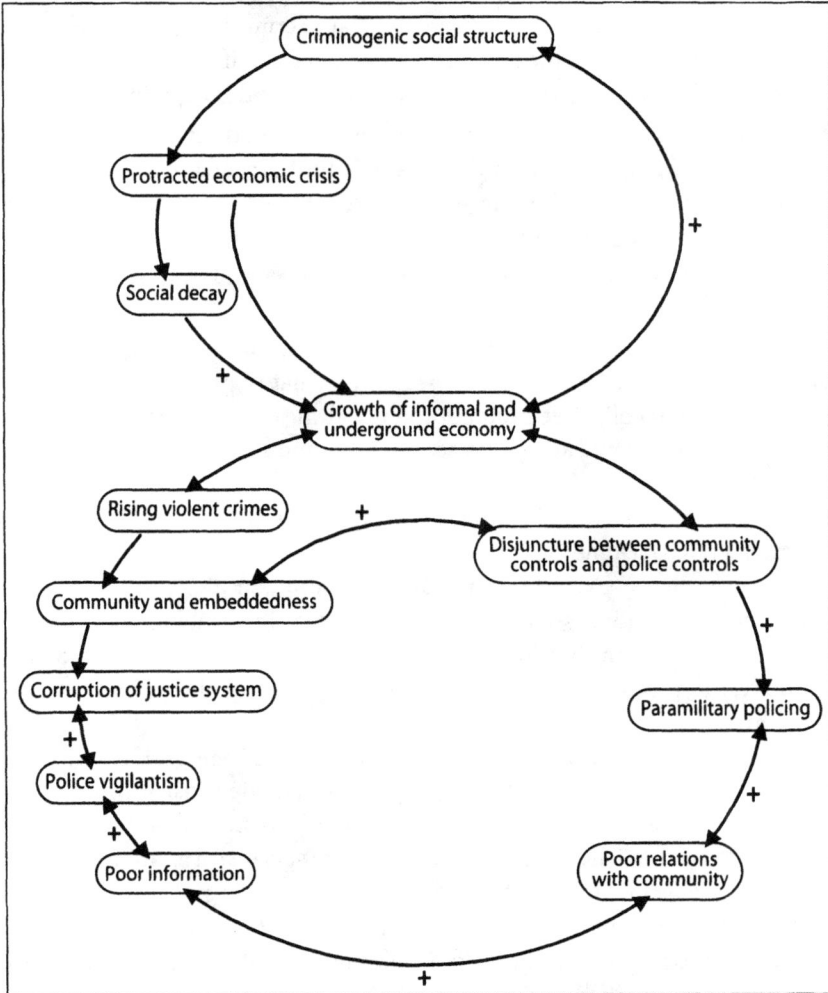

community toward the police and the police toward the community described above, which contribute to the impunity enjoyed by the more successful street criminals.

Recently, CBP as a concept has come in for greater critical scrutiny [Fielding 1994; Riechers and Roberg 1990; Goldstein 1987]. A number of problems have been identified at the conceptual level (and many more in its application):

•   It is too state intrusive and expansive of the police role in society. CBP is seen as extending the police role beyond law enforcement to norm enforcement, thereby giving the police too much power in the society [Riechers and Roberg 1990].

- It is soft on crime [see Skolnick and Bayley 1986:50–58]. Research shows that it is more successful at reducing the fear of crime than the rate of crime. Nonetheless, it has shown successes in reducing specific categories of crime in specific types of communities [Trojanowicz and Bucqueroux 1990].

- It assumes community and a civic-communitarian tradition. But societies are tending to be more individualistic and atomized. On this basis, Manning [1984, cited in Riechers and Roberg 1990] criticizes it as a vain attempt to recapture a lost past.

- It erroneously assumes a congruence between law and community norms, and community and police values.

These objections are not exhaustive. They simply show that while the general direction in which CBP points may be fruitful (that is, putting police-citizen cooperation and collective problem solving at the centre of policing), it has limitations, some would argue very serious ones, and should not be uncritically applied.

Jamaica has a record of community involvement in policing. The district constables (DCs), Home Guard, and Neighbourhood Watch are all institutions of citizen policing [see Harriott 1994]. Running parallel with these state institutions is, as discussed earlier, a tradition of informal justice in some of the inner city communities of Kingston and Montego Bay and isolated rural areas in the eastern end of the island that have not always been socially integrative.

These forms of community involvement have all been problematic. The DC was a colonial imposition, an extension of an alien institution among an alienated people, and was never integrated into and made accountable to the community. The Home Guard was more successful as an instrument of crime management, but it became politically partisan and, as a result, was eventually overcome by the political resistance that it attracted within the JCF and the society more generally. Neighbourhood Watch, the latest in this tradition, was launched in the mid 1980s. It is the broadest in participation but the most limited in its scope of action, being simply "the eyes and ears of the police". At the end of 1992, there were 300 Neighbourhood Watch groups in Jamaica. This represented some 15 percent of all community based groups in the island. Most of these groups were located in the KMA [Harriott 1992]. They rapidly multiplied in response to the increasing incidents of crime and the declining confidence of citizens in the ability of the police to protect them. By the end of 1996, there were 445 such groups [JCF *Annual Report* 1996:22].

Although they enjoy a close relationship with the police and are often initiated by the local community relations officers, the Neighbourhood Watch groups have not developed as simply passive adjuncts of the police. They actively lobby the Ministry of National Security and the JCF for better service and tend to be critical of some of the shortcomings of the Force. At their national conference in 1993, they were critical of the police force for its differential responsiveness along class lines and its breaches of confidentiality by transmitting received information to criminals.[19]

There is a growing recognition of the limitations of the Watches in the context of poor police responsiveness. The national conference of 1993 effused a low self-evaluation and feelings of impotence. "We watch the criminals, but can't do anything about it," they lamented. This outcome has two connected sources: the uncritical transplant of the concept as applied in the USA/UK, and the influence of the old professional model of policing. The Neighbourhood Watch remains an imitative transplant (as opposed to a transposition) from the USA where the police have the capacity to make quick responses and the citizen has easy access to firearms. In this context, citizens may be asked to simply be the eyes and ears of the police. But neither of these conditions obtains in Jamaica, thus there has been a call for members of the Watch to become DCs. This is an attempt to give them a capacity to intervene. Community groups have tremendous potential for social crime prevention and problem solving. Despite the problems, the Watches suggest the existence of a significant social base for a CBP type of project.

It is against this background that the Alexanderville experience is best examined. The duties of the CPOs are to patrol, respond to emergency calls, assist in intelligence gathering, settle disputes, service Neighbourhood Watch and police youth clubs, maintain contact with crime victims, counsel juveniles, lecture at schools, and provide fora for the police to meet with interest groups to discuss and implement solutions to local problems.[20] With such a wide range of duties, it is inevitable that some will be de-emphasized. Moreover, some duties are conflicting. For example, some problems such as drug distribution have to be openly confronted in association with the citizens. This may conflict with the intelligence function, which may involve confidence building with the main offenders. These conflicting duties tend to generate considerable tensions as they are not simply contending priorities but, rather, duties that place the CBOs in conflicting roles.

CBP, as practised in Alexanderville, is less oriented on substantive policing and more focused on community relations. Its main substantive crime control work is in the area of settlement of domestic disputes (perhaps guided by the erroneous view that most homicides are a consequence of domestic disputes) and some efforts at social crime control. It is perhaps too early to judge, but CBP has had no apparent effect on the crime rate and, although there has been some success at incident solving, there has not been any attempt at problem solving.

Despite these limitations, there are some indicators of the potential of CBP for advancing policing in the Jamaican context when compared with the traditional mode. This is best depicted in the new levels of collaboration with the people in the following case, in which a resident of the community stole a refrigerator from the community clinic operated by the local Baptist church. This crime constituted a serious violation of community codes, since the clinic is a socially valued service and the church a sacred symbol. The CIB and other such units were unable to make any advances in the case. Unlike these units, the CPOs received the support of the people and were told where the refrigerator and the offender could be found. After the negotiation of an informal settlement (on the initiative and to the satisfaction of community representatives), the offender was made to do community service.

This type of case would normally have been handled by the community don, as it represented a breach of community norms and threatened the continued provision of a valued service to the community. The outcome in such a case might have been different – perhaps even resulting in a gang war. If CBP, as practised here, simply retakes this ground from the dons, then it would have made an important contribution, as this protector function is an important source of the social power of the dons. It accords them the moral legitimacy to use coercive force.

These simple successes of cooperation in incident solving are helping to positively transform the attitude of the CPOs to the people (and may yet lead to problem solving). But this has come at the price of adaptation to, and acceptance of, community norms as the parameter of police action (which police officials may not be willing to accept). For example, there were no arrests for dealing in drugs by the entire staff of the local police station, despite the existence of at least 11 crack houses in the community. CBP generally claims a good record on the treatment of victimless crimes. Its handling of the drug dealing in the inner city communities of the USA is often celebrated as the biggest success of CBP in crime control and improving the quality of life in these communities [see Skolnick and Bayley 1986]. No attempt has been made to mobilize the community against the crack houses in Alexanderville, despite the strong cultural resistance to cocaine in these communities.

The effect of CBPs on police-community relations has been positive. It has helped to reduce the incidents of police brutality, false arrest, and community vigilante action in response to some types of matters. The community, however, continues to receive mixed signals from the JCF since CBP coexists alongside the "hard policing" of the special squads. The latter is stimulated by the high level of violence, and the former by the need to clean up the resulting alienation. Such an approach runs the risk of the CPOs being seen as a community relations sideshow or, worse, simply intelligence agents on whose information these central units act.

Citizens' involvement in the project is narrowly structured. A consultative committee provides this function, but it is mainly composed of persons who are associated with the community through their professional or business activity but who do not live in the community and are socially not representative of it. The consultative committees ought to simply cap what is a wider process of participation and, through this, the building of consensus on how best to police the community, which ought to occur in the daily activities of the CPOs. This is the essence of the democratic content of community policing.

But these activities have been more about simply multiplying the number and types of contact with the citizens than real consensus building. This is reflected in the ineffectiveness of the consultative committee that operates in Alexanderville. Thus, there is very little real community input into policy, priority setting, problem solving and a deficit of police accountability to the community. That the forms of contact with citizens and the concept of community policing as observed in Alexanderville are emptied of their democratic and consensus-building content should not be surprising as, from his or her experience in the Force, the typical constable becomes steeped in authoritarian practices and thus must be expected to have great difficulty fitting with the style of community policing.

Although most communities enjoy a tradition of civic activism, in Alexanderville, as in Normanville, this has declined (due to greater individualism and fragmentation) and most organized activity is canalized by the political parties. This has meant that police have had to either work with, and run the danger of being co-opted by the party system, or mobilize the associations it is supposed to partner; or alternatively, avoid community mobilizations (as was done) instead of working with selected individuals – usually business persons and church leaders. Either direction is problematic for CBP; both present it with problems of credibility and reduce the problem-solving capability of these structures that are supposed to operationalize police-citizen partnership.

In Alexanderville, the Kingston Restoration Company (KRC, an independent, credible, and resource endowed organization) initially facilitated the development of police-citizens fora. But these were not sustained. It is perhaps too early to make a general judgement, but it is evident that adjustments to this project are needed.

Despite these problems, the experience suggests that good policing not only improves citizen-police relations and offers possibilities for more effective crime control but may also help to transform the communities. Police reform may facilitate community reform. By reducing the dependence on "protectors", it may assist in bringing the more positive social forces to the fore and strengthen their role in the leadership in these communities.

Conclusion

Ultimately police effectiveness rests on the active associative participation of the citizens, especially the most victimized. This cannot be achieved without structured consultation with, representation by and accountability to them, indeed, a reordering of the power relations between police-state and citizen and a reordering of the power relations within the inner city communities. In a democratic ethos, legitimacy must rest on democratic principles. CBP, if nothing else, at a conceptual level, recognizes this. But in practice this has so far been lost to an incipient paternalism. A concerted remodelling of the general style of policing remains a challenge for the future.

In a large number of jurisdictions, the average citizen enjoys a fair measure of equality before the law (or at least an appearance of this), although this may stand in contrast to his or her material inequality. In Jamaica, the average citizen must face both an evident inequality in how he or she is treated in the criminal justice processes and material inequality.

This is particularly problematic at the level of attitudes and the affective orientation to the Force and justice system, and the development of alternative institutions on alternative principles. Social order in these communities has been related to the assertion of power by a dominant party. The weakening of the party system partly accounts for the greater fragmentation and disorder in the communities of the urban poor. The police by themselves have had great difficulty coping with these communities as order and stability cannot be maintained by force alone. More open opportunities, greater respect for people as individuals and greater social justice more generally are some of the important bases of lasting stability. Change in the model of inner city policing consistent with these values is vital, if these communities are to be reclaimed rather than remain extrastatal islands beyond the law.

As this and previous chapters exploring the nature of the crisis of policing in Jamaica suggest, the necessity of reform is great and the character of the changes profound. It is to an examination of the attitudes of the members of the Force to such a reform project that we now turn.

Section III

The Reforms

6

Attempts
at Reform

This chapter provides a critical evaluation of the aims, their operationalized derivatives, and the methods of executing the current project to reform the JCF. The factors favouring the initiation of the reform programme and the intellectual sources of the project are further examined. Some of the elements of this reform programme are not new. They carry with them considerable historical baggage, which conditions the attitudinal biases towards them. The current process is therefore placed in the context of previous attempts at reforming the JCF.

The aims of the current programme of police reform are set out in the Wolfe [1993] and Herst [1991] reports. In his first written communication to Commissioner Trevor MacMillan, the minister of national security and justice, Mr Keith Knight, indicated that these reports had the general approval of the administration and would provide the script for a programme of action during his tenure.[1] The aims of this project were generally to improve the efficiency and effectiveness of the JCF. Efficiency concerns are narrowly managerial and simply seek to increase the present outputs (patrols, number of arrests, cases cleared up) using fewer units of resource without necessarily having regard for social utility and the quality of justice. While efficiency concerns are narrowly technocratic, effectiveness is more foundational and is indicated by the extent of achievement of socially useful goals and satisfaction with the services provided [see Blau and Myer 1987:139–61]. In the Jamaican context effectiveness is prior to efficiency and entails commitment to democratic values including the rule of law (substantive and procedural), distributive justice and general issues of police rectitude.

In pursuit of effectiveness, the reforms were intended to reduce the abuse of power, improve the relations between the police and the public, control corruption, and depoliticize the Force [Wolfe 1993:17]. This was to be effected by improving discipline, ensuring greater openness and accountability within the Force (providing evidence that the system of internal control works), organizing rewards on the principles of performance and ability rather than political affiliation and personal empathy, showing greater respect for human rights and civil liberties by operating within the law, and improving the quality of the managerial personnel and the resources available to the Force.

These aims were largely cast in a negative way – although a vague reference to a "civil model" of policing and professionalization can be found in the *Report of the National Task Force on Crime* (otherwise called the Wolfe Report [1993]). The reform package seeks to tackle the negative manifestations of the existing mode of policing, but fails to provide a coherent positive perspective on change. The latter requires a critique of the existing mode of policing, not just its negative expressions, as these we have tried to show are inherent and unavoidable accompaniments of this mode. Although their progressive character cannot be denied, these are, nevertheless, system-refurbishing and reinforcing, not system-transforming reforms.

The Historical Background

The reform of 1993 was the third effort at police reform since 1834, and the second at reforming the JCF in the 130 years since it was established in 1867.[2] These reforms have all followed, albeit somewhat distantly, in the wake of similar reforms in Britain. The first of these efforts was initiated in 1866 and, in effect created the JCF. The central objective of this reform project was to ensure tighter control of its constables and to improve their capability and reliability in controlling the population and safeguarding the security of the colonial state. This was to be achieved by "improving the quality of its recruits", militarizing the Force, and making policing a full-time salaried occupation.

These reforms were influenced in their content by the Peelian reforms, which inaugurated the London Metropolitan Police in 1829. Both occurred in the context of protracted public order problems and other threatening phenomena associated with profound social changes and the responses of the mass public to these changes. State control systems tend to respond to perceived threats and may even reinvent themselves in the face of these threats, as was the case with the JCF. The 1866 reform of the Jamaican police occurred in the context of the postemancipation efforts to control the former slaves, and to regulate the newly emerging labour market by excessive taxation and restrictive land control measures, which were made more oppressive by the conditions of economic crisis. This conflicted with the struggles of the newly free black population to create new economic and social spaces independent of the plantation. The upshot of this was the 1865 Morant Bay Rebellion, which revealed the incapacities of the "old police". This is more fully discussed elsewhere [see Harriott 1994].

Similarly, the creation of the London Metropolitan Police occurred in the context of the public order problems (rioting by the displaced and dislocated urban populations) and rising crime rates associated with the social changes induced by the Industrial Revolution [Reith 1943]. But, unlike in the case of the JCF, the creation of the London police was influenced by the need to avoid the violent excesses of the military suppressions, which typified the handling of the mass protests at the time, by inventing a politically sensitive institution that would be more measured in the use of coercion to maintain public order. The model of policing applied in Jamaica – despite the excesses in the suppression of Morant Bay – was stripped of the citizen protective aspects and the safeguards available to accused persons in England (after 1836), of its decentralized and more civil character, and was instead more directly modelled on the Royal Irish Constabulary (RIC). The RIC model was clearly regarded as being preferable for the control of the colonial populations as it was militarized, armed, subjectively controlled (with Catholics in the ranks but Protestants as officers), practised differential enforcement against the Catholics and was exempt from the British tradition of minimum force and political independence [see Jefferies 1952:30–31; Weitzer 1995].

By the turn of the century, the state of the JCF was again regarded as problematic and, in the tradition of the British, a commission of inquiry was established [see Thomas 1927]. The central issue from the standpoint of the authorities was again the poor quality of men and, from the standpoint of the men, racism. The first was "solved" by the importation of white Irish NCOs, thereby compounding the second. This period did not introduce any new elements when compared with the reforms of 1866. It simply strengthened British control of the Force by completing the process of whitening the ranks of the NCOs. It may thus be regarded as a continuation of the reforms of 1866 (albeit after a considerable hiatus) rather than a distinctive period of reform.

The second programme of reforms (of the JCF) was initiated some 85 years later, under the leadership of Commissioner Calver. It entailed reducing the arbitrary practices in the management of the Force by the formalization and standardization of procedures, reordering the criteria for promotions and making performance prior to seniority (this was speedily aborted after the first objections), and eroding race exclusion at the upper echelons of the Force [see Renny et al. 1951]. These reforms followed an earlier movement in Europe and America for the professionalization of their police forces and were part of a wider programme of reforming the colonial police forces in preparation for independence.

The third reform project occurred in the postindependence period as part of the broader programme of social reforms initiated by the democratic socialist movement of the 1970s. It sought to complete the Jamaicanization of the leadership personnel (which began in earnest in the 1950s and intensified immediately after Independence in 1962), but its central thrust was the civilianization of the Force. While fully succeeding in the former, the achievements with regard to the latter were more limited. This latter element of the reforms was largely negative in its orientation, seeking to alter the more insufferable aspects of paramilitarism, such as obligatory residence in the police barracks, which were associated with the colonial era. The professionalization initiated during the reforms of 1952 was not continued, however, rather, politicization was intensified [Harriott 1994].

With the exception of the 1865 reforms, all attempts have been weak, incrementalist correctives to the existing model, which remains paradigmatic. Moreover, they are usually considered long after they have become accepted practice in the British police services. CBP is the most recent example of this. Even then, all such reform programmes were either domesticated or truncated. Successive reform efforts therefore face an increasing accumulation of unresolved and even more intractable problems.

This postindependence neglect, or lack of any sustained commitment to police reform, may be explained by the continuities in national security policy. The role and style of the police remained unchanged. The design of the political élite with respect to the JCF was simply to gain control of the Force. From this narrow perspective, decolonization was simply equated with personnel changes rather than a re-engineering of the institution.

This continuity, with the consequent reluctance to engage the Force in any fundamental reforms, is associated with a deep fear among policy makers of police resistance to reform. The police force is a powerful, armed institution capable of constraining and even removing governments, with a reputation for jealously guarding its perceived institutional interests and treating reform efforts as condemnatory. In Jamaica, in 1968 and again during the 1970s, police resistance not only stymied the process of police reforms but also played an important role in the electoral defeat of the respective JLP and PNP governments [Harriott 1994]. There is thus some experiential foundation for this fear.

Serious efforts at reform therefore have to be propelled by external popular pressure. In a highly segmented and easily polarized society such as Jamaica, broad multiclass and multiparty support for such programmes is needed. This has been absent, particularly among the upper classes whose social insecurity tends to induce considerable tolerance of police abuses of the policed masses.

The reform efforts of the past were motivated primarily by issues of power and control, either over the Force as an instrument of political power or over the population. Only in the 1990s has the concern with crime control become central.

Past reform efforts share the following features: they are usually imposed by governments as responses to public dissatisfaction and to pressure for police reform. These pressures, at times cross-pressures from different sections of the society, may be interpreted as ambiguous, as the cross-pressures may sometimes appear to run in different directions. For example, in response to what is perceived as a greater threat from criminal violence, some may urge a stronger, less legalistic force; while other sections of the population, in response to the excessive use of lethal violence by the police, may be demanding reform in a more democratic direction and with stronger controls. Regardless of the direction urged, as the impetus for reform usually comes from outside the Force (indeed, outside the entire security establishment), in response, the Force tends to adopt a defensive posture that retards the development of internal change agents and casts doubts on their authenticity, thereby ceding intellectual and operational leadership of these processes to agents external to them. With some exceptions, the actual reforms have tended to be more symbolic than substantive and, as will be discussed later in the text, are limited by the politicization of the reforms and the associated internal political resistance.

Sources of the Reforms

As noted earlier, the reforms are a response to the deep legitimacy crisis enveloping the Force. The approval rating of the police had declined from 67 percent in 1987 to 40 percent in 1991 [Stone 1991b:6]. The JCF was regarded by the majority of the population as corrupt, ineffective, uncivil, excessive in its use of violence and abusive of the rights of the people [Stone 1991a].

It may be argued that, despite the myth of a golden era of policing (during the postwar preindependence period of 1945–62), the level of confidence in the JCF among the policed had always been low. Therefore, on the hard definition of legitimacy, a crisis would have obtained from the pre-independence period. In other words, the 1991 data may arguably be interpreted as simply representing the intensification of an old trend, not a crisis.

However, what makes 1991 a turning point is the generalized and multifaceted nature of the critique of the JCF – that it was ineffective in controlling crime, corrupt, uncivil in its interaction with citizens, abusive of its powers, too violent, unjust in its treatment of suspects and so forth. Unlike in the 1970s and 1980s, majority opinion now rated it negatively on all these issues [Stone 1991a].

Consistent with theoretical expectations, survey data show that popular evaluations of police forces tend to be more negative among high-contact groups, which are usually those at the lower end of the status hierarchy. By 1991, however, this pattern had changed; negative perceptions were found to be uniformly distributed among all social groups, regardless of the level of contact with the police. Indeed, negative opinions were now slightly stronger in the middle strata [Stone 1991a]. Thus even on the soft definition of legitimacy, whereby élite approval is regarded as the decisive indicator (regardless of the rating of the majority or the policed), the Force would still be regarded as being in a crisis.

This state of crisis was recognized by some senior officers of the Force and was openly discussed in the internal backstage fora of the JCF. In a discussion paper circulated to the officers under his command, one such officer commented as follows:

Our effectiveness to deal with crime, criminal activities and the fear it has generated, has been openly criticized. The impact of the police services are perceived as ineffectual. The morale of the personnel is waning. The image of the Force is at stake. We must reduce crime and criminal activities and in so doing reduce fear in the communities. We need to regain our stature. We need to initiate, revitalize and motivate personnel to give quality service to the public. We need to rebuild our image if we are to be an effective organization. [Martin 1993:2]

It was in this setting that the Herst and Wolfe inquiries were commissioned. If, as in the British tradition, they were intended to dissolve the problem, they certainly did not succeed. The depth of the crisis and its continued affirmation in dramatic events, such as the Constant Spring case discussed earlier, served to intensify public pressure and élite lobbying to have the recommendations in the reports implemented.

The programme of reforms sought to attend to the main dimensions of the legitimacy problem. These include:
- a credibility and accountability deficit,
- political and class partiality,
- abuse of authority on human rights issues, and
- ineffectiveness in crime control.

Improving Credibility and Accountability

The efforts to improve the credibility of the Force included three elements – leadership renewal, improving discipline and controlling corruption. However, prior to restoring the credibility of the JCF, the credibility of the reform process itself needed to be established. Leadership was vital to this project, as the internal operational leadership may easily frustrate or effectively advance what was and is a top-down process. This factor is particularly important in the case of the JCF, which is highly centralized and operates on the principle of command and control. Moreover, the problems were so deep that its capacity for self change under a self-created leadership would have been seriously doubted by the mass public.

The appointment of Trevor MacMillan, a former army colonel and head of the Revenue Protection Division (RPD)[3] (the first outsider since Independence to hold the post of commissioner), reflected the deep crisis of confidence in the leadership of the JCF. He brought with him a reputation for incorruptibility and political and class impartiality, which was acquired during his army career and renewed during his tenure as director of the RPD. He represents the best of the Independence generation of middle class professionals who, infused with a spirit of optimism, willingly engaged the problems of the country through disinterested public service. At the time of his appointment, after over 40 years in security, he was still largely free of the cynicism that is, understandably, so prevalent and is indeed an occupational hazard in the security forces, and still retained this spirit of service and optimism. He eschewed the anti-intellectualism of his predecessors and possessed an intellectual openness to questioning the fundamentals of the system of policing that prevailed and the strength of character to risk failure in departing from the mind-numbing routines and rituals of the Force. Physically, he presented an image of discipline, contrasting with the corpulence of his predecessors, and, unlike them, was invariably seen in uniform. But most of all, he was free of the political baggage of departmentalism, the pandering to special interests and the personal debts to colleagues that are usually accumulated in order to get to the top in a power culture.

To transfer the credibility and moral authority of the leadership to the organization required behaviourial change, most of all restoring discipline and reducing corruption.

Restoring Discipline and Reducing Corruption

A major achievement of the period was the improvement in discipline within the Force. On a superficial level, this was reflected in more consistent enforcement of the dress code of the Force, a more orderly arrangement of office furniture, and so forth.[4] More substantially, it involved greater internal accountability at all levels of command.

The threshold of tolerance of corrupt and incompetent behaviour was sharply lowered. During 1994 and 1995, some 572 allegations of misconduct and criminality among members of the Force were investigated. If we assume one allegation per person, it was found necessary to investigate (often in response to complaints by citizens) some 10 percent of the Force [JCF *Annual Report* 1995:11].

During the period under review, there was a sharp increase in the frequency of internally initiated disciplinary charges against police offenders. This increased by approximately 100 percent in the first year of the reforms. However, as reported in chapter 3, there was no change in the structure of offending. This suggests that while supervisors seemed to have supported the call to restore discipline, they did not respond to the new priorities. Thus indolence and unresponsiveness to requests for service to the public largely remained unpunished. They simply intensified the old patterns of punishment. Little behaviour modification should therefore have been expected. The data from the Charge Book for the Internal Courts of Enquiry indicated (by a high frequency of incidents of insubordination and disrespect for supervisors and managers) that reasserting their authority was clearly problematic and required a greater resort to coercion and the removal of many of these officers, as the supervisory leadership had clearly lost its moral authority.

There was a significant renewal of the officer corps during the period under review, with approximately 15 percent of it being replaced.[5] Some 25 percent of the officers retired, were sent on secondment, or transferred from sensitive, high-opportunity or high-contact line positions to the Inspections Unit (which was then viewed as a sort of pre-retirement home for corrupt or incompetent officers). These were replaced by some 35 young, better educated and better trained officers via an Accelerated Promotions Programme or performance criteria, or both.

By introducing three new elements, the treatment of corruption departed from the traditional symbolic approach: officers were no longer effectively exempt from surveillance and sanctions; the most serious and incorrigible offenders now faced the prospect of having their careers terminated; and the creation of new institutions that allowed the JCF to more consistently treat with the problem. An Internal Affairs Division was formed in 1994. It represented a shift from reliance on "news carrying" to proper investigations, thereby safeguarding members of the JCF from the caprice of their superior officers and self-interested others, as well as providing a more effective agency for acting on reports from citizens. Prior to this, corruption was investigated by the highly politicized Special Branch and was mainly used as a pretext to remove politically undesirable personnel from sensitive posts or as political revenge. It was therefore never a serious threat to corrupt constables.

The treatment of corruption, however, while resulting in more responsible behaviour at the managerial and senior supervisory levels, remained a very problematic issue inside the Force. The institutionalized nature of this corruption and the deep involvement in these practices by many of the "frontline crime fighters" and politically connected personnel, who sought to use their political influence to insulate themselves from sanctions, meant that any thorough anticorruption campaign necessarily involved the complex and prickly process of depoliticization.

The depoliticization of the Force was a central issue of the reform programme, as autonomy is cardinal to the project of professionalization. This idea has its ideological roots in the doctrine of administrative political neutrality and a notion of how democracy ought to work. Parties, as representative of the people, translate their mandates into public policy. These are then executed by a politically neutral bureaucracy, which is not expected to frustrate the will of the people and that of their political representatives.

In contrast, in the political model of policing that obtains, these two clear domains of power are not discrete. This model tends to generate constant conflicts as the boundaries of these two domains are constantly renegotiated, particularly during periods of change. More so in this case, as depoliticization was not treated as part of a broader goal of transforming the governance of the Force but was narrowly cast as a struggle for empowering the commissioner of police and disempowering the minister of national security.

The legal framework was altered to more clearly define and limit the role of the minister and to exclude his involvement in operational matters and safeguard this as the sole province of the commissioner. Practically, this meant amplifying and extending the power of the commissioner to apply sanctions – subject to political oversight via the Police Services Commission. Promotions and assignments became less determined by political considerations and more by performance. For many party activists within the Force, their careers seemed to have been effectively ruined or truncated by having been passed over for promotions, removed from strategic posts, and having to endure the associated loss of status.

A peculiar difficulty for the reforms, then, was that a process initiated by the government has resulted in some of its strongest supporters being the greatest losers of that process. This resulted in systematic lobbying of the political directorate to veer from the course.

This political interventionism nevertheless served as a system of accountability, as citizens (affiliated to the ruling party) were able, via their political representatives, to impose disciplinary measures on abusive police operatives. However, this weakening mechanism of accountability was to be replaced by a more representative system of local control with the launch of citizen consultative committees. This idea (which was imported from England via the British advisors) had considerable potential for adding a new dimension to the governance of the JCF, but instead has been merely symbolic.

The committees operate at the parish level and were originally intended to consist of community organizations, representatives of the state bureaucracy, elected representatives and citizens [Ministry of National Security and Justice 1993:8]. In reality, at the parish level, they are small committees (of six) composed of the custos and senior bureaucrats from the local state institutions, under the effective leadership of the police representative for the area. They therefore remain unrepresentative, nonparticipatory, unaccountable, and remote from the problems of the communities. This arrangement represents an unsatisfactory resolution of the tension between community inclusion and professionalism. Stripped of any substance, it is thus unable to aid problem solving, protect the rights of the citizenry, or help to break with the class justice associated with the criminal justice system.

Respect for the Law and Civil Liberties

Since Independence, the JCF has been progressively confronted with an ideologically constructed tension between law and crime control. As shown earlier, the Force has developed a reputation for resolving this tension in the direction of "crime fighting" [see Chevigny 1991; 1995]. Indeed, the phrase "law enforcement" was absent from the active lexicon of the Force, with the more legally distanced phrase "crime fighting" adopted as a comfortable substitute. Such a resolution is incongruent with professionalism, which entails concern not just with narrow crime control ends but also with means, that is, with issues of rectitude.

New measures were introduced to restrict the use of force. New internal rules of engagement were adapted, which prohibited "the use of firearms against persons except in self-defence or the defence of others in the face of threats of death or serious injury". An exception to this is allowed in the case of a fleeing felon if two conditions are met: "all other means of effecting an arrest have been exhausted, and the police reasonably believes that the escape of the felon will pose a significant threat to human life should escape occur"[JCF 1995:Appendix A, 1–2]. This marked a significant shift from the previous guidelines of 1990 laid down in *Force Standing Orders* 2248 [JCF 1990] (this represented the first revision of the colonial guidelines of 1949), which allowed the use of deadly force to protect property, not just endangered lives, and to unconditionally stop fleeing felons.

Although unaccompanied by changes in the law, these guidelines provide the standards for internal administrative evaluations, which are now required in every instance of the use of deadly force by police personnel, and which may lead to internal disciplinary measures and impact on career outcomes. This is perhaps the first instance of self-imposed police guidelines being ahead of the law and reflecting a real commitment to the principle of minimum force. Consistent with the new approach, access to automatic rifles was restricted. Detectives were not permitted to carry them unless accompanied by uniformed constables, and in some uniformed branches of the Force attempts were made to withdraw the M16 rifles. This was accompanied by vigorous pursuit of breaches, particularly in the use of deadly force.

Institutionalized vigilantism was discouraged and dismantled. The rule of law was defended in the face of pressure from within the Force and the security establishment, and from elements within the established parties, opinion leaders with regular access to the press and the mass public, to revert to illegal methods. The best example of this was perhaps the criticism of the commissioner by the leader of the Opposition for being too legalistic and not acting on evidence of factual and/or reputational guilt. This was occasioned by his reluctance to act against 13 alleged gunmen whom the leader of the Opposition wished to have excoriated from his constituency.[6]

The police began to show greater respect for the law and reduced the use of deadly force. While in the early 1990s the number of justifiable homicides had steadily increased, after 1993 both the number of police killings and police killed began to decline. The number of police killings further declined from 123 in 1993 to 100 in 1994, and the number of police officers killed from 10 in 1993 to 6 in 1994 [Table 4.1]. During 1994, offenders from whom guns were recovered and who had even shot at the police (including, in one instance, a police killer) were not summarily executed but were instead arrested. This is even more significant as it is occurring in the context of a rising rate of violent crimes. In 1995 there was some increase in the number of police homicides, reflecting the growing resistance to the reforms, and in the latter half of 1996, following the termination of Colonel MacMillan, this increase gained momentum, reflecting popular encouragement of this trend and a speedy return to old ways.

Vigilantism is only the worst expression of a more generalized denial of the rights associated with citizenship. Impressionistic evidence suggests that during the period under review, the police became more civil and there was a general improvement in the treatment of the public and of suspects. In order to discourage the practice of using arrest as an investigative tool and to remove its effect (the holding of suspects for lengthy periods without charge), in each police division an inspector was assigned the responsibility to ensure that all arrests were justified.[7] These improvements were facilitated by the repealing of the Suppression of Crimes Act and, perhaps more importantly, by Force policy and by improved internal accountability.

There remains a divergence of views, both within the JCF and the mass public, on the use of force in the present context. Thus, despite the changes in the law, abuses such as holding suspects without charge for lengthy periods and searches without warrants have continued. As cases are lost by the Crown on procedural grounds, one would expect either behaviour modification on the part of the police (in adjusting to the new legislative regime and to conform to the conduct norms required of them, by improving their investigative skills and so forth) or, as was the case, attempts to lobby and agitate for the de facto restoration of their (emergency) powers and a more permissive leadership.

This more rights-regarding and legalistic mode puts greater pressure on an already overloaded court system. The reforms, therefore, ought to be extended to the judicial system, otherwise the confidence of the police in the reform process will be further undermined, and the insistence on the priority of respect for the law over crime fighting will be seen as out of touch with the violent realities of Jamaica and as being soft on criminals. The more rights-regarding and legalistic mode also placed new demands on police personnel, necessitating an improvement in the capabilities of the Force.

Improving Capability

The drive to improve the capability of the JCF was deeply influenced by the association of professionalism with the mastery of technology. On the "professional model", however, the use of this technology is usually designed to more efficiently manipulate the existing core strategies of the police (such as patrol and investigation) than to aid new innovations.

Efforts to improve the capability of the JCF have involved four elements. The first of these involved the use of computer applications to improve the information systems of the Force. This was and remains limited by the low level of education of the senior supervisory personnel and their reluctance to learn (the latter being conditioned by their advanced age and proximity to retirement).

This limitation necessitated improving the quality of the personnel, the second element of reform, and was pursued by the accelerated promotion of younger, better educated and more competent officers. They symbolize elements of the new values (promotions on merit, hard work, respect of the law) on which a more responsive and effective JCF must be built. They now constitute a core (but not a critical mass) of change agents.

Training programmes at the level of both the officers and the other ranks were redesigned to acquaint responsible personnel with the application of computer technology to departmental management and policing. There was a broadening, beyond the transfer of policing skills and basic knowledge of the conditions under which arrests may be made for violations of the law, to a return to human rights sensitization.[8] Consistent with this, to correct the overreliance on coercive methods of investigation (hostage taking and other methods of applying direct pressure to suspects) and on witnesses, training programmes were designed to better acquaint investigators with basic criminalistic techniques. This, of course, required an upgrading of the forensic laboratory. There was also considerable discussion of the impact of problems derived from the social environment. However, with the possible exception of the Accelerated Promotions Programme, the rudiments of social scientific knowledge needed for effective policing have not been systematically introduced into the curriculum.

The third element was organizational rationalization. Motivated by the need to improve the efficiency of the JCF, the hierarchy was flattened somewhat by phasing out two ranks – that of acting corporal and of assistant superintendent. The JCF nevertheless remains among those forces with the tallest hierarchies. A strong commitment to the existing paramilitary principles remains, even while attempting to eliminate their effects.

Excessive centralization retards initiative and contributes to a reluctance to assume responsibility and to ineffectiveness. On the other hand, allowing incompetent and corrupt divisional officers greater autonomy resulted in some negative effects, such as the issuing of firearm licences to drug dealers.[9] This presents a dilemma. Decentralization is needed for improved effectiveness (and is an imperative of professionalization), but since the reform process derives its energy from the top, and given the level of corruption and resistance, centralized control was required to ensure the advance of the process. The old centralizing tendencies have therefore persisted, with the continued formation of special squads and units – the Mediation Unit, community policing, the special unit to investigate white-collar crimes, and the strengthening of the Rape Unit. Decentralization is needed to overcome irrationalities, allow better service delivery, and to broaden and extend identification with the change process.

Fourth, as noted earlier, the resource base of the Force was significantly improved, with an increase in the size of its fleet in the order of 100 percent. This has heightened police visibility. This improved capability, however, has had no noticeable impact on the crime rate, which has continued to rise. For 1994, the rate of violent crimes increased by 3.5 percent. The number of murders increased 6 percent (690); shootings, 11 percent (1,251); rape, 8 percent (1,070); and robbery, 1 percent (5,461) when compared with 1993. Nor has there been any positive change in the cleared-up rates from violent crimes (murder 43 percent, down from 44 percent).

The enduring nature of the trends in violent crime should alert us to the difficulties facing the process and the professional model itself. A general feature of the reforms is their limited scope and perspective: greater rectitude, but limited change in the systems of accountability; depoliticization, but within the existing mode of governance; organizational change, but within the existing organizational principles of paramilitarism; improved police-community relations, but no change in the style of policing that generates the conflicts with the community. These limitations inhere in the professional reform model itself.

Criticisms of the Professional Reform Model

The content of the reforms described above differs little from that applied in the USA in the 1920s – the redefinition of the mission to focus on crime fighting; improving the quality of personnel and training; military type discipline; greater application of the emerging criminalistics and communications technology to policing; reconstructing the image of the police; and depoliticization [cf. Sparrow, Moore and Kennedy 1990:34–37; Johnson 1976].

After a 50-year period of reforms (1930–80) on the basis of this reform model, the police forces in the developed countries, including the USA and UK, remain plagued by problems similar to those of the JCF. The limitations of this model became apparent (in the developed countries) as early as the 1970s. It has been criticized for:

- Its failure to control crime effectively
- Its goals (to control crime and maintain order) and methods being too narrow to help win back the social and physical spaces lost to criminals and thus to help in improving the quality of life of inner city residents
- The reduction of the ties between citizen and police
- An insulation from political accountability that tends to make the police less responsive to the needs of the people
- A certain structural woodenness and poor adaptability; this is particularly disadvantageous in a dynamic environment [see Moore 1992:111–19; Sparrow et al. 1990:44–50]

From the standpoint of the developing countries, the resource demands of the model are unsustainable. It now costs approximately US $90,000 to keep a two-person patrol car on the road for one year.[10] The model demands an ever-increasing police density, regardless of its impact on crime. Even the developed countries are finding the calculus of police resource demands on the traditional professional model beyond them [Bayley 1994:54].

The professional reform model was applied in Jamaica well after the high point of the managerial reform movement, which was such an important complement to the professional reform model. It was thus not accompanied by the questioning of the managerial principles and structures of the paramilitary model, or of Taylorist influences on police structures with which the managerial movement was engaged [see Roberg and Kuyendall 1990]. The elements of "managerialism", which were transferred to the JCF via English police officers, were thus largely emptied of this critical content and narrowly focused on concerns with efficiency [cf. Herst 1991].

This reform model represents an attempt to ground the legitimacy of the JCF in technocratic expertise (and the law). This is problematic for the JCF because of the low level of technological and criminalistic applications, and the generally low level of education of constables, including officers. While this technocratic principle is seen as entailing a redefinition of its relationship with government, allowing greater autonomy, by the same logic, it also ensures autonomy from the people and avoids reconstituting citizen-police relations, which are the foundation on which effectiveness in crime control must ultimately rest.

Moreover, policing is dependent on the collaboration of the citizenry at every stage of the process – report, investigation (the provision of information) and criminal prosecution (as witnesses). It is therefore best done with their consent and cooperation. In the current context, participation would seem to be a necessary condition for consent. This makes it rather difficult to legitimate police work on the professional principle only, as this principle is, by definition, exclusionary. The failure to properly appreciate this point is rooted in a similar failure to grasp the importance of the symbolic issues in restoring the legitimacy of the JCF and, in particular, the issue of correcting the problem of the symbolic representation of the police in popular consciousness as being repressive. Recognition of this point would place the issue of changing the style of the JCF more at the centre of the reforms.

But perhaps the most serious criticism from the viewpoint of the Jamaican experience is the failure to control crime. The ideology of professionalism limits citizens' participation in crime control to that of relatively passive observers, thereby weakening their own efforts in this regard by excluding rather than harnessing the power of the people. Of course, such inclusion need not degenerate into populist policing, as occurred with the Home Guards of the 1970s. This experience still invokes intense emotions as it is associated with party political abuses, but correctives to these problems can be found.

The main thrust of the criticisms of the reform model is that it avoids changing the fundamentals by ignoring the value related problems that are at the root of the crisis in the JCF, the essence of which is captured in the present style of policing. It is, after all, these value related problems that find expression in police-citizen encounters.

In the field of policing there are no successful models that can simply be replicated. But both local and international experiences with CBP are instructive as they point in the direction of new styles of policing based on a more democratic value system. For Jamaica, and perhaps other countries that inherited colonial constabularies, such a model must involve reshaping the fundamental relationships that structure police work – namely, police-government, police-citizen and, internally, police manager-operative, High Command-divisions and so forth – and following from this, developing appropriate institutions.

Conclusion

The reform programme was progressive but limited by the restorative vision that informed its elaboration and its negative character. Attempts at reform were not sufficiently attended by an awareness that considerable innovation and experimentation was required as part of the process in an effort to develop an appropriate model or style of policing that was consistent with democratic values and fitting for the realities of Jamaica. Relations with the public and their confidence in the police improved, although this improved authority was more attached to its leadership than to the Force, and to the particular office holders associated with the reforms than to the office.

The reforms have had no measurable impact on the rate of violent crime, however. Although this was perhaps an unrealistic expectation, it reveals the limits of the professional reform model and of policing as an instrument of crime control. Since crime control is regarded as a central function of the police, it is taken as a measure of its ineffectiveness. Legitimacy, even on our soft definition, particularly if it is to be diffused, is a function of effectiveness.

The reforms also sought to restore police legitimacy on the basis of the old processes of manipulating what people know and believe about the JCF and the masking of the particularistic interests served by it. But as shown earlier, in the changed environment, these modes of acquiring legitimacy are now bankrupt.

That the reforms have involved structural and personnel changes (a veritable purge of the upper echelons of the JCF is underway) has generated sincere disagreements, as well as self-interested winners and losers. The responses to the process have thus been quite varied. It is to these that we now turn.

7

Attitudes
to Reform

Since Independence, the majority of the members of the police force have been supportive of the movements and programmes for social reform [Harriott 1994]. With the exception of the period of Jamaicanization of the JCF in the 1950s and 1960s, which involved the replacement of foreign officers by Jamaicans, the record of support by members of the Force for change within their own institution has, however, not been as positive. Police forces are reputed to be highly resistant to change, yet programmes of police reform are unlikely to succeed without considerable support from within the police forces that are the objects of these reforms.

In this chapter, the attitude of police personnel to reforming their own institution is examined. It is well known that there may be some incongruence between attitudes and behaviour, as some persons may make a distinction between their ideal and actual selves. However, in general, it is reasonable to assume that attitude conditions behaviour and may thus be used to anticipate the likely responses to reform. Indeed, such responses may be expected to find their justification in beliefs and attitudes. If the ideas, which provide culturally approved justifications for the existing harmful practices and for the resistance to changing them, are diffused throughout the Force (and enjoy wide appeal in the society), then a deeply entrenched resistance to change should be anticipated.

First, the attitudinal orientations towards reform and the extent to which these are ideologically rooted in coherent belief systems are explored. The logic of the analysis will proceed by examining the degree of coherence across the following conceptually constituted scales or subscales representing dimensions of them: the attitude to the sources of crime (ASC); the attitude to law enforcement (ALE) or the nature of the state disciplinary processes that it is felt the offender should be subjected to; the attitude to citizens' rights (ACR); the attitude to style of policing (APS); and the attitude to reforming the JCF (ARJCF). A coherent ideological perspective implies either a greater susceptibility or resistance to reform, rapid and sharp polarization and higher levels of conflict.

The nature of these perspectives is then analysed for the political values informing them. From this, the dispositions toward reform are discerned. The programmes of reform, as will be shown, may be based on a restorative paramilitary model, the professional reform model, or a civil reform model such as CBP. Finally, on the basis of this analysis, the main cleavages and the relative balance of power between the coalition for change and the defensive coalition are determined.

The technique adopted is principal components analysis, which is a form of factor analysis. This technique yields the best linear combination of variables in the sense that the particular combination of variables would account for more of the variance in the data than any other linear combination of variables. The conceptually constructed scales are examined and reconstituted empirically. They are reduced to factors that represent the dimensions internal to the scales, which are then analysed for the ideological orientations of the subjects. From this, the character of support and opposition to reform are inferred. The analysis develops by first examining separately how the attitude sets measured by the four scales are structured. Reporting the aspects of the preliminary analysis may seem unnecessary to some readers, but as it adds useful details and helps to reveal the logic of the process, it was decided to proceed in this way.

Attitudes to the Treatment of Crime

Studies of the attitudes of the operatives and professionals in criminal justice systems indicate that attitudes to crime can positively contribute to crime control measures and criminal justice reform programmes [Ortet-Fabregat and Perez 1992:193]. Similarly, perspectives on crime and how it ought to be treated may be reasonably expected to condition attitudes to policing and, by extension, attitudes to police reform. Thus, the proper point of departure for an analysis of the attitudinal orientation towards police reform is an examination of attitudes to the sources and treatment of crime.

The majority opinion within the JCF located the primary sources of crime in socioeconomic factors rather than individual attributes, supernatural predeterminations or political permissiveness (excess freedoms), although notable minorities were of these views. More specifically, high levels of unemployment (70 percent), lack of opportunities (40 percent) and, more generally, "defects in Jamaican society" (51 percent) were seen as the main criminogenic factors – along with a relaxation in internalized discipline, which is attributed to a weakening of the institutions associated with the process of socialization (93 percent).

Examination of a pairwise correlation matrix of the seven variables composing the ASC revealed two groupings of weakly associated variables. Principal components analysis, after varimax rotation and based on the mineigen (or Kaiser) criterion, resulted in a two-factor solution, presented in Table 7.1 below.[1] The variables associating criminality with individual attributes, that is, with biological and supernaturally determined destinies coupled with a permissive political environment loaded onto the first factor (labelled INDIVID), and those associated with a defective socioeconomic structure loaded onto the second factor (SOCIOEC) [Table 7.1]. Preliminarily, this must be taken as the first sign of an ideological cleavage.

If crime is seen as a natural or supernatural rather than social phenomenon, then there are implications for the menu of policy approaches for treating it. The authoritative use of force to suppress crime is likely to be seen as the most important and perhaps the only worthwhile corrective. This explains the strong association and loading of both sets of variables onto the same factor [Table 7.1]. The acceptable limits of the use of force to control crime becomes less of a morally significant issue, with the police force being given greater licence for unnecessarily violent conduct. On the other hand, if crime is seen as a consequence of distorted economic development and an unjust social structure, the perplexing issue of how to best approximate just policing in an unjust setting arises.

Table 7.1 Factor Matrix – Attitudes to Sources of Crime

Item	Factor Loadings		Communality*
	INDIVID	SOCIOEC	
Individual sources			
Genetic disorder	.64846	–	0.679181
Destiny	.62288	–	0.702513
Sociopolitical sources			
Excess freedoms	.59801	–	0.386163
Decline of discipline	.27089	–	0.761945
Socioeconomic sources			
Defects in Jamaican society	–	.44434	0.441164
Unemployment	–	.51540	0.530206
Lack of opportunities	–	.60384	0.606126

*This value indicates the amount of variance of a variable that is shared by at least one other variable in the set.

Attitudes to the treatment of crime and criminals are consistent with beliefs about the sources of crime. As crime is seen by the majority as a social phenomenon (the outcome of unemployment and lack of opportunities), their prescriptions for its treatment are primarily social. Data from the attitude survey revealed that some 45 percent favoured social interventions in the form of greater opportunities for inner city youth, 45 percent for improved police effectiveness (mainly by community participation in policing), and in these initial responses, only 7 percent supported an intensification of the traditional applications of coercive measures and harsher punishments.

The apparent low levels of support for harsher physical punishments might be misleading. The population tends to favour harsh punitive treatment of offenders, and the police are no different in this respect. What the data really suggest is that the police, unlike the population, are perhaps less confident in the putative instrumental value of these punishments as social defence. These punishments are rather supported as expressions of retributive justice. For example, while our survey found that only 5 percent of the members of the JCF believed capital punishment was an important instrument for crime control, the vast majority of the Force (76 percent) was supportive of it (as is the case with the population, of which a stable majority of between 80 percent and 85 percent has consistently supported the death penalty [Stone 1982:56; 1991a]), with some 59 percent being supportive of extending its use.

The data on the social sources of crime are quite remarkable, given the high levels of cynicism common to law enforcement operatives, who, in the course of their professional lives, have to contend with the worst of humanity. For them, it is quite easy and reasonable to make less generous conclusions about the sources of this phenomenon and to locate it in greed, innate aggression and other such attributes associated with particular individuals, if not human nature itself.

Attitude to Citizens' Rights

There were two dimensions to this scale. The first is represented by those indicators designed to measure attitudes to the rights of citizens to influence the political process by open dissension and organized protests (POLITIC). The second is represented by those indicators that measure attitudes to rights codified as procedural laws that protect individuals against arbitrary police intrusion, limit and set rules for police procedures and treatment of suspects (PROCGARD)[Table 7.2]. The first is usually directly confronted by the police in public order situations and the second in the prosecution of the criminal law.

Generally, police opinion is fairly supportive of those political rights that are protective of interest articulation and, more generally, participation in the political process. Active political opposition is seen by them as a legitimate part of the political process. Majority opinion (62 percent) supported the right to political dissension and to influence the political process. This attitude is based on beliefs about democratic procedures in constituting governments and their association of this with social progress (the state facilitating access to education, health care and other social goods). These rights are not so much valued as good in themselves but, rather, as instrumental goods. Therefore, they have to be validated by their effect on the material aspects of the quality of life and thus may be attacked on this basis as impediments to effective crime control.

Table 7.2 Attitude to Citizens' Rights

Items	Factor Loadings		Communality
	PROCGARD	**POLITIC**	
Legal procedural safeguards			
The police should not be allowed to enter homes without a warrant	.75542	–	0.586175
Suspects should not be detained for more than 72 hours	.60940	–	0.543420
The deportee act is too restrictive of the rights of citizens	.39296	–	0.247428
Political			
People should be allowed to protest against government	–	.52964	0.289887
To reduce crime, citizens should be prepared to sacrifice some of their freedoms	–	.60020	0.424161
The state should provide better legal aid service	–	.49343	0.323212

Interestingly, the police do not regard the protection of these rights as their responsibility and duty. This discourse only arises in their public pronouncements as justification for public order action – usually the clearing of road blocks, as (it is argued) this form of protest action denies others their freedom of movement. They are, at best, ambivalent on the role of the police in protecting citizens in the exercise of their rights [Harriott 1994]. To many of the young and more reformist officers (who are relied upon as change agents, but who are still schooled in the traditional watchman notion of policing), this is most definitely not the prerogative of the police [Focus Group 1995]. And, as discussed earlier, entitlement to these rights is not accorded to all simply as individuals and citizens but is determined by status and is attached to status related notions of personhood.

Not surprisingly, then, the police tend to be regular violators of citizens' rights and the procedural laws crafted to safeguard these rights. These illegal practices are treated as protective of the society, which is prior to the individual rights of the "dangerous" and socially marginalized. (This is why the society, particularly its élite, is so comfortable with, and indeed, from time to time encourages, the police in these violations.) A happy coexistence thus obtains between these practices and the beliefs on which they are based on the one hand and equally strong beliefs and respect for a democratic protocol of governance on the other. This fragmentation suggests a primacy of order as a political value that casts doubts on the reliability of any democratic commitment.

Individual rights, as codified in procedural law and presented as constraints on police work, were still supported by a minority. On the two fundamental issues of the inviolability of the home and habeas corpus, minorities of 38 percent and 40 percent, respectively, were supportive. Support of some rights are conditionally related to the difficulties they are perceived as presenting for police work.

Attitude to Law Enforcement

The politically inconsistent attitude set of support for social crime control conjoined with, at best, a conditional respect for citizens' rights, signifies the complex, but in some aspects progressive, orientation towards law enforcement. The first impulse of the majority of the Force in treating with crime is to recommend social intervention, not law enforcement. This may be seen as implying the devolution of responsibility and blame transfer or, more generously, as a recognition of the complexity of crime and the limits of policing in preventing and controlling it.

Police tolerance of some types of violations of the law is consistent with this attitude. While class differential policing has been a historical feature of the style of policing of the JCF, this is softened by a recognition of the power of community norms, which finds expression in a reluctance to enforce some of the more unpopular laws (especially those applying to the use of cannabis, illegal occupation of land and street vending).

This downwardly directed policing, which is colonial in its origins but reinforced by the rigid class structure, finds its justification and logical ideological outcome in authoritarianism. This will be revisited later in this chapter, but as a single indicator, the idea that laws must be enforced even if they are wrong is a good measure of this. On this indicator, 18 percent exhibited an authoritarian tendency, which approximates an earlier measure of this tendency [see Harriott 1994].

The disregard for due process is similarly oriented ideologically. As is evident from Table 7.3, the indicators of authoritarianism and the measures of lawlessness and support for vigilantism all loaded on to the same factor. This disregard for procedural law is more acutely and actively expressed as vigilantism. Support for police vigilantism among members of the JCF has not only been high, as noted earlier, but also stable. In 1991 some 54 percent of officers [Harriott 1994:324] and 38 percent in 1994 ($p < .00004$) of the officers and 44 percent of the Force as a whole favoured the summary execution of gun criminals. This extends beyond police vigilantism to support for citizen initiated vigilantism as well. This support for vigilantism is anchored in a view (held by 50 percent) that the criminal justice system is ineffective and obstructs the work of the police. The ideological drift of this justifiable critique is unmistakably counterdemocratic. Driven by retributive notions of justice, majority opinion within the JCF tends to be supportive of harsher punishment of violent offenders (85 percent), including more extensive use of the death penalty, and favours extending it to gun crimes, thereby formally recognizing the existing police code.

Table 7.3 Attitude to Law Enforcement

| | Factor Loadings | | |
Items	RULELAW	PUNISH	Communality
Rule of law			
Summary execution of criminals	0.73583	–	0.61508
Vigilante justice is sometimes appropriate	0.52363	–	0.49649
The criminal justice system usually obstructs the work of the police	0.41994	–	0.49669
The law should be enforced even if it is wrong	0.27295	–	0.79968
Law breakers should be given stiffer sentences	0.50547	–	0.48176
For some crimes the death penalty is the most appropriate sentence	0.49942	–	0.46891
Gun criminals should receive the death penalty	0.67873	–	0.68402
Punishment			
Some criminal laws are unenforceable	–	0.50517	0.35607
More noncustodial sentences for minor offenders	–	0.57605	0.60977
Possession of small quantities of ganja should be decriminalized	–	0.76208	0.58441

Again, this appears to be inconsistent with the data on sources of crime and the social interventionism that most seem to favour. It certainly suggests that, perhaps for the majority, there is not a coherent liberal or authoritarian ideological perspective, and that these attitudes to law enforcement are perhaps based on pragmatic notions of an unhappy necessity.

Police Style

This inconsistency (strong on general political rights, but weak on rights related to police procedure and the rule of law) is reflected in the attitudes to police style. It is reconciled by the notions of citizenship and personhood (explored earlier) that rights are associated with social and more specifically occupational status. These inconsistencies are becoming increasingly problematic for the criminal justice system and most institutions of the society, which claim, in their legitimating rhetoric, to rest on universalistic principles.

Despite the problems associated with it, there is considerable support for the watchman style, and in particular the paramilitary model, within the JCF. A majority (59 percent) of the Force felt that police forces tend to be most effective when organized on paramilitary principles, with only 24 percent disagreeing and the remaining 17 percent being unsure. More conditionally, 68 percent felt that the paramilitary model was situationally appropriate for the Jamaican environment, given the high level of criminal violence. These attitudes present some difficulty for any programme of reform involving a change in the style of policing. It is therefore worthwhile examining, in some detail, the attitudes of the members of the Force to the core aspects of the style of policing.

As with the attitudinal dispositions regarding the reform of the structures of the Force, and the attitudes to law enforcement discussed earlier, there are notable inconsistencies in the attitudes to the style of policing. These may be interpreted as important signs that the changes that the members of the Force are willing to permit may be bounded in scope by the existing style of policing. For example, majority opinion favours the "net fishing" tactics associated with paramilitary policing but admits to its ineffectiveness. And consistent with the paramilitary ideal, members generally support the closed character of the Force, but are somewhat ambivalent on the issue of male exclusivity and tend to be supportive of greater female inclusion. Support for male exclusivity may be taken as an indicator of strong adherence to the existing style of policing. Yet support for greater female recruitment was higher (38 percent) than opposition to it (34 percent), particularly in the lower ranks where only 29 percent supported the preservation of male exclusivity ($p < .0015$). This greater degree of openness in the lower ranks is not due to the larger proportion of women in these ranks, as on controlling for sex, male support for increasing the proportion of females in the Force and elevating them to positions of greater authority and rank was greater than that of women. Perhaps this ambivalence may be explained by the increasing integration of women into the archetypical paramilitary units such as the Mobile Reserve and special tactical squads such as the Special Anti-Crime Task Force (SACTF), and, with this, their assimilation into the existing action oriented male dominated culture. Opening the Force to women above the 10 percent threshold may thus seem less threatening to the existing mode of policing.

This commitment to paramilitarism may be expected to vary across the different sections of the Force based on their functions, with the strongest support for it being located in the central operational units (Mobile Reserve and SACTF), which operate in a highly confrontational style, and the weakest support in intelligence/investigations where work is more individualized and less violent. The existing operatives in the powerful operations units have a vested interest in the preservation of this style of policing as the valorization of their skills and experience is tied to it.

To effect a more parsimonious analysis, the indicators of police style were reduced by creating new variables representing its main dimensions, that is, aggressiveness, participation and selectivity, by which is meant attitudes to tactics that are discriminating at the group level but nondiscriminating at the individual level, such as house to house searches.[2] This was done in the first instance by simply aggregating the indicators. The values of these new variables range from 1 to 25 for aggressiveness, 1 to 20 for citizen participation, and 1 to 15 for selectivity. The higher scores represent support for the paramilitary ideal. We take as cutting scores of 15, 12 and 9, respectively, with scores above these representing a paramilitary orientation. These variables are then cross-tabulated with rank and function.

A positive attitudinal orientation toward the paramilitary model of policing was not uniformly exhibited across all of its dimensions. This affirmation was above the cutting scores for aggressiveness and selectivity, but below for citizens' participation among all ranks and functional units. As expected, support for some dimensions of paramilitarism varied with rank, but with regard to function this variation was negligible. Attitudinal predispositions favouring paramilitarism as a general principle tended to increase with rank. When measured in terms of belief in its effectiveness, paramilitarism enjoys the strongest support (67 percent) in the higher ranks. However, examination of the attitudes of members of the Force on specific dimensions of paramilitarism revealed a more differentiated picture. Support for aggressiveness was directly related to rank but was fairly evenly distributed across the different functional units, being strongest in Traffic and among General Service personnel rather than among constables involved in Operations as was expected. A strong association between selectivity and aggressiveness would logically be expected, yet this relationship was an inverse one – with the officers returning the lowest scores, that is, being least supportive of "net fishing" type tactics. The Intelligence personnel were most supportive of this, perhaps because their units tend to be a major beneficiary of these tactics which tend to yield few convictions but much information. The citizen exclusionary aspect of the style is least supported by all groups.

That a supportive attitudinal orientation to paramilitarism in its tactical mode (represented by aggressiveness and selectivity) is not restricted to some units or functions but is fairly evenly generalized across the Force is consistent with the generalized expressions of its practices to most functions. Most functions (Intelligence, Investigation, Operations) have become dependent on the tactics associated with it.

Table 7.4 Attitudes to Style by Rank and Function

	Dimensions of Style					
Item	**Aggressiveness**		**Selectivity**		**Participation**	
Rank						
Officer	16.6111	(2.5569)	10.0000	(2.0864)	17.3333	(1.8787)
NCOs	15.8264	(2.6906)	10.2975	(2.6281)	18.0950	(2.7772)
Ranks	15.2049	(2.9298)	10.9580	(2.2648)	18.1847	(2.4940)
Population	15.4692	(2.9295)	10.6917	(2.4191)	18.1291	(2.5871)
Function						
General Service	15.6071	(2.8936)	10.6888	(2.4683)	18.1837	(2.5709)
Operations	15.4217	(2.7108)	10.8675	(2.2144)	18.1566	(2.6582)
Investigation	15.1111	(2.8936)	10.5741	(2.6127)	18.2407	(2.4375)
Intelligence	15.5517	(3.2797)	11.1371	(2.4889)	17.8966	(2.4690)
Traffic	15.6905	(3.2572)	10.9762	(2.4543)	18.1905	(2.7783)
Administration	15.4016	(3.0893)	10.5118	(2.2917)	17.9453	(2.7844)
Population	15.4446	(2.9440)	10.7186	(2.3960)	18.1287	(2.5986)

N = 665–666

Aggressiveness = Sum (λ69, λ70, λ71, λ76, λ77)

Selectivity = Sum (λ72, λ73, λ74)

Participation = Sum (λ61, λ79, λ80, λ82)

Note: The standard deviations are in the brackets.

The pattern of support by rank is consistent with the view among the officers that it ensures better internal control. It also ensures control over the citizenry. With this style of policing, tremendous power and privilege are concentrated at the top, with little real accountability. Commitment to this style may have more to do with power than crime control effectiveness. The extent to which these attitudes to the style of policing are anchored in deeper beliefs will be explored later. However, the data presented thus far suggest that (with the exception of a minority of some 20 percent) paramilitarism is not anchored in deeper political-ideological values. For the majority, its justification rests on its putative effectiveness in ensuring internal discipline and in managing violence, that is, its pragmatism.

The colonial version of the watchman style of policing is characterized by the primacy of order as a political value. Order is regarded as prior to justice and even law. The latter is reconciled to freedom via notions of obligation (which can only be entered into by free citizens). Historically, this style is thus firmly anchored in an authoritarian spirit and logic. As in most ex-colonial societies with a conservative élite, change to a more just social order often entails political mobilizations outside the established channels, and some conflict and disorder is usually associated with these processes. In this context, the fixation with order is thus a source of conflict between the police and citizens.

In the JCF, however, according to the survey data, while crime fighting takes priority over law, order is not valued over freedom and neither is law over justice. This suggests (and will be demonstrated later) some ideological fragmentation – for authoritarian principles in the Force and in crime fighting, but not for their wider application to the polity as a whole. We will return to this later.

The factor solutions are consistent with the above analysis. The variables loaded on to three factors representing the main dimensions of the construct (its organizational principles, tactics or the selectivity issue, and the nature of the relationship with the people). The data are thus not empirically reducible to the construct style; there was no such single underpinning factor [see Table 7.5].

Table 7.5 Factor Pattern Matrix of Attitudes to Police Style

	Factor Loadings			
	1	2	3	Communality
Organizational dimension/aggressiveness				
Police forces are most effective when organized on paramilitary principles	.83236	–	–	0.84463
Paramilitary model as situationally appropriate	.88384	–	–	0.84575
Tactics/selectivity				
Detaining people *en masse*	–	.43515	–	0.38738
House to house searches	–	.52978	–	0.49997
Stop and search without suspicion too frequent	–	.66338	–	0.56898
Use of the military in crime fighting	–	.26104	–	0.37031
Police violence	–	.46204	–	0.30842
Participation				
Citizens' participation	–	–	.41444	0.45131
Military like training of police	–	–	.31953	0.82335

Factor 1: as expressed in organizational structures

Factor 2: style as tactics

Factor 3: as an expression of power relations with the citizenry

Attitude to Reform

Against this background, the attitudes to reform of the JCF may be described. Here attitudes toward changing the fundamental relationships of internal and external control, the organizational principles that give expression to them (centralization, openness), and the relations with citizens (accountability and participation) are considered the core indicators or the more deeply held dispositions towards reform. A positive attitude to changes in these relations in a more democratic direction may be taken as an indicator of a willingness to accommodate a shift in the power relations (and style of policing) in return for greater effectiveness.

The indicators were designed to measure not just the attitudes to the immediate existing arrangements but also the structural principles on which they are based; for example, responses were elicited towards the existing hierarchical structure (the number of ranks) but also more abstractly in ways that allowed an examination of attitudes to the principle of hierarchy itself and to the military command model. The attitudes to these basic principles were more deeply excavated by exploring the responses to civil alternatives in which the internal relationships of command and control would be replaced by collegiality and team cooperation, and police relations with the people based on their active participation as responsible agents in the system of policing.

A commitment to changing the essential relationships is measured by attitudes to mode of governance, style and internal structures. The mode of governance, and the degree of political intervention it allows, is usually seen as a prime source of many of the problems that beset police forces (such as corruption and ineffectiveness). This is particularly true of highly centralized forces such as the French police forces [cf. Horton 1995]. In ex-colonies such as Jamaica, the political élite tends to exploit and compound the colonial heritage of concentrated power. Police perspectives on this problem, while favouring greater autonomy, need not support a more decentralized configuration and democratic accountability. Indeed, greater police autonomy of the political administration, in the context of highly centralized power structures and low levels of accountability, cannot but result in less responsiveness to the public.

Majority opinion seems to favour change, with only 14 percent reporting having a deep fear of reform. Opinions within the Force appear more diverse, more variable, when members are interrogated for the character of the changes they are willing to support. The ambiguities and contradictions in attitudes to change, such as favouring the existing paramilitary tactics but doubting its effectiveness or being critical of existing organizational structures and yet unsupportive of structural change, may suggest that opinions are not deeply held. It could also indicate, seeing that they were least ambivalent on issues of openness, popular accountability and control, a reluctance to restructure the system of power and control associated with the present style of policing.

A reform model that did not seek to alter the style of policing would perhaps meet the approval of the majority.

Consistent with the preservation of the structures and power relationships, attitudes to change seem to be primarily conditioned by the "bad eggs" theory, which explains the problems of the Force in terms of the attributes of the individual, not structures. Conceptually, this narrows the vision of change to the shuffling of personnel. Large majorities willingly supported improving the quality of recruits (84 percent) and excoriating the bad eggs (88 percent), and a significant minority (34 percent) supported a purge of the officer ranks.

Ideological Fragmentation

The analysis may now proceed to including in the same procedure all 53 variables which compose the five scales. First, some of these variables were recoded to ensure that the response categories were conceptually consistent; then the data set was standardized using Z-scores in order to give it greater stability. Factor analysis assumes fairly strong associations among clusters of variables; therefore an initial step is an examination of the correlation matrix of all the variables included in the analysis. This correlation matrix of the standardized variables yielded a fairly high proportion of correlations of 0.2 or greater. More rigorous tests of the extent to which this precondition (of strongly associated clusters of variables) is met are the Kaiser-Meyer-Olkin measure of sampling adequacy (KMO), which compares the magnitudes of the observed correlation coefficients to the magnitudes of the partial correlation coefficients, and the Barlet Test of Sphericity, which tests the hypothesis that the correlation matrix is an identity matrix [Noruisis 1994:50–52]. The KMO (0.65311) was above the minimum level considered acceptable (that is, 0.5) and the Barlet Test of Sphericity, which yielded a large value (446.50821) and a p value of .00000, indicated that it was unlikely that the correlation matrix was an identity. These outputs suggested that it was appropriate to proceed with the factor analysis.

The output of the principal components analysis reported in Table 7.6 below yielded 21 factors with eigenvalues greater than one. These factors or indices explain 60.2 percent of the variance in the data set, with none of them singly accounting for more than 6.5 percent of the variance in the data set. A relatively large number of factors was anticipated by the weak correlations between the standardized variables, which suggested that there were many dimensions to the data set. For this reason (and to assist with the next stage of the analysis), some of the variables returning a small proportion of the variance on the principal components analysis were retained. The number of factors (for extraction) was determined by the Scree Test, and variables with a factor loading of 0.25 and above were retained [Table 7.6].

Table 7.6 Principal Components and their Variance

Variable	Communality	Factor	Eigenvalue	% of Var.	Cum. %
λ1	1.00000	1	3.76344	6.5	6.5
λ3	1.00000	2	3.50145	6.0	12.5
λ22	1.00000	3	2.65648	4.6	17.1
λ23	1.00000	4	2.25793	3.9	21.0
λ24	1.00000	5	1.83833	3.2	24.2
λ25	1.00000	6	1.73142	3.0	27.2
λ26	1.00000	7	1.57316	2.7	29.9
λ27	1.00000	8	1.53574	2.6	32.5
λ28	1.00000	9	1.51638	2.6	35.1
λ2	1.00000	10	1.45921	2.5	37.6
λ11	1.00000	11	1.36168	2.3	40.0
λ12	1.00000	12	1.33857	2.3	42.3
λ13	1.00000	13	1.30746	2.3	44.6
λ14	1.00000	14	1.25354	2.2	46.7
λ15	1.00000	15	1.23283	2.1	48.8
λ16	1.00000	16	1.16272	2.0	50.8
λ19	1.00000	17	1.14906	2.0	52.8
λ20	1.00000	18	1.10737	1.9	54.7
λ21	1.00000	19	1.08782	1.9	56.6
λ30	1.00000	20	1.04924	1.8	58.4
λ31	1.00000	21	1.04597	1.8	60.2

Various methods have been proposed for this type of exercise. Here, varimax rotation has been used in such a way as to maximize the sum of the variance of the squared loadings within each column of the rotated loading matrix. Using the mineigen criterion, 12 factors were initially retained. Nine of these were anticipated and were readily identifiable constructs. At this point, three variables, which accounted for negligible variance and which were of little conceptual value to the analysis, were removed, and the remaining 50 forced into a 10-factor solution, which was found to better fit the conceptual expectations. The resulting factor loadings are presented in Table 7.7. These factors represent an empirical reconstitution of the scales presented earlier, but still approximating them, as the constructs represented by these factors are but dimensions of the scales with which the analysis began. The constructs from the initial design were thus largely empirically validated. These constructs are (1) summary punishment (SMPUNISH), (2) openness (OPENNESS), (3) critique of structural principles (STRUCTUR), (4) citizens' rights (RIGHTS), (5) purge or removal of incorrigible elements (PURGE), (6) paramilitarism (PARAMIL), (7) decentralization and reduced hierarchy-structural reform (DECENTRL), (8) citizens' participation and accountability to the public (PARTICIP), (9) female inclusion (FEINCLU) and (10) social crime control (SOCIALCR).

Table 7.7 Varimax Rotated Factor Matrix

	SMPUNISH	OPENNESS	STRUCTUR	RIGHTS	PURGE
λ11	.66762	.13036	.09566	.17277	−.08248
λ13	.62969	.06901	−.00452	.11980	.08629
λ15	.44004	.01409	.20280	−.00974	−.13034
λ35	.41522	.26233	.27600	−.03670	.07233
λ23	.39574	−.03907	.06875	.05220	−.00025
λ53	.38528	.01604	.05355	.32738	−.02766
λ14	.37456	−.11667	.14022	.00722	−.17923
λ16	−.22749	.20868	.03139	−.18252	−.00606
λ66	−.28073	.63854	−.06062	−.01112	−.15182
λ65	−.22067	.61527	−.13377	−.09163	−.10884
λ67	−.09682	.55391	−.01099	.22586	.11426
λ36	.19510	.39063	−.02532	.14162	−.11724
λ34	.37580	.38776	−.04077	.18791	−.06589
λ68	.11503	.35383	.08211	.02464	.23197
λ58	.19471	.31510	.05676	.15507	.07288
λ26	−.03117	−.01156	.61298	−.04519	.09172
λ27	.21141	.04337	.55144	.09969	−.12673
λ19	−.01708	−.07633	.52562	.11349	−.02951
λ25	.26188	.03533	.46941	−.08830	.12694
λ54	−.01989	−.10835	.40957	−.06496	.04384
λ30	−.05639	.04531	−.37318	.16164	.07116
λ28	.07656	.28231	.32529	.05387	.19421
λ22	−.02842	−.05699	−.00281	.51202	−.12177
λ74	−.19993	.12699	.09734	.49963	.05949
λ31	.22933	−.08252	−.12275	.49133	−.18560
λ73	.02845	.22582	.03911	.47654	.03580
λ72	.02286	.07389	.01947	.46908	.10157
λ20	−.19700	.17292	−.00537	.37866	.09389
λ33	−.01175	.01349	.06107	−.03813	.63382
λ32	−.05370	.03931	−.03989	.06673	.59450
λ78	.05325	−.06832	.06012	−.10148	.40949
λ79	−.11016	−.07495	−.13620	−.08223	.40290
λ24	−.14083	−.03795	.35198	.07328	.38618
λ77	−.13795	.31381	.10456	.10577	.37062

Table 7.7 continued

	PARAMIL	DECENTRIL	PARTICIP	FEINCLU	SOCIALCR
λ70	.83229	−.07359	.01930	.04652	.28988
λ69	.81565	−.03859	−.03565	.09301	.12540
λ60	−.11445	.71267	.03083	.14288	
λ62	−.00274	.52610	.05446	.04896	.20161
λ49	−.00663	.50227	.21111	−.08368	−.23083
λ12	.05426	.35918	−.14833	−.16788	
λ46	.05066	.08339	.72294	−.07944	
λ47	.02118	−.12542	.52304	.00857	
λ45	−.05755	.15460	.45654	.12373	−.15569
λ43	−.03953	.01669	.40651	−.10535	−.12648
λ48	−.08150	.33510	.34368	.16315	.17272
λ63	.15308	.05180	.07498	.73692	
λ64	.08262	−.01395	−.15440	.72464	
λ2	−.31696	.04324	−.00111	.25959	.68767
λ1	−.21930	−.01691	.07305	.38096	.59729
λ3	−.30743	.15944	.06476	.26795	.45375

The 10-factor solution provides a fair representation of the variables included in it, as it explains 25 percent to 66 percent of the variance of each of the variables in the model as is indicated by the communalities [Table 7.8]. However, each factor accounts for but a small proportion of the variance in the model. This ranges from a high of 7.2 percent for factor 1 (SMPUNISH) to 2.6 percent for factor 10 (SOCIALCR). Only 41 percent of the total variance is attributable to the model [Table 7.8]. For the rest of the analysis, we proceed using these empirically validated constructs.

From the standpoint of this study, identification of the main attitudinal cleavages is of considerable importance, as these are the markers of the issues that are likely to generate the most intense and enduring conflicts and which (with the attitude structure being as complex as the data suggests) are likely to be the main fault lines, not just between coalitions but also within them, given the rather diverse coalition for change. These cleavages are indicated by the way in which the factor scores are grouped.

Those identified were lawlessness versus respect of individual rights; openness versus closed institutional structures; and purging of the ranks versus moderate personnel changes, public versus self and traditional modes of accountability, and participation versus managerial exclusion. The treatment of corruption is also an important cleavage point, but this is absent from the analysis here due to the difficulties with these data (described earlier in

Table 7.8 Communality of Variables (Final Statistics)

Variable	Communality	Factor	Eigenvalue	Percent of Variable	Cumulative Percent
λ1	.57121	1	3.61776	7.2	7.2
λ12	.32632	2	3.18134	6.4	13.6
λ13	.50852	3	2.51902	5.0	18.6
λ14	.26813	4	2.14175	4.3	22.9
λ15	.32896	5	1.83788	3.7	26.6
λ16	.24773	6	1.57834	3.2	29.8
λ19	.31220	7	1.54904	3.1	32.9
λ2	.50972	8	1.47155	2.9	35.8
λ3	.33296	9	1.44726	2.9	38.7
λ22	.34359	10	1.31718	2.6	41.3
λ23	.20535				
λ26	.43069				
λ27	.44267				
λ28	.31844				
λ25	.40345				
λ30	.25909				
λ31	.41176				
λ32	.41670				
λ33	.52502				
λ34	.49892				
λ35	.38957				
λ36	.31196				
λ43	.40509				
λ45	.40760				
λ46	.60178				
λ47	.44402				
λ48	.39879				
λ49	.41972				
λ53	.27056				
λ54	.37212				
λ65	.47784				
λ66	.50060				
λ67	.39042				
λ68	.25392				
λ62	.42128				
λ63	.66460				

chapter 3). It is indirectly reflected here in the divergence of opinion on the degree of personnel changes required – a purge, or the removal of a few bad eggs. These issues are all fundamentally related to any attempt at changing

the style of policing. A more legalistic approach, informed by the professional reform model, would be confronted by the cleavages demarcated by the issues of summary punishment and internal accountability; while a service oriented approach would be confronted by issues of participation and public accountability. All reform models would have to negotiate the issue of the degree of personnel changes considered acceptable.

Of great importance to the management of the reform process is the identification of the most important cleavage points. If summary punishment and vigilantism (SMPUNISH) is the factor accounting for most of the variance, then it is not difficult to see that any reform project that attempts to negatively sanction these practices (and corruption more generally) and erect new control institutions is likely to generate considerable conflict. These are profoundly moral issues and thus likely to generate greater intensity of feeling. Moreover, in the context of reform, they are essentially control issues and are (correctly) seen as placing greater constraints on the powers of the police over citizens. As a result of this, from the viewpoint of the individual constable, they are perhaps the most threatening of the issues. Polarization is likely to occur most easily around these issues. Since a strong power culture obtains within the JCF, the more salient issues (which are already morally charged) are even more likely to generate intense feelings and therefore sharp conflicts with the potential for splitting the coalition for change.

Ideological coherence would further increase the potential conflict intensity levels. However, as the factor solution suggests, the attitudinal structure is rather complex. The reduction of the data to far fewer factors would have been indicative of it being structured by coherent ideologies. However, the relationships between the constructs represented by the scales were specifically not reducible to a libertarian-authoritarian axis. There was no such undergirding structure to the attitudinal dispositions. While there are obvious secondary tendencies to coherent ideological perspectives of a libertarian and authoritarian character, the analysis suggests a somewhat ideologically fragmented attitude set. In fact, none of the factors accounted for more than 8 percent of the variance [see Table 7.6].

The analysis thus revealed a more complex attitudinal structure than is usually encountered in studies of the political beliefs of mass publics which usually succeed in reducing these beliefs and attitudes to core ideologies [cf. Evans, Heath and Lallijee 1996]. Earlier studies of the police have tended to report similar results, emphasizing their authoritarianism [Skolnick and Bayley 1986; Waddington 1982; Colman and Gorman 1982; Niederhoffer 1969]. The implications of these findings for the direction or directions of the reform project favoured by the members of the Force may now be explored.

Direction and Commitment to Reform

The general ideological orientations may be expected to anticipate the preferred options for police reform. However, the lack of ideological coherence suggests that the different tendencies may each opt for reform programmes that might not be consistent with their attitudes to the prior issues discussed above. The perspectives on police reform must therefore be directly mapped rather than inferred.

The first clues regarding the orientation on the direction of police reform may be sought in the attitudes to the existing style of policing. This entails how the core issue of the relationships of control (relations with the political administration, the policed and the law) discussed earlier are defined. The critique of the existing style of policing and the ambivalence associated with it (measured by the responses to the positive alternatives) suggest approaches to change that may lead in different directions, to support for different reform programmes.

Logically and empirically, three approaches to reforming the police may be discerned. These are not all clearly defined and discretely bounded but are sufficiently distinct, conceptually and politically, as emergent trends within the Force. They are a re-energized paramilitary model, the professional reform model, and a civil reform model with a strong service reorientation.

The first, refurbished paramilitarism, is empirically evident from the factor analysis (PARAMIL). It is an unmistakably conservative position marked by support for the structural principles and tactics associated with the existing paramilitary model. Its reformism is limited to a clean-up of the Force by purging the bad eggs and strengthening it in terms of manpower based on the existing structures and style. This orientation could reasonably be expected to correlate most strongly with summary punishment over law (SMPUNISH), and order over freedom (RIGHTS). An authoritarian perspective on crime control, which would favour a strong state and rely heavily on the police force as the primary instrument of policy, rather than on social interventions and community initiatives, is logically associated with such a perspective.

Support for the professional reform model is described by a rule-bound orientation, a respect for procedural law and citizens' rights anchored in notions of equality before the law. Its point of departure is the core issue of control. The centrality of the law in this approach finds its purest expression in the idea that the police ought to be accountable only to the law. The proponents of this model are thus highly critical of the systems of control of the JCF. The popular view among the population, that the mode of governmental control of the JCF allows a heavy-handed partisan political manipulation of the Force, resonates widely throughout the JCF and particularly among those most supportive of this model. Some 64 percent of the Force were of the opinion that the JCF was too politicized (with only 15 percent disagreeing with this). They therefore tend to support greater limitations on the powers of the minister responsible for the JCF and a professional model of greater police self-regulation and autonomy. The paramilitary model is distinguished from the civil and service oriented model of reform by its rejection of popular participation [Table 7.9].

A positive attitude to the service oriented approach is characterized by support for engagement in social crime prevention and control, popular involvement, systems of accountability to the public, decentralized structures and so forth. As discussed in chapter 2, majority opinion within the JCF regards the Force as being too centralized, too hierarchical and too closed, but is at best cautious about structural reforms that would entail radical decentralization, further flattening the hierarchy and opening up the Force. Such a structural configuration is a condition for responsive and effective service delivery and a change in the style of policing to a less adversarial and more civil and service oriented model.

This service oriented approach represents a sharp shift in the style of policing and the present power arrangements (both within the Force and externally in its relationship with the people). As a tendency it is weak but nevertheless evident as a set of ideas, albeit not well formed.

The factors associated with reform are used as source variables and correlated with the attitude measures (using newly created variables) representing them with the three orientations on reform identified above. The partial correlation coefficients (controlling for length of service, which is strongly and positively associated with rank and age) are reported in Table 7.9.

As logically anticipated, SUMPUNISH and PURGE correlated most strongly with the paramilitary restorative approach to reform. Citizens' rights, participation and female inclusion all showed weak negative correlations. Support for the service oriented model correlated best with citizens participation and decentralization of the organizational structures, while support for the professional reform model correlated best with DECENTRALIZATION and OPENNESS. If one tendency favours a purge for revitalizing the old structures, but is supportive of summary action and punitive policing, while the other main reformist tendency favours greater openness and accountability, tensions must be expected. Interestingly, all tendencies are weak on citizens' rights and female inclusion [Table 7.9].

The Power Configuration of the Coalitions for and against Change

In this section we try to determine the relative influence of the coalitions for and against the reform process. This entails a numeric balance, but also

Table 7.9 Direction of Reforms

	Respondents Favour		
	Paramilitary Restorative	Professional Reform Model	Civil Reform Model
Attitude Measures	R	R	R
DECEN	–.0447	.4618	.3050
RIGHTS	.0014	.0118	.1529
PARTICIPATION	–.0412	.1070	.3437
SMPUNISH	.5426	.1344	–.0814
OPENNESS	–.0778	.2291	.0943
FEINCLU	–.0549	.0472	.1827
PURGE	.5401	.0677	.1827

a qualitative dimension reflected in the characteristics of the groups – such as their location in the hierarchy and function – which indicates their relative importance in the structure, the power resources at their command and their ability to influence organizational outcomes and the general course of events. Rank is particularly important to any such evaluation, given the hierarchical nature of the institution.

Simple univariate methods are used to explore the attributes on which reformers and conservatives differ. Unlike the previous section, which focused the analysis on the dependent (attitude) variables, here the analysis turns on the independent variables (rank, length of service, function and sex). This allows identification of the potential centres of resistance and support for reform.

An index of attitudes to reform composed of measures of attitudes to police style and relations of control, and the extent of personnel changes, is taken as the grouping variable. Its values range from 6 to 28, with a cutting score of 17 used to differentiate reformists from conservatives. The lower end of the index (that is, values tending to 6) represents conservative positions, and the higher end, a reformist attitudinal predisposition. The means may be taken as a measure of the intensity of the commitment to reform. These vary between 18 and 20, which are only slightly above the cutting score – indicating generally weak or low intensity pro-reform positions [Table 7.10].

Location in the hierarchy and in space are important in power considerations. The first is more obvious and was discussed earlier. Senior NCOs and officers tended to be somewhat more hostile to the process. This may be accounted for by the change in promotions policy, which replaced seniority by capability and performance as the main criteria in the evaluations for promotion. This resulted in many young persons (their former subordinates) being promoted over them. The second, spatial proximity to centre of power (particularly for a highly centralized organization and system of government), allows participation in events that more decisively influence the ultimate outcome of the reform process. In terms of the spatial location, those constables in the rural areas tended to be more supportive than in the urban (although those born in the city tended to be more reformist) [Table 7.10].

Table 7.10 Group Means on Attitude to Reform for Selected Independent Variables

	Mean	Std. Dev.	DF	Sum of Sq.	Mean Sq.	F Ratio	F Prob.
Area of Work							
KMA	18.468	3.988	1	232.186*	232.186	14.3745	.0002
Rural	19.645	4.046	671	10,838.464†	16.153		
Sex							
Male	19.278	4.143	1	4.622*	4.622*	.2802	.5967
Female	19.042	4.047	664	10,952.472†	16.495†		
Education							
Low	19.668	3.985	1	9.822*	9.8219	.6005	.4387
High	19.509	4.670	670	10,958.886	16.3565		
Length of service							
< 10 years	18.958	4.149	1	11.391*	11.391*	.6911	.4061
Other	19.218	3.966	671	11,059.259†	16.482†		
Rank							
Officers	18.667	5.076					
NCOs	19.276	4.135	2	13.727*	6.864*	.4177	.6587
Other	19.017	3.955	662	10,893.331†	16.430†		
Function							
Operations	18.819	3.849	5	166.376*	33.274*	2.0502	.0698
Admin.	18.781	4.381	663	10,757.919	16.226†		
Intelligence	20.552	2.898					
Traffic	20.333	4.177					
Investig.	19.379	3.773					
Gen. Services	18.913	4.177					

* Between group   † Within group

Education and age may reasonably be expected to have a significant effect on attitude to reform. However, education had no effect on attitude to reform. This may be explained by the fact that at the time of the survey, all constables with higher levels of education had acquired this after serving many years in the Force and were already fully assimilated by the police culture before undertaking these programmes of higher education. As a general rule, education was thus not a change agent.

After area of work, length of service (a good proxy for age) and sex were the two variables exhibiting the greatest differences in group means. The younger constables and the females were most supportive of the reforms. These are not very powerful groups, although the younger constables enjoy considerable influence via the Police Federation.

The significance tests for the equality of group means (the F test) indicate that, with the exception of area of work (AREAWORK), the differences in group means may all be explained in terms of sample error [Table 7.10]. Thus attitudinally, there seems to be little differentiation between reformers and nonreformers along the lines of our independent variables. It would not be possible to predict which groups are likely to be most reformist based on a profile of their social and institutional status. Opinions were fairly randomly distributed – in what is still a basically socially homogeneous institution. On the basis of attitudinal predispositions, no distinct power centres would have been expected to quickly develop within the JCF.

Conclusion

The attitude structure of the members of the JCF on issues of crime and crime control is characterized by equivocation and ideological fragmentation. This is quite different from the depictions of the police in the early literature as ideologically rigid authoritarians.

This change would seem to suggest a greater opening for police reform, as such fragmentation is unlikely to be associated with strong convictions and high levels of certainty regarding the type of reforms that are appropriate, and would be expected to lower somewhat the level of emotional intensity on the issues. While in a power culture, conflict is constant and is usually generated by even very petty issues, if the outlook of the members of the Force is, in fact, essentially pragmatic, then they may be expected to more willingly submit any programme of reform to the test of practice.

From this discussion of attitudes, the analysis next proceeds to a discussion of the behavioural responses to the reforms. This is the subject of the next chapter.

8

Resistance
to Reform

Reforms are usually initiated by the political directorate and frustrated by the state bureaucracy. Armed with procedural instruments, the administrators typically engage in a war of attrition that slows the momentum of change and frustrates the process until the reformers lose influence and power [Mills 1992]. Externally imposed reforms are therefore unlikely to realize their objectives without a critical mass of internal change agents and a favourable balance of power. Thus, in the case of the JCF, one of the oldest, most closed state institutions in Jamaica, an outsider had to be inserted at the top of the chain of command in order to initiate and give impetus to the process of reform.

In this chapter, the interaction between the different advocacy coalitions and the outcomes of this process are analysed. Building on the attitude data from the previous chapter, the emergence and character of the defensive coalition and the development of resistance are described as a dynamic process. The reasons for its success in somewhat domesticating the process are then discussed.

In a highly politicized institution such as the JCF, reforms are expected to generate conflicts. Where the change process is led by an outsider, even greater conflicts are to be expected, as this introduces greater uncertainty about the process and constitutes a negative statement on the competence of its senior officers and their commitment to change, and generally connotes a negative evaluation of the regenerative capacity of the institution. Past reform processes encountered considerable resistance and were stymied, deflected or modified to fit the parameters set by the old guard conservatives of the Constabulary. In this tradition, the JCF had successfully stonewalled the recommendations of the Herst Report [1991], and by every indication the Wolfe Report [1993] would have met a similar fate. This was signalled by the defensive treatment of these reports. The Herst evaluation [1991] was regarded as highly confidential with its circulation narrowly restricted, while the Wolfe Report [1993], which was made available to all, has not been read by most officers.

Despite the overwhelming public support for the reforms and the appointment of Colonel MacMillan, public dissension among senior officers developed at the inception of the process.[1] This dissension quickly matured into a fairly well articulated opposition, which eventually succeeded in removing the commissioner from office and somewhat domesticating the reform process. How and why did the process generate these outcomes in the short period of three years?

Reliance on Coercive Power

The system-reinforcing perspective on reform as a sanitizing and restorative process was directed at purging the bad eggs who were seen as corrupting an essentially sound institution and system of policing.[2] This viewpoint has had a fairly wide appeal outside and inside the JCF.

The reforms thus began with a sweeping attack on corruption. Rather than timidly probing at its margins and targeting its petty forms (such as traffic related transactions) for symbolic public relations image-refurbishing purposes, action was directed against the drug-trafficking networks and drug related corruption within the Force.

As noted earlier, the Canine Division, in which drug related corruption had become institutionalized, was almost completely purged. Some 30 percent of the total staff complement of 42 were transferred to a specially created, highly visible and publicly stigmatized unit with no effective function.[3] Suspected drug dealers and facilitators of drug trafficking in other sections of the Force were similarly relieved of duties that afforded them opportunities for corrupt accumulation, and were "sidelined" to nonoperational, low opportunity posts. Referring to the restrictions associated with his new assignment, one such officer indignantly remarked, "As far as I am concerned, this is house arrest."[4] The response to these sanctions was most dramatic among members of the CIB, as the consequences included loss of their status as detectives (being returned to uniform duties), celebrated "crime fighters" and models for young constables.

In addition to corruption, the targets were expanded to include the abuse of police powers and managerial incompetence. As with the treatment of corruption, there was a departure from tradition and the expectations of the members of the Force. This is illustrated by the willingness to admonish lawless crime fighting. Actions resulting in unjustifiable homicides were censured, not only when done in an off duty and private capacity as in the past but also in the execution of their duties, for which institutional protection was expected and often received.

Based on evaluations, a number of incompetent officers (who had been promoted on seniority, their political affiliations or other ascriptive criteria) were removed from their posts and replaced by younger, better educated, more competent and more innovative officers. The constables attached to the CIB were particularly offended by this. As investigators, the intellectual demands of their work are perhaps greater than in most of the other specializations, yet they tended to return the worst performances on the internal examinations and evaluations.[5] At the time of writing, some 58 percent of CIB personnel had not received any specialized training as investigators.[6] This might be alarming, but it is not surprising. The freedom from uniforms, additional perquisites, off duty access to guns, greater autonomy and a generally higher status made the CIB a prize posting. In a small society, such postings were often treated as rewards, or they may be associated with the strategic positioning of allies in games of empire building and struggles for political control of the Force. As a corrective, non-CIB officers were posted to manage the department.

This imposition was perceived as a threat on two grounds. First, as a peculiar instance of lateral entry, whereby non-CIB personnel would be able to move directly into the department as officers on the basis of managerial rather than investigative competence. In effect, it introduced the managerial principle as one basis of officer selection, on the assumption that, with the exception of the line officers, specialized police operational skills (while being useful) were not necessary or sufficient for managerial roles. This gave new meaning and a rather threatening twist to the process of professionalization. Second, a logical extension to this would be the opening up of the Force to outside appointments at various levels below that of commissioner, much in the American tradition of having two streams, one of line officers and the other of managers recruited directly from the civilian population [see Alpert and Dunham 1988]. This was particularly threatening to the more incompetent and typically suspicious officers and senior NCOs who were only too painfully aware of their managerial inadequacies.

The difficulties associated with these attacks on incompetence are perhaps best exemplified by the handling of jail breaks. The police have had considerable difficulty keeping prisoners in their jails.[7] This was particularly evident in the case of some of the drug-rich prisoners.[8] It was thus often unclear whether some of these escapes were due to incompetence or corruption. Perhaps for this reason, swift action was now directed at the responsible officers. This level of accountability (albeit singularly and coercively imposed rather than collectively and cooperatively established) was hitherto unheard of. Punishment, in the rare cases when it had been considered, was much less severe and directed at the lowest operatives rather than the supervisory and managerial staff. To many in these ranks, the new approach seemed harsh and unjust, given the porosity of the jails and the contrasting manner in which this transgression was treated in the past.

In this approach, change is effected primarily by the negative use of coercive power. These types of action were limited in their effectiveness as the existing structures and web of relations positively encouraged some of the forms of police deviance that the disciplinary actions were intended to control. The targets of these actions therefore enjoyed considerable support and empathy among their peers. For example, despite its general support for the commissioner and the reforms, the Police Federation interceded on behalf of the "narco cops". This ultimately encouraged resistance.

As the scope of action widened, so did the targets. More daringly, coercive power was now being directed at the formerly untouchable managerial/officer and supervisory/NCO ranks. This break with tradition in wielding coercive power in support of new levels of accountability served to broaden the resistance to reform at the managerial levels of the Force. However, this resistance was initially blunted by the degree to which the officers were discredited within the Force. The attitude of the lower ranks to the plight of the incompetent officers was most colourfully expressed by one constable who, although obviously not impressed with the commissioner, felt that the rank and file members of the Force should "Let them [the officers] suck salt through [meaning 'from'] the MacMillan spoon."[9]

From corruption and incompetence, the campaign further progressed to issues of negligence and poor service delivery. This widening of the range of targets of the reforms, with no indication of the principles that would have disciplined the process of target setting and set clear limits on the scope of disciplinary action, served to increase the level of uncertainty and feelings of vulnerability among the officers. Although these actions appeared threatening to many of the officers, they generated popular support externally. To the mass public this was taken to mean a greater responsiveness on the part of the commissioner and a willingness to act on their complaints. This stimulated increased appeals to him for redress against police abuse. Within the Force, this was seen as a tactic for instigating and concentrating the wrath of the public against its members. This wrath, they felt, was further amplified by the artful manipulation of a willing press, which they believed had occurred in the Flankers case that was discussed earlier.

The Flankers incident was the first and only major confrontation between the police and the people during the period under review, however. Its handling, including the prompt response from the High Command, listening to the people at the site of the event and speedily taking action against the offending personnel, set the tone for the duration of the period. Subsequently, appeals to the police authorities against their operatives came to typify such instances. This represented improved confidence in the willingness and capacity of the police to police itself and was a positive reversal of old patterns whereby external control agencies, such as the Police Public Complaints Authority, were established in response to the loss of credibility of the police authorities and of the capacity of the JCF for self-regulation.

By its negative sanctioning of corruption and abuse of police powers, the new police administration signalled that it was not prepared to cover up corrupt behaviour, not just on matters to do with pecuniary gain, but also not in aspects related to the traditional policing bias against the poor. This indicated a potential for a shift in power and an intention to shape a new dominant coalition within the Force. The consequence of these developments was a growing tension between the reformers and the defensive coalition, which set the stage for early polarization and resistance to the reforms.

The Strategy and Tactics of Resistance

This resistance rapidly developed despite evidence from the attitude data that suggested significant internal support for the reforms. The intensity of the crisis and the extent of external pressures for change had led many within the Force to accept the need for reform. But the rapidity with which the resistance developed was also conditioned by the rapid pace of the reforms, or at least the signalling by the commissioner of the seriousness of his commitment to this project. In 1994, one year after the programme of reform was initiated, 72 percent of the members of the Force reported that the reforms already had a significant impact on their unit or department. At this point, when the sanitizing character of the reform programme was already evident, some 24 percent of the Force described themselves as being supportive of fundamental change, 71 percent for incremental change and 4 percent for no change. These data may suggest that, initially, the resistance was supported by a small minority, but they were not an isolated group, as the vast majority of the Force (the 71 percent) provided a pool from which support could be drawn as mistakes were made and the process seemed to exceed, or threaten to exceed, the boundaries of incremental change.

Consistent with the "bad egg" theory of the problems of the Force, reform (for the typical constable) is more associated with expunging these elements than with altering the fundamental relationships and structures. The orientations on reform described above are thus largely equated with the degree of personnel changes that they find acceptable. These data are presented in Table 8.1, with items ordered from least to most radical. Considerable support existed for a purge of the bad eggs at all levels of the Force. Some 34 percent felt that "in order to create a good force, at least half the officer corps should be replaced", while another 17 percent were "neutral" on this issue. The attempt to purge the officer corps therefore had a substantial basis within the Force. There were, however, divergent definitions of what constituted a bad egg. To many, if one was regarded as socially useful, as was the case with the crime fighters, then despite their corrupt behaviour, they were not considered bad eggs. This more restrictive definition confounded the reformers. Interestingly, the Force's view of its corrupt members is similar to that of the closed homogeneous urban communities to their criminals. The police, like the members of these communities, do not extend this view to outsiders. Instead, they tend to adopt a dualistic view of outsiders, or nonpolice, as simply friend or foe, good or bad. The sociological foundations of these perspectives on deviance by members of the group are in some respects quite similar. Controlling such deviance is perhaps equally difficult. A merger of the JCF and the JDF is seen as one solution to this problem of controlling the police. Support for this position goes well beyond the "bad egg" theory to the view that the JCF ought to be reconstructed. It connotes the subordination of the leadership of the JCF to that of the military leadership in any such new institution. It is quite a statement on the level of awareness of the nature of the crisis of the JCF that a notable minority of 14 percent agreed with this [Table 8.1].

In response to the reforms, the defensive coalition sought to engage the process in a war of attrition, with the objective of neutralizing and ultimately removing the commissioner, and to either constrain the reform movement within system-supportive parameters or to stymie the process. These aims represented the positions of two different (at times diverging, at times converging) trends within the defensive coalition. These aims were met by depriving the coalition for change of the main power resources to execute the reforms and in the process accumulating the power to block the process.

Table 8.1 Attitudes to Personnel Changes (percentage)

Items	Agree	Neutral	Disagree
Purge "bad eggs"	88	5	8
Purge majority of officers	34	17	49
Purge majority of the Force	8	11	81
Merge the JCF and JDF	14	8	78
Create a new police force	4	6	90

In pursuit of this strategy, the tactics adopted by the defensive coalition included attacks on the competence of outside change agents, the use of protective myths, information control, and legal defensive manoeuvres. The forms of resistance used in executing the above tactics changed in combination and grew in intensity as the process progressed. Initially, when popular support for the reforms was at its zenith, there was resort to legal and bureaucratic manoeuvres. Later, in a more offensive mode, resistance included malingering in concert with political networking and propagandizing within the Force, which, in the final phase of the struggle to remove the commissioner (July to September 1996), developed into an aggressive campaign on the police radio communications network.[10] The defensive coalition had orchestrated an increasingly sophisticated and tactically astute campaign. These tactics are not peculiar to the JCF and have been used widely within public bureaucracies to resist change [see Mintzberg 1989]. Each is discussed in turn.

Many change agents were in some sense outsiders. The labelling of them as such served to undermine their authority (as experts) and frustrate their efforts. Within the JCF, policing is seen by most as an almost mystical existential reality that may only be understood via the direct encounters experienced by being a constable. The only authentic authorities on policing operations *and* policy in a particular environment are therefore policemen (and perhaps policewomen) who have done police work in that environment. The outsider was thus, by definition, incompetent. This was aimed at all externally imposed change agents, including the British advisors who were former police officers but not Jamaican, but most of all it was aimed at Commissioner MacMillan, and served to deny him the option of harnessing further outside support via a more open policy of direct officer recruitment or via secondments from the army. Fierce opposition to the direct entry programme sustained over two decades made policy makers and the ministry reluctant to pursue this option. It was not until after the termination of the tenure of Colonel MacMillan, when the reforms seemed less threatening, that the ministry forced a small number (11) of direct entrants into the officer ranks for the specific purpose of enforcing the Money Laundering Act and Assets Forfeiture Act of which the US government was a powerful advocate and which required technical expertise that could not be found within the Force or at lower entry rank offerings.

The British advisors were targeted as the source of unpopular measures, such as the rules governing use of violence and access to weapons, based on the principle of minimum force. They were, of course, highly vulnerable to attacks of being out of touch with the realities of the Jamaican environment or trying to transmit an irrelevant set of experiences (exceptions were perhaps made for those who had served in Northern Ireland).

Commissioner MacMillan was, of course, the foremost outsider. Despite its paramilitary tradition, the JCF (it was argued) was unlike the army and could not be managed in a similar way. MacMillan's outsider attributes were taken as the source of what was regarded as his problematic leadership style. This was characterized by an uncompromising stance and a perceived arbitrariness on disciplinary matters, which were associated with his military background, and his insistence on adherence to law over crime fighting, which was attributed to his middle class liberalism. He was propagandized as a Trojan horse for a military takeover of the JCF. As evidence of this, it was claimed that the military was being positioned to take over the leadership of the JCF by transferring some 50 of its officers into key command posts in the Force, and that Military Intelligence was being used for intelligence gathering on police officers.[11]

More self-interestedly, the real threat posed by Colonel MacMillan was seen as the blocking of the career paths of police officers. His appointment was interpreted as holding the prospect of an opening up of the post of commissioner to wider competition, and thereby precluding the appointment to this post of career police officers who enter the Force at the base of the rank structure. This view was echoed by a highly respected former commissioner who, in a speech to a police audience, argued that the constable could "no longer aspire to the top post" and likened the appointment of Colonel MacMillan to a "reversion" to the colonial years "when the Force was run by expatriates".[12] The outsider threat was magnified and depicted as directed against the personal interests of every constable. Moreover, on the same principle on which an outside commissioner could be appointed, similar appointments could be made in other managerial posts. The idea, that what was needed was a cadre of professional managers, was particularly threatening, as it seemed to elevate managerial expertise over policing expertise and experience.

These attacks on outsider competence sought to challenge the authenticity of the change process by presenting it as coercively imposed by alien agencies. This applied not just to the outsiders, but to the young, rapidly promoted and, by extension, inadequately acculturated reformers in the officer corps, who were depicted as inexperienced and their youth cited as proof of their unworthiness of such authority (not fully assimilated insiders). Those resistant to change argued that police work, and police management in particular, were not (and perhaps ought not to be) "professions" that schooling prepares one for, but rather crafts acquired by experience and the in-service tutelage of more experienced craftsmen and women, a world-view formed from lived experiences, and a social being acquired by years of willing assimilation into the police subculture. The absence of grey hairs was thus a sure sign of one's unpreparedness for the rank of officer.

A second defensive tactic was the use of protective myths. Myths about the heroic accomplishments of the crime fighters were spun to resist the removal of corrupt detectives and the insistence on the primacy of the rule of law over crime fighting. Many of these crime fighters are police personnel who had gained notoriety as being corrupt, excessively violent and politically biased in the execution of their police duties but who are celebrated within the Force (and some politically homogeneous communities) for their toughness, bravery and action orientation. One of the great myths of the Force is that these crime fighters are able to control the crime rate and that the rate of violent crime continued to rise during the period of the reforms because the crime fighters were removed from the front line of the "war" against crime. The suggestion is that they are able to control the rate of violent crime by their aggressive social cleansing. Thus, despite their shortcomings, they were considered invaluable members of the Force. Their disciplining and redeployment by the reformist leadership, it was argued, had lowered morale, initiative and willingness to take risks among all members of the Force. The consequent lower police output, it was felt, was thus being exploited by criminals.

While, as pointed out earlier, there are some advantageous aspects to the corrupt activity of the crime fighters, contrary to this myth, they tend to contribute handsomely to the accumulated legitimacy problems of the Force. They are usually sources of conflict within the Force and between the Force and the people, with their actions serially embroiling the police in political disputes. This myth further served to defend not just the particular crime fighters but the style of policing that created them. It is underpinned by a deep cynicism about human nature and Jamaican society (which was discussed earlier in the text). The crime fighters are considered effective and heroic figures because they are seen as responsive to the policing needs of poor communities in a manner more or less consistent with the norms of these communities, and are competent in the use of violence directed in a protective rather than repressive direction (from the standpoint of particular groups).

This crime-fighting myth resonated within the Force and society, as the notion of being in a special situation of societal vulnerability to violent crime (making it necessary for citizens to give up some rights and for the police to fight by any means) had gained currency within the Force, the political élite, opinion leaders with platforms in the news media and the mass public, as noted earlier in chapter 3. Such views were reflected in the poor rating given the leadership of Colonel MacMillan on the issue of crime control. Some 35 percent of the Force felt that under his leadership the ability of the JCF to control crime had declined, another 30 percent felt that it had remained the same, while only 30 percent felt that it had improved (the remaining 5 percent did not wish to offer an opinion). The continued increase in the rate of reported violent crimes was erroneously attributed to the control on crime fighting imposed by the reforms, although this has been an enduring trend since 1962.

Indications are that the upward trend in the rate of violent crimes was perhaps accelerated by higher rates of reporting due to the increased public confidence in the Force. This is particularly true of reported rapes, which seem to be highly sensitive to changes in police attitudes. Making the cleaning up of the Force the focus of the reforms, and treating it as a stage of a linear process that must precede improved effectiveness in crime control, meant that the point at which the reforms made a positive impact (improving public confidence in the Force) became self-defeating, as this had the effect of generating higher reporting rates that in turn were seen as the most important measure against which the worth of the reforms was ultimately judged. Reform therefore came to be seen as morally directed (against the police rather than the criminal) and as an end in itself without any utility as the rate of violent crime continued to increase.

Given the extent of the reforms required and the anticipated difficulties in executing them (even if this linear thinking was avoided), the reforms were unlikely to have had an immediate, positive impact on the crime rates. And even then, the continued increase in the rate of violent crime points to the limitations of the professional reform model, indeed, the limits of the effect of policing in general on crime rates.

Nevertheless, the claim that the crime fighters were able to exert a controlling influence on violent criminality should not be dismissed without examination. Their connection to the underground affords them privileged information and the ability to use informal levers to assist in the control of violent crime. In some communities they operate in active collusion with the local dons. This alliance, perhaps even bonding, is not difficult to understand as both correctly consider themselves special agents of social control who have similar responsibilities and shared normative beliefs. The attack on corruption within the Force may thus have resulted in the loss of the short-term advantages of crime fighting as practised by these detectives. However, while organizational dislocations associated with change are usually likely to negatively affect short-term performance, reform is largely about investing in the future, and this was perhaps a necessary price that had to be paid. While the police leadership did succeed in somewhat immobilizing the crime fighters, it was not able to remove them, in part due to how information may be controlled within the organization.

Information control and the exploitation of the secrecy norms of the Force are routinely used to frustrate external and internal accountability [Harriott 1994]. The police subculture as a source of resistance to change is well documented [Van Maanen 1989; Blumberg and Niederhoffer 1985:141;

Niederhoffer 1969:109–60]. The veil of ignorance and its acceptance by the public protects the Force from public scrutiny. In no other organization is the difference between front stage (to use Goffman's language) image manipulation and backstage realities greater. This allows image manipulation, for example the myth of the bad eggs, which is not just designed to reproduce legitimacy but also to avoid necessary reforms.

Colonel MacMillan was regarded as too open. Rather than masking the abusive behaviour of the Force, he committed the sin of opening the Force to scrutiny by the press, with the latter becoming a more effective instrument of police accountability and control. Information control was used internally to resist change by withholding, filtering and distorting messages directed both upward and downward. Information from the High Command, which was relayed at regular meetings of the officers, was consistently withheld and not acted on. This had become so bad that in the latter part of his tenure the commissioner insisted on having at least three persons present at all meetings attended by him and that everything was recorded.[13] This did not prevent distortions or inaction. To compound this problem, some middle level commanders ensured that every unpopular action that they took was presented as the personal wishes of the commissioner.[14]

The manipulation of upwardly directed information is an old tradition in the JCF [Harriott 1994]. In the context of resistance, this tradition, the code of secrecy, primary group loyalty and protectiveness on which it is based may be fully exploited. Delay and distortion are standard techniques. This is best illustrated by the Savanna-la-Mar events of 29 May 1996[15] and the Hopewell events of April 1997.[16] In both cases citizen protesters were shot by the local police, who in order to mask their culpability, knowingly sent distorted reports to the Police High Command. In the case of the Hopewell events, citizens resorted to a roadblock (a popular form of protest) in an effort to have the authorities make good their commitment to install a reliable water supply system. Six to eight protesters were shot by the local police, who, in an effort at cover up and damage control reported to the High Command that only one person had been shot.[17] These events served to advise the public pronouncements of the commissioner and consequently to discredit him somewhat, as the injured protesters were later paraded in the media.

This problem usually leads to distrust of the formal channels, and consequently, attempts are made to bypass the chain of command and to resort to the use of informal channels. Both measures in turn usually create even greater distrust. It was in this context, for example, that the belief that Military Intelligence was being used as the primary source of information on members of the Force gained credibility and the spectre of military oversight of the police was believed to loom large.

Operating on an individual level was the type of information control associated with the creation and guarding of monopolistic preserves of specialized skills and knowledge. There is generally a reluctance to transfer technical knowledge gained from training abroad, particularly in highly specialized areas such as the detection of fraud. The acquisition and privatization of such knowledge are assisted by the empathic and political relationships that ensure that specialized knowledge is restricted to a few personally and politically loyal persons who can then be strategically positioned in the organization. This in part explains the odd training patterns in the JCF, whereby the same persons are repeatedly sent on similar courses [see MacMillan 1994]. As these skills are usually associated with strategic positions, it assures privileged access to sensitive information, which in turn affirms one's importance and status in the organization and guarantees against transfers during periods of change. Moreover, by withholding knowledge, the privileged keepers of these secrets may embarrass young officers and make them appear incompetent.

In the early defensive phase, there was less scope for the successful use of these tactics. Thus, the defensive coalition resorted primarily to legal tactics aimed at frustrating any attempt at a purge. This was pursued by individuals, groups of affected persons, and by representative associations (as in the case of the Police Officers' Association). It was employed defensively against disciplinary actions ranging from forcible leave, as in the case of Deputy Commission of Police (DCP) Harper;[18] transfers, as with the Canine Division[19] and the Immigration Department in Montego Bay;[20] suspensions, as in the case of Inspector Roache whose actions precipitated the events at Flankers discussed earlier in the text;[21] refusals to renew the contracts of allegedly corrupt persons; dismissals;[22] and was even attempted in an effort to block nonpunitive means of effecting personnel changes, in particular the proposal to offer early retirement to older members of the Force.[23]

Even the Internal Courts of Enquiry offered considerable scope for frustrating the disciplinary process. The commissioner is not empowered to order internal trials without the approval of the Police Services Commission (PSC), which at times was a source of inordinate delays of "months, sometimes years" [MacMillan 1994]. This requirement, which was designed to protect the rights of suspects, allowed considerable scope for the political protection of corrupt personnel or simply the exploitation of the ineffectiveness of the system. Constables were able to delay their trials by manipulating the judicial process, "resulting in enquiries taking up to three years to be completed" [MacMillan 1994].

Constables below the rank of inspector may be dismissed only on a conviction by a Court of Enquiry, but this is subject to review by the PSC.

There were instances of persons dismissed for "gross misconduct" who were reinstated by the PSC, not on the basis of successful appeals but, rather, on the reluctance of the PSC (as a principle) to support dismissals, thereby frustrating the attempt to arraign and remove the bad eggs [MacMillan 1994:46].

As Commissioner MacMillan was considered the driving force of the reforms, if his actions could be slowed, as indeed they were, then the chances of the individuals who were subjected to the disciplinary processes surviving his three-year tenure would have been considered good. This partly accounted for their reluctance to exit the Force. This institutionalized resistance, or "natural" blocking power of the structures, favoured the defensive coalition and from very early tended to frustrate the change process.

In March 1996 there were 200 cases of interdicted police personnel before the Jamaican courts which had accumulated since 1990.[24] A significant number of these cases were still being processed after seven years, with few being completed in less than three years. The political cost of these kinds of delays to the reform process was great and the economic cost constituted a strain on the finances of the Force. For example, until the outcome of the trial, the accused constable remains on 75 percent of his or her salary while suspended, and if acquitted is paid the remaining 25 percent.

These court battles became a lasting feature of the tenure of Colonel MacMillan. Every disciplinary action was challenged on legal grounds in order to depict him as arbitrary, hasty in his judgements, and quick to punish and even dismiss his men on the basis of dubious intelligence reports and the observation of consumption patterns incongruent with known earnings, rather than legal standards of proof of corruption or criminality. As an outsider, he was perceived by some of his officers as a carrier of the strong antipolice bias in the society. According to one officer who was a target of these actions, the commissioner was "acting like a civilian coming in to discipline the force".[25] This apparent disregard in wielding coercive power at internal targets was also explained in terms of his social characteristics and military background. More seriously, these actions were seen as the outcomes of the lack of empathy and poor judgement expected of an outsider – in this case a triple outsider on grounds of colour, class and profession – who was out of touch with the realities of policing. This theme resonated within the Force.

This first line of attack was thus directed at delegitimizing and constraining the use of the coercive powers of the commissioner, and certainly at preventing any extension of these powers to include the managerial prerogative of terminating the employment of constables, which was then being publicly debated. Having succeeded at this, in the final phase of the resistance, the commissioner was sharply criticized for the failure to control the rate of violent crimes, which was then attributed to his misplaced priority of disciplining the JCF and the moral crusading directed at it, which constrained the police in their war on crime.

Given this sharp polarization within the Force, the reformists were left with three options. First, to accelerate and radicalize the reform process by purging the managerial ranks and re-engineering the Force. This option required the full support of the government and will be discussed later. The government, however, was reluctant to support it. Second, to continue the war of attrition. On this trajectory, the tensions tended to take on a destructive dynamic, leading to increased mutual intolerance, with the commissioner becoming more exclusionary and increasingly reliant on the external elements in his coalition for change, such as the British advisors, and on those officers elevated during his tenure. This would in turn force more confrontationist approaches on the part of the representative associations within the Force. It is not difficult to see, especially with hindsight, that the likely outcome would have been the commissioner becoming increasingly frustrated, as was the case, and eventually either resigning or having his contract terminated (as occurred), with the Force possibly returning to its old ways of conducting business. The third option was to retreat and attempt to reconstruct a broader internal alliance for change. This latter course required considerable political concessions to the defensive coalition and might have entailed risking the moral integrity of the process.

The Shift in Favour of the Defensive Coalition

In a power culture such as that which obtains in the JCF, the outcome of any reform programme having implications for the power arrangements within the Force rests on political mobilization. This involves accumulating power and constructing coherent coalitions. The conditions for this, in the belief structure and ideological trends in the Force, were discussed in the previous chapter. There it was argued that the positions of the majority are not deeply anchored in coherent ideologies and systems of beliefs. One would therefore expect delicate and constantly shifting coalitions, with their relative stability being conditioned by national party politics. The defensive coalition consisted internally of the leadership of the Officers' Association and the older officers and NCOs, and externally of former officers and, later, sections of the political leadership of the ruling party.

Control of the representative associations usually reflects the shift in party alignment in the country. During the period under review, this generally favoured the ruling party. However, the police affiliates of this party were not homogeneous in their attitudes to reform. While the Police Federation, which represents and reflects the positions of the rank and file of the Force, tended to be supportive of the reforms, the Police Officers' Association waged an unremitting battle with the commissioner. The latter became a useful instrument for the defensive coalition, but was frequently neutralized by the split in the officer corps and the dilemma of casting itself in opposition to the policies of a governing party to which most of its leaders were affiliated.

While the commissioner enjoyed tactical autonomy, managerial autonomy was only partial. Finances, which had always been an important source of control of the security institutions, were fully retained by the Ministry of National Security and Justice. This power resource, and reward power generally, was virtually monopolized by the political leadership, thereby making their role in the process and their inclusion in the coalition for change vital to any successful outcome.

Initially, the defensive coalition suffered from a number of handicaps that reduced its effectiveness: their association with corruption had compromised their moral authority; the natural internal opposition (of old guard conservatives and corrupt personnel) was split along party lines with opposition supporters being largely neutral or supportive of important aspects of the process and of the commissioner; and the leadership of the reform process by a government that they largely supported. This split the pro-PNP old guard and moderated their resistance to the process. This reality also tactically conditioned the personalization of their resistance to the process by targeting the commissioner.

For the defensive coalition, the challenge was to rupture the coalition for change, such that those for system reinforcing reforms would realign themselves and thereby isolate those for system change. This was a dynamic process, with shifting patterns informed by the internal processes as well as party politics. Such a shift was sufficient to oust the commissioner and to turn the course of events, even if only temporarily.

The response of the Force to the process at the end of the first year (1994) suggested that majority opinion among all ranks tended to positively evaluate the reforms and the performance of the commissioner. Discipline, public support, the rationalization and creation of greater opportunities for promotion attracted the most positive evaluations, while crime control and issues related to internal control and power relations (anticorruption, depoliticization) attracted the most negative evaluations [Table 8.2]. Nevertheless, as reported in Table 8.3, there was a notable correlation between perceived improvements in internal discipline and perceived improvements in public support (.358) for the Force and its capability to control crime (.363). This was the logic of the reform process and justification for the strong internal disciplinary actions that the reformers tried to communicate.

Table 8.2 Evaluation of Outcomes of the Reform Process 1994 (percentage)

Item	Better	Same	Worse
State of internal discipline	75	21	3
Ability to control crime	35	30	35
Party activism within the JCF*	40	31	29
Party manipulation of the JCF*	52	30	18
Public support for the JCF	70	21	9
The promotions process/officer level	51	34	15
The promotion process/other ranks	34	34	32

* For these items, better = reduced

Table 8.3 Correlation Matrix of Eight Performance Items

	DISCIP	CRIMEC	PARTY	POLMAN	PUBCON	PROMO	PROMOR	PROMOA
λ111	1.0000							
λ112	.3631	1.0000						
λ113	.0910	.1234	1.0000					
λ114	.0575	.0326	.6583	1.0000				
λ115	.3581	.2785	.1673	.0937	1.0000			
λ116	.1846	.1596	.1415	.1170	.1218	1.0000		
λ117	.1620	.2127	.0556	.0407	.1165	.2729	1.0000	
λ118	.2294	.1085	.1081	.0698	.1896	.2629	.2046	1.0000

The variables above are ratings of the performance of the commissioner on the following indicators:

DISCIP – discipline within the Force

CRIMEC – ability to control crime

PARTY – party activism within the Force

POLMAN – political manipulation of the Force

PUBCON – public support for the Force

PROMO – promotions at the officer level

PROMOR – promotions at the level of other ranks

PROMOA – accelerated promotions

Three issues of control have been central to the debates within the Force. These are the control of corruption, depoliticization and, as would be anticipated from the earlier discussion, the limits on crime fighting. Some 52 percent of the Force expressed opposition to the commissioner's treatment of corruption. There is a high correlation between attitude on this issue and generalized opposition to his administration. Of those opposed to his handling of this issue, 71 percent were generally opposed to his administration ($p < .0000$). Opposition to the constraints on crime control and depoliticization tended to increase with rank, while opposition to the handling of corrupt personnel was strongest in the lower ranks [Table 8.4]. This opposition in the upper ranks was weakened by the considerable disrespect and even hostility to these officers shown by their subordinates.

Table 8.4 Opposition on Control Items by Rank (percentage)

Rank	Crime Control	Corruption Control	Political Manipulation	Promotions Process
Officer	55	18	41	24
Inspector	36	15	43	25
Junior NCOs	32	26	31	17
Constables	31	28	25	13

$N = 660$

Essentially, the resistance was rooted in policy differences; narrow self-regarding concerns (loss of status, authority and perquisites); reorientation of the reward systems such that skills once valued (enforcer type skills) were now devalued and education and professional services once devalued were now highly valued, and most of all, the efforts to remove the rewards derived from corruption and service to the political parties; disruption of old power bases and equilibria, with implications for drug related corruption and national political competition (election rigging, ability to offer criminals and political thugs protection from the justice system); and objections to the leadership style of the commissioner.

Within and beyond the broad aggregation for change, real differences on important policy issues emerged. Perhaps most important was the issue of crime control discussed earlier. The disputes on this reflected deeper attitudes to the nature and objectives of the reform programme itself. Crime fighting is associated with the traditional paramilitary style of policing and a reluctance to change the basic relationships of control within the Force and with the people. By its indifference to the means of achieving this end, the Force reflects a dubious commitment to the rule of law and the democratic process. However, in the face of a growing rate of violent crimes, the Force quickly recoiled from any openness to, or effort at, changing this style of policing.

Self-regarding concerns were of great importance as a source of resistance to professionalization. The reforms brought dislocations for many who were beneficiaries of the existing patterns of policing. The exposure of incompetent officers who knew and worked the system, or who were "carried" by their more competent subordinates, was resented. With promotions restructured, the patronage and politics that served to shore up this old system was disrupted. Resistance by the crime fighters (who were the stars of this decaying style of policing) and the indolent who were accommodated by it (identified by Muir [1977] in his insightful discussion of individual policing styles as "avoiders") would have been expected. To the crime fighters, their skills were being undervalued, perhaps negated, by the new requirement to observe due process. Their status was accordingly devalued and, with their new posting away from the front lines of the war on crime, their opportunities for corruption were minimized. Avoiders suffered scrutiny for incompetence, the inability to advance on seniority alone, and the loss of quietude and predictable routines.

Depoliticization was particularly problematic as many progovernment officers did not enjoy the anticipated career advances that usually accompany the installation of their party as the government. At the level of the internal struggle between the advocacy coalitions within the Force, depoliticization upset the power equilibrium and threatened to reconstruct a new dominant coalition for professionalization, thereby also threatening the traditional system of subjective party political control of the Force inherited from the colonial era. In the face of this threat, the interests of the old guard and the political administration appeared to converge.

The meaning of the objections to the leadership style of Commissioner MacMillan is best understood against this background. The objections to the content and direction of the reforms were aggravated by the difficulties associated with the cascading character of the process and found expression as objections to the leadership style of the commissioner.

Managing the Process of Change

Four approaches or strategies in managing the change process have been identified. These are shuffling the structure, the cascade, political networking, and a collaborative process [Heckscher, Eisenstat, and Rice 1994]. *Shuffling* involves cutting layers of supervision and transferring their responsibilities downward in the organization. The *cascade* entails "opening up information but not power". Goals are developed at the top, then "sold" to others in the organization. The values of the institution are changed from the top down via a directive process. *Political networking* involves private ad hoc consultation and coalition building. Here only the top knows the goals of the project, and support for change is equated with support for the leader. The *collaborative approach* is one of consensus building by an open and inclusive process. This tends to reduce resistance. While the first two strategies are linear the latter two are not [see Heckscher, Eisenstat, and Rice 1994: 137–45].

Using these categories, a combination of shuffling, the cascade and elements of political networking was adopted. There was, however, greater shuffling of individuals than of organizational structure. The shuffling of the organizational structure was restricted to the phasing out of two ranks. This was not sufficient to alter the internal relations and organization of work, nor to force their reconstruction on a new team-collegial or decentralized basis. Political networking efforts to develop linkages into the networks of opinion leaders was potentially self-defeating and limited by the goal of depoliticization.

The strategy adopted was influenced by the goals of the reform project (that is, attempts to change behaviour without changing the structures and system of sanctions that frame those behaviour patterns) and the instruments for behaviour modification available (negative coercive power). Such a (restorative) project need not have been inclusive. However, had it been conceptualized as change in structures and power relations in order to ensure more effective crime control, a more participatory approach might have been encouraged.

The reform strategy contributed to the resistance. Though the collaborative approach is the ideal, it makes the dubious assumption that all have an interest in change, or at least are not blocking change. This assumption hardly applies to the JCF, as it would represent an underestimation of the problem of corruption and the spirit of self-interested conservatism regarding the reform of that institution. The approach of the commissioner thus had some realism and justification to it.

It would be somewhat misleading to present the reform process as being as planned and coherent as described above. Indeed, part of the problem with the process was that there was no coherent authoritative perspective on the reform of the Force. The absence of a clear authoritative perspective contributed to the personalization of the process and to widely differing and unreasonable expectations (for example, the criticism at the end of year two that the reforms were not having a significant impact in reducing the crime rates), which eventually hastened the setback of the process.

With the setbacks, the government, which had initiated the process, began to recoil from it. This was most evidently expressed in its volte-face on the efforts to purge the old guard officers. Decisive to the outcome of the reforms and this first political battle was the removal of these officers. The government had given an undertaking to provide an attractive inducement to all persons age 55 years or older to retire by offering them a "golden handshake" with the full benefits they would have received had they retired at age 60 [see Knight 1994:29]. The commissioner had acted on the assumption that this would have been honoured, but the government reneged on its offer, ostensibly on grounds of costs.

In reality, the change of heart represented a political shift in the position of the government. Too many of its valued supporters had been negatively affected by the reform process, and as a result, there was a consistent lobbying of members of the government to put a brake on the process. Disciplinary action, directed against some of the more reform minded senior officers who were known to be affiliated to the ruling party, was decisive in precipitating a shift from dissension to opposition and a recoil from the process by sections of the Force who were supportive of system reinforcing reforms. The removal of a particular officer marks this turning point in the process. He represented the best of the old guard with all of their warts. He was a senior ranking officer, a highly decorated crime fighter, highly connected and valued politically, reform minded and supportive of Commissioner MacMillan from the inception of his tenure, yet steeped in the sexism and protective codes associated with the police subculture. His removal was taken as signifying an overreaching of the reform process.

There was thus an accumulation of a critical mass of dissidents and losers of the process (most of whom were posted to the Inspections Branch of the Force) who could not be removed from the Force. The opportunity to purge the officer corps had been lost, and a significant number of alienated but influential officers at the highest levels of command was now a new reality that had to be contended with.

The reforms served to undermine the system of subjective control of the Force, which is based on ministerial control of reward power. The emergence and deepening of the nascent coalition for change threatened a loss of ministerial control of the reform process and the Force, as well as the prospect of the process moving beyond system-reinforcing to system-undermining reforms.

This prospect seemed to have split the élite. The PNP, which represents the new black entrepreneurs who have accumulated their wealth with the direct aid of the political system and who remain dependent on it, naturally recoil at any prospect of reforming the wider political system. The party tends to be more supportive of social reform and tends to view the political process as a lever for effecting this. In contrast, the economic élite (with the support of sections of the political élite) has tended to be more supportive of political rather than social reform (as a path out of the crisis). This approach is naturally more appealing as it deflects the debate away from the issue of social injustice (and the need to reform the economic and social structures) and allows the economic élite to scapegoat the political élite and its maladministration as the sole source of the crisis. The economic élite associates stability and the hope of development with reducing the power of the political administration. With these countervailing interests and pressure, neither social nor political reform (and with this substantive police reform) is likely to be successfully effected.

Commissioner MacMillan and police reform became victims of the government's recoil and its desire to more tightly manage the reforms. Thereafter, the process was deprived of resources, thus making the commissioner seem ineffective and generally making it difficult to get things done. For example, training courses, which were seen as vital to the process, had to be aborted. This issue of control and the scope of police autonomy, therefore, became central in the termination of Colonel MacMillan's tenure as commissioner of police.

Without a credible policy broker, the deterioration in the relationship between the commissioner and the minister of national security and justice, which personified the split in the reform movement, proved exceedingly difficult to repair. Any such reform process, which must generate considerable conflicts within and between shifting coalitions, needs credible brokers. Unfortunately, there were no institutional players able to fulfil this role. In a winner-take-all political system (such as that of Jamaica) where power is highly concentrated and the structures do not facilitate compromise as a normal part of the political process (the Opposition being largely excluded) – as is the case with the governance of the police force – any such broker would have been ineffective. This situation narrowed the scope for collective choice, resulting in an easy personalization of the problems. Consequently, as issues of power underlay the disputes, simple problems became increasingly difficult to resolve.

The shift in the position of the government occurred despite the robust popular approval of the commissioner and support for the process. Even after his removal and during a campaign to discredit him, the Anderson poll reported that 83 percent of the population felt that he had done a "good job" and only 2 percent that he had done a bad job.[26] This was significantly higher than his 62 percent approval rating at the beginning of his tenure.[27] No other government or state official, and certainly no past commissioner of police (the most unpopular institution), could boast such an approval rating.

Conclusion

The reform process encountered considerable institutionalized resistance. This is entrenched in the structures that obstruct anything that deviates from the routine and protect the status quo. These structures are organizational, legal and cultural. Given the entrenched nature of the system of subjective control of the police force, things are, in the main, done by informal networks. Relying on the mechanisms of the formal system to effect change (more so system changing reforms) is to court defeat. The institution becomes a very stiff and formal bureaucracy whenever it encounters the new. This institutionalized resistance was exploited by the defensive coalition.

Given the profoundly political nature of the Force, such reform projects cannot be successful if narrowly conceptualized as administrative processes. Success depends on the ability of the reformers to build and sustain new and dominant coalitions for change. Ownership of the process was located by many constables exclusively at the top at the level of the commissioner, who was erroneously regarded by some as imposition on a reluctant government by representatives of the economic élite. There was wide but diffused approval of the process in the society; it was thus easily over-turned.

9

Conclusion

In this final chapter, the general limits on the process of police reform and their implications are discussed, and the policy options are considered. In exploring these options, the impetuses toward and dangers associated with an authoritarian solution, along the lines of the increasingly alluring Singaporean model of crime control, are considered and, in contrast, the outlines of a more democratic model of policing are elaborated. The chapter concludes with some general comments on the difficulties of formal social control.

No developing country with the vulnerabilities that Jamaica exhibits can reasonably expect stable development while maintaining such persistently high rates of violent crime, a developing tradition of urban gang warfare and lawlessness. Indeed, societies that must contemplate such considerable strain on their social and political institutions need legitimate institutions capable of managing major conflicts and serious social problems in socially constructive and perhaps democratic ways.

The state of the police and the criminal justice system more generally, are important variables in this process. There is a clear need to strengthen these institutions and, more broadly, the capacity of the state to deal with the problems of law enforcement in the changed and rapidly changing environment. Indeed, the prospects are for further development and increased sophistication of organized crime. Such phenomena must be expected to thrive in an environment where people in all layers of the social hierarchy exhibit a behavioural pattern of indifference to means and gross disregard for state authority and where there is a general waiving of negative sanctions, as is the case in Jamaica. The more developed criminal networks that already operate internationally in different environments have to contend with more resource endowed and technologically advanced police services and have been forced to adapt to these conditions in order to survive. The Jamaican criminal justice system is now trying to catch up with these advances in the social organization of criminals. While the character and direction of this strengthening of the police and criminal justice system may not have been decisively resolved, the situation clearly urges reform.

The reforms during the period 1993 to 1996 may be considered a case of "successful failure". Heckscher describes this as a pattern of initial support for change, followed quickly by stalled innovation [Heckscher, Eisenstat, and Rice 1994:133]. There is demonstrable evidence of some successful outcomes of the reform process. Public confidence in the leadership of the Force was improved. This was evident in the high approval rating of both Commissioner MacMillan and his successor Commissioner Forbes. A public opinion survey conducted by the Stone organization in May 1997 recorded a 71 percent approval rating of Commissioner Forbes who was also associated with the leadership of the reforms.[1] This approval is fragile, however, and still narrowly indicates an approval of the individual occupying the office (who is seen as representing change and thus as a critic of the system) rather than an approval of the system of policing and of the JCF as an institution. Achieving the latter, as has been argued, requires a recognition of the broad criticisms of the political values that find expression in the nature of existing police-citizen interactions, and a commitment to altering the style of policing.

The process of change during the period under review demonstrated the political viability of reform and, in so doing, strengthened the foundations for further change. A generational shift has been partially effected in the officer corps with a significant number of younger reformist officers and NCOs being positioned in its lower levels. It failed, however, to establish a new dominant coalition that could safeguard and further advance the changes. The reforms simply forced the old guard on the defensive and subdued the old practices momentarily, only to have them re-emerge after the balance of power had been altered and before the new leadership could consolidate itself.

The Limits of Reform

The political environment conditions the outcome of the reform process. The particularistic principles on which social goods are allocated in the society, and which unfortunately also extends to the criminal justice processes, are outcomes of the sharp social divisions, the strength of group identities and the consequent articulation of social and political power in the society. To be successful and enduring, the scope and character of the reform project must thus be broad enough to help to alter this configuration of power.

There will be limits on any change process, even innocuous, non-threatening, incremental and narrowly managerial processes aimed at greater efficiency and that leave the basic power arrangements untouched. Regardless of the destination of the change process, the political environment may be profoundly enabling or limiting. As the Force is deeply permeated by the political parties, police behaviour is highly influenced by them. The prospects and limits of reform will vary with the shifting political alignments and the balance between advocacy coalitions.

The leadership of the political élite is thus vital to the outcome of the process. Ministerial support, as well as a measure of bipartisan support, is necessary for its success. Otherwise, resistance and the consequent divisions within the police force eventually find expression in the national politics and vice versa. The process of developing the programme of reforms is usually itself a determinant of the extent and character of the political support for the programme. In the existing reform project, bipartisan support was more forthcoming as the process involved wide consultations (although the police were excluded) with a cross-section of the population [Wolfe 1993] and was not clearly appropriated by either of the political parties. Yet for reasons already discussed, sections of the political élite remain opposed or, at best, ambivalent in their attitudes to fundamental reforms. This is driven by a fear of loss of control and the possible effects of this on the political structures.

Reform projects are confronted not just by the negative power of some sections of the élite but also the negative power of the different groups within the JCF. This negative power is amplified by the cohesiveness of the Force and by the character of the police culture. As Manning observes, the features of the organization that contribute to its cohesiveness and integration, such as the patrimonial modes of loyalty and secrecy norms, are also those that make the organization most resistant to reform [Manning 1977:338]. The capacity to readily exercise this power is facilitated by the high level of organization of the various formal associations within the Force, such as the Police Federation, Police Officers' Association, ISCF Association, District Constables' Association, and, of course, the informal party networks within the Force.

While among the police resistance to reform may not be rooted in a coherent social ideology, or in even developed views about crime control, it is informed by a deeply cynical view of human nature (which is more intensely expressed in their views of Jamaicans) that tends to weaken the commitment to democratically oriented change. This kind of perspective presents great obstacles to partnership between police and citizens in poor communities, to service, accountability to community structures, and any democratically oriented reforms. These issues help to frame the policy options.

Policy Options

The political directorate is confronted with three standard and logically possible policy options. These are reform termination, maintenance and reform succession.

Even though the limits of policing in its present mode are evident, termination of the reform project remains an option (made feasible by the successes and consequent space created by the reforms). However, in the long run, preservation of the status quo, or even incremental reform limited to some inconsequential aspects of the Force, holds little possibility for stability and successful crime control. Given the dynamic nature of the environment, the immediate consequence of reform termination would be a reversal of the progress achieved.

The implications of such a turn of events are worthwhile considering. First, policing issues are becoming more internationalized (drugs and firearm trafficking, migration, policing international criminal organizations). In this context, the performance of the police is potentially a source of international conflict on these issues. For example, performance on drug interdiction and eradication is linked, via the US certification process, to issues of trade and aid. This is a source of tension in the relations between the USA and a number of Latin American countries [see Tokatlian 1994; Perl 1994]. In the Caribbean, and Jamaica in particular, failure to improve the effectiveness of the police services now has implications for jurisdictional control within our sovereign territories. The recent demand by the USA, during the negotiation of the Maritime Counter Narcotics Agreement, that its coast guard be given policing powers within Caribbean jurisdictions, even allowing it to at times act independently of Caribbean police services, is more difficult to rebuff if Caribbean police services remain ineffective.[2]

Second, the Force had become integrated into the machinery and machine politics of the parties, thereby, until quite recently, posing a direct threat to the integrity of the electoral system. The Force has not been fully retrieved and, under these conditions, could easily revert to such a compromised state. With this, its capability for managing serious crime and disorder would become questionable.

Finally, with any retrogression of this sort, the ineffectiveness and negative reputation of the JCF could serve to further shift resources to the military and encourage its increased involvement in policing (particularly drug interdiction) and consequently increasing the relative influence and power of the military in the political life of the country. A course of policy termination would likely involve an incremental descent into further lawlessness, with the police and military having to increasingly, and with increasing ineffectiveness, rely on the authority of force rather than the force of authority.

Policy Maintenance

Policy maintenance, or a continuity of the programme of reforms on the professional reform model, is a more attractive option to policy makers. Although limited by its negative agenda, this approach still has considerable progressive potential in the Jamaican context. It offers possibilities for further consolidating the legitimacy gains if greater attention is paid to issues of distributive justice – of fairness and equal treatment of citizens regardless of their social status – and if anticorruption measures are more consistently adopted.

Policy maintenance largely rests on the assumption that the Force is capable of self-change. And the recent experience suggests that this is rather doubtful and is, at best, highly problematic. Moreover, as was argued earlier, even if such a reformation was fully implemented, the Force would remain relatively ineffective in controlling crime. Both the police and the population would eventually become impatient with it (as has occurred in the recent past) because of this incapacity. A programme of reform succession should therefore be considered.

Reform Succession

A positive programme of reform is required. Such a project (as noted earlier) may take either of two main directions: an authoritarian approach or a deepening of the service model of democratic policing.

If the present reform project fails to yield significant crime control results, then the case for a Draconian disciplinary approach to crime control and a corresponding authoritarian reconfiguration of the criminal justice system is likely to become more appealing. As an approach it should therefore be taken seriously.

The authoritarian approach is inspired by the Singaporean model. Singapore has been attractive to the élite and to policy makers in developing countries such as Jamaica, not just as a model of economic development but also as a model of social control. The latter has had some independent appeal, but more so when presented as a necessary aspect of an integrated development project. In other words, the model finds its justification in the anticipated development outcomes rather than narrow public safety outcomes.

Singapore has enjoyed rapid economic development with low crime rates. This has been achieved by developing an elaborate system of surveillance of its citizens, a strong police force and a very punitive justice system. The system of surveillance of the population requires all citizens to be registered with their photograph and fingerprints captured in the process, and be required to carry national identification cards at all times. This is coupled with a dense network of citizen committees that operate at the community level and in close association with the police. A number of legal instruments give the police extensive powers. The Internal Security Act gives them the power to detain suspects without trial. This power is principally directed at organized crime but is also used against internal political dissenters and social activists. The powers of the judiciary were similarly extended as trial by jury was abolished, as well as appeals to the Privy Council in England, and a wider menu of harsh punishments introduced for a wider range of crimes. The Arms Offences Act, for example, prescribes mandatory caning for a number of offences. Prime ministerial control of the judiciary is robust and is designed to make it politically responsive. This is accomplished via the power to have all judges fired [see Buendia 1989:279]. There is state-police intrusion into most aspects of social life and the criminalization and repression of most forms of deviance.

The success of the model is seen as being based on a trade-off between economic and physical security on the one hand and social and political freedoms on the other. Clammer correctly noted that the fundamental point in understanding Singaporean successes in social control is not the peculiarities of their culture (the submission to authority associated with Confucianism and so forth) but, rather, that it is underpinned by their successes in economic development [Clammer 1998:151]. This is the essential point to be grasped by those seeking to import this model. This is not to suggest that economic development is a precondition for effective social control but that, for this particular mode to succeed, some developmental dynamism must accompany it. And here the Jamaican record has not been particularly good. Thus, the likely trade-off would simply be greater physical security for less freedom. The primacy of order in a context of social exclusion, downwardly directed law enforcement and systemic injustices is less acceptable.[3] It is a bitter pill without the sugar coating of economic opportunity. The application of the Singaporean model in such a context would therefore require even greater coercion and carry a greater risk of degeneration of the Latin American or, rather, Brazilian type where there is a high and increasing level of social violence (Columbia, Peru, Guatemala) and formal state control is characterized by lawlessness, but the state structures continue to take a democratic form [see Chevigny 1995]. Of course, an important difference in the case of Jamaica is that the state does not have a comparable capacity for the delivery of violence; a more likely prospect along this course is therefore a Haitian type scenario where the general state structure and form of government also degenerate. Indeed, such a course would nurture the seeds of degeneration that are already present in the links among crime, politics and the police and the excessive use of force, pervasive corruption, party manipulation of the police and the general abuse of power associated with it.

The effectiveness of the Singaporean model of crime control also seems to rest on the interconnections between the formal state control institutions and the informal mechanisms of control, and the synergies derived from this. This is perhaps where Asian values are of some relevance, as the model is likely to work better in more collectivist cultures than in the more individualistic, westernized societies, such as Jamaica, where the power of socially controlling communal or even familial pressures are much less efficacious. This is a secondary point. But it implies that to achieve similarly low crime rates in the latter type of country (especially where there is a low level of development and weak or nonexistent welfare systems) would therefore require stronger and more coercive state control structures.

If this analysis of the core problems is correct, then the approach to reform cannot be simply to give the existing system of policing, or a more authoritarian variant of it, more power. Yet this is what is entailed in the Singaporean model, as it is essentially a process of removing the restraints on the institutions of state that employ armed coercive power, and energizing and concentrating this power. With this type of project, boundaries are difficult to establish and patrol. It is indeed a slippery slope.

Democratic reform of policing (along the lines of the service model) is also not without its problems and risks. But the objectives of any positive reform process ought to be fixed on improving the police effectiveness in crime control, the *quality of justice* and, consequently, the quality of life of the people. This is best done in a manner informed by the democratic principles of citizen responsibility, participation and equal treatment of all.

Following Johnson, democratically oriented police reform may be defined as reforms designed to enhance public influence on policy and make the police more responsive and accountable to the public [Johnson 1988:61]. In an era of universal secondary education, a communications revolution and an increasingly developed public opinion, the legitimization of any state institution that directly affects the lives of the citizenry in the way that the police do is difficult, if not impossible, without some public accountability and popular participation. While Johnson correctly emphasizes popular participation, and the literature on community policing details many ways in which this participation may productively occur, such reforms would also necessarily entail fidelity to the rule of law, adherence to principles of distributive justice (as difficult as this might be, given the nature of the social structure, the unequal distribution of social power and small size of the society), greater openness, police involvement in social crime control, citizen responsibility and perhaps support for the development of authentic local institutions capable of conflict resolution. This latter point is perhaps not essential to such a policing reform project; but providing easier access to just mechanisms of conflict resolution is a facilitating condition for a less repressive and statist mode of social control, and for new police-citizen relations.

Such a model would alter the functions of the police, the power relations between police and citizen, decentralize the organizational structures and transform the internal relations of the Force in order to ensure better service delivery and problem solving. This would represent a more civil model and would mark a radical break with the paramilitary political control model of the colonial era. The range of reforms would thus span the political (the structure of governance), operational (the style of policing) and administrative management of the Force (competence, efficiency and resource management).

In making the structure of governance more democratic, what must be emphasized is the need to develop control mechanisms, which, while being anchored in the principle of ministerial policy direction, are more broadly accountable to Parliament and to the community. This is likely to yield the benefits of reduced party manipulation of the Force. The process of depoliticization of the police force is more fully discussed elsewhere [Harriott 1994]. But central to the success of this process is placing the power to reward constables more directly in the office of an independent but accountable authority. This approach could be reinforced by further legal reform to empower citizens to better protect themselves against police abuses and the provision of enabling institutions such as a public defender. Together, both would provide improved channels and accessible means of securing redress. The introduction of such reforms is a necessary condition for a less repressive and statist mode of social control, and a facilitating condition for new police-citizen relations and a change in the style of policing.

In essence, the major challenge facing the Force is to evolve an authentic consensus-building style of policing suitable to Jamaican conditions. This would entail redefining the role of the police in order to highlight their duty to protect the constitutional rights of citizens and, generally, their service and citizen-protective functions. For example, protecting freedom of movement for women would seem to imply reducing the risk of rape. To secure these rights and freedoms, an appropriate style would need to emphasize crime prevention and partnership with citizens in problem solving.

Great difficulties are likely to attend any such effort as the sharp social divisions in the society make it difficult for the police to aggregate the various demands placed on them and to respond in consensus-building ways. The different social classes tend to have different ideas about police priorities and enforcement practices. For example, enforcing the laws regulating night noises or vending in public places tends to generate considerable conflict, and attitudes to these problems tend to be structured by class positions. However, these types of difficulties are not insurmountable if democratic principles are consistently applied.

The principle of openness is a natural companion to accountability and helps to build trust – on the basis of greater public access to accurate information on Force activity. It also yields an additional benefit. The application of these principles (in combination) tends to facilitate more effective service delivery. This is a general truth that applies well beyond policing to good governance in general. Robert Putnam, in a work that has been celebrated for its rigour and sound methodology, makes the case that effective government is best explained in terms of civic community or the participation by people in community activities and governmental affairs. This, he argues, cultivates a willingness to compromise and more responsive government [Putnam 1993].

Effectiveness in the delivery of service and in law enforcement, however, also requires direct regard for the managerial and supervisory needs of the Force. Some of the more open American (and European) police services have resolved this issue by having a clear administrative stream responsible for resource management that is discretely separated from the line officers [see Alpert and Dunham 1988]. Professional civilian managers (or police officers with managerial competencies) are allowed to operate in the administrative stream and to bring the level of managerial competence and more participatory style needed.

The application of these principles to policing, and thereby redefining relationships between the police and the citizen, is hardly likely to be consistent and secure if they are not also applied to the internal relations within the Force and to the treatment of its constables. For example, in the Jamaican context, fairness as a principle of distributive justice means, among other things, correcting for the downward direction of policing and upward responsiveness in service delivery. It means treating people equally. This principle should, for example, also apply to the treatment of women within the Force. If constables are treated fairly, they are more likely to treat citizens fairly. Similarly, the principle of participation should also apply to the internal relations and management style within the Force. Indeed, some police services are already moving in this direction. It is only to the extent that democratic practices prevail inside the Force that it will be able to meet the challenges of democratic policing.

Democratic policing requires a more democratic police force and also a more democratic society. Stable advances in police reform are best accompanied by change in other societal structures, although the latter is not a precondition for the former. The JCF responds to the pressures generated by the social and political structures; it responds to how social power is articulated. Central to this project is a shift in the distribution of power between police and citizen. Harnessing the collective energy required to succeed will depend on a willingness to engage in power sharing.

We have argued that social compliance cannot be reliably established on the basis of simply expanding the coercive power of the state and police-military power in particular, although these institutions ought to be strengthened and made more effective. Rather, it is suggested that social compliance be sought via greater consensus regarding the style of policing and the quest for greater legitimacy of the institutions of control, a legitimacy based on shared values and a redefinition of the power relationship with the citizenry. Moral authority and willing compliance are derived from this.

The intensity of feelings of moral obligation to support the state institutions of social control are related to the extent to which these institutions are just and effective in their operations; the degree of social integration and inclusion; the extent to which the population believes that it has a stake in the society and its development; and, objectively underpinning these, the extent to which worthwhile legitimate economic opportunities are created and made accessible to the majority of citizens. Willing compliance is less likely in a condition where many are outside the labour force and socially marginalized, and a high proportion of the labour force is engaged in individualistic own-account activity that sets them in competitive survival type relations (rather than relations of interdependence), as is presently the case. From observation, such individualistic and fiercely competitive modes of making a living hardly engender feelings of social responsibility and social obligation among the citizenry.

Reform is an investment in the future; the benefits are usually not immediate. Radical reform commonly has the most disruptive consequences, particularly if a "sunset approach" to the implementation of such a reform programme is adopted. The sunset approach entails dismantling of the Force (possibly in a phased way) and its reconstruction. As early as 1991, Stone [1995] advocated this approach. It has the distinct advantage of offering a good opportunity to break the culture associated with the existing style of policing, and to avoid being trapped by the patterns of action encouraged by the existing system. It would, however, generate considerable conflict and disruption. Regardless of the approach to process and destination, of great importance to the outcome is the recognition that the journey of police reform is a long one and must be pursued consistently rather than in reactive and opportunistic ways. Reform is, after all, not just a moral imperative but, if we may be permitted the language of survivalism, it is also a necessity.

Appendix

Survey of the Opinions
of Members of the JCF
on Police Reform

Attitude to Crime Scale

On a scale of 5 to 1, where 5 is strongly agree; 4, agree; 3, neutral; 2, disagree; and 1, strongly disagree, please state your attitude to the following statements.

λ1. Unemployment is the most important cause of crime.　5 4 3 2 1

λ2. Property crimes such as burglary are due more to lack of opportunities than to greed.　5 4 3 2 1

λ3. Crime is more often due to defects in Jamaican society, than character defects in the offender.　5 4 3 2 1

λ4. Crime in Jamaica stems mainly from a breakdown of discipline in the society.　5 4 3 2 1

λ5. Crime is largely due to an excess of freedoms in the society.　5 4 3 2 1

λ6. Most hardened criminals are destined to be that way.　5 4 3 2 1

λ7. Most hardened criminals were born (genetic) to be that way.

λ8. In order to reduce crime, the top priority of the government should be to:

    a.　create more economic opportunities for youth in the inner city areas　7

    b.　increase the size of the JCF　6

    c.　depoliticize the JCF　5

    d.　impose curfews, roadblocks, etc.　4

    e.　resume hangings　3

    f.　improve community participation in fighting crime　2

    g.　increase the powers of the police　1

    h.　other　0

Attitude to Law Enforcement

λ9. People breaking the criminal law should be given stiffer
sentences.   5 4 3 2 1

λ10. For some crimes the death penalty is the most appropriate
sentence.   5 4 3 2 1

λ11. Gun crime offenders should receive the death penalty.   5 4 3 2 1

λ12. There should be more noncustodial sentencing for minor
offences.   5 4 3 2 1

λ13. Gun criminals should be summarily executed.   5 4 3 2 1

λ14. Vigilante justice is sometimes appropriate.   5 4 3 2 1

λ15. The criminal justice system usually obstructs the work of
the police.   5 4 3 2 1

λ16. The law should be enforced even if it is wrong.   5 4 3 2 1

λ17. The possession of small quantities of ganja should be
decriminalized.   5 4 3 2 1

λ18. Some criminal laws are often unenforcible.   5 4 3 2 1

Attitude to Citizens' Rights

λ19. People should be allowed to organize and to protest
against government.   5 4 3 2 1

λ20. Excepting during a state of emergency, the police should
not be allowed to enter private homes without a warrant. 5 4 3 2 1

λ21. The police should be allowed to detain suspects without
charge for more than 72 hours.   5 4 3 2 1

λ22. The Deportee Act is too restrictive of the rights of the
individual.   5 4 3 2 1

λ23. In order to reduce crime, citizens should be prepared to
sacrifice some of their present rights and freedoms.   5 4 3 2 1

λ24. The state should provide a better legal aid service.   5 4 3 2 1

Attitude to the Reform of the JCF

λ25. The JCF is too politicized.   5 4 3 2 1

λ26. The JCF is too hierarchical; there should be freer
exchange of information across divisions.   5 4 3 2 1

λ27. The JCF is too centralized; too much power is
concentrated at the JCF High Command.   5 4 3 2 1

λ28. Most police personnel tend to adopt too adversarial an
approach in their professional contacts with the public. 5 4 3 2 1

λ29. How do you rate the public image of the Force?   5 4 3 2 1

λ30. The poor image of the Force is caused by:

    a. the press   6

    b. inadequate defence of the Force by its leadership   5

    c. a few "bad eggs"   4

    d. the improper behaviour of many of its personnel   3

    e. failure of the High Command to ensure discipline   2

    f. other   1

λ31. Attempts to change the Force will only make things worse. 5 4 3 2 1

λ32. To get a good Force it is necessary to improve the quality of recruits.   5 4 3 2 1

λ33. To get a good Force it is necessary to purge the "bad eggs". 5 4 3 2 1

λ34. To get a good JCF it is necessary to replace at least half of the Force.   5 4 3 2 1

λ35. To get a good Force it is necessary to replace at least half of the present officer corps.   5 4 3 2 1

λ36. To get a good Force, a new Force should be created.   5 4 3 2 1

λ37. The JCF should be merged with the JDF.   5 4 3 2 1

λ38. Do you think the Force should remain as is, undergo some change, be fundamentally changed?

    a. basically remain as is   4

    b. some change   3

    c. fundamental change   2

    d. other   1

Control and Accountability

λ39. Have you ever been brought before an internal court on disciplinary charges?

    Yes 1   No 2   (if no, skip to λ40)

    b. How many times   _____

    c. When was the last time (to the nearest year)?   _____

    d. What were the charges on the last occasion?   _____

    e. What was the outcome?

        guilty 1   not guilty 2

λ40. An Internal Affairs Unit charged with the responsibility to investigate corruption within the Force has been formed. How do you feel about this?   5 4 3 2 1

λ41. Most police personnel can easily evade the systems of accountability to their supervisors.   5 4 3 2 1

λ42. Community consultative committees will help to improve the ability of the Force to fight crime.   5 4 3 2 1 λ43. The citizens' consultative committees should receive regular reports on the performance of the Force within their area.   5 4 3 2 1

λ44. Consultative committees should set the operational priorities for the divisions.   5 4 3 2 1

λ45. The JCF should be more accountable to the public.   5 4 3 2 1

λ46. The JCF Act should be changed to reduce the powers of the minister.   5 4 3 2 1

λ47. How do you feel about the present method of appointing the commissioner of police?   5 4 3 2 1

λ48. The commissioner of police should be appointed by:
    a. an internal board   4
    b. external independent   3
    c. bipartisan committee   2
    d. other   1

Recruitment and Bureaucratic Culture

λ49. The ranks of A/Cpl and ASP are being phased out. Do you agree or disagree with this?   5 4 3 2 1

λ50. The hierarchy should be further flattened by reducing the number of remaining ranks.   5 4 3 2 1

λ51. Decision making at all levels should be more participatory.   5 4 3 2 1

λ52. Which of the following do you think (a) is and (b) ought to be the main factor in promotions?

	(a) Is	(b) Ought
a. seniority	1	1
b. level of formal education	2	2
c. experience	3	3
d. managerial competence	4	4
e. performance	5	5
f. other	6	6
g. politics	7	7

λ53. How do you feel about increasing the age limit for new entrants to the Force to 40 years?   5 4 3 2 1

λ54. How do you feel about the proposal that the age of retirement be lowered?   5 4 3 2 1

λ55. More effort should be made to activate the direct entry programme.   5 4 3 2 1

λ56. The divisions should be allowed greater autonomy or
independence.   5 4 3 2 1

λ57. The JCFHQ should not interfere in operational planning
at the divisional level.   5 4 3 2 1

λ58. The divisions should be allowed greater scope for
long-term (strategic) planning.   5 4 3 2 1

λ59. More females should be recruited to the Force.   5 4 3 2 1

λ60. More females should be promoted to the senior ranks
(that is, above superintendent of police).   5 4 3 2 1

λ61. More civilians should be employed in the Force.   5 4 3 2 1

λ62. Civilian employees should be given wider responsibilities
within the Force.   5 4 3 2 1

λ63. The post of CP should remain open to persons from
outside the Force.   5 4 3 2 1

λ64. It should be made easier for gazetted officers to be fired
for nonperformance.   5 4 3 2 1

Police Style

λ65. A police force functions most effectively when it is
organized along paramilitary lines.   5 4 3 2 1

λ66. Given the level of violence in Jamaica, the police need
to be organized along paramilitary lines.   5 4 3 2 1

λ67. The military aspects of recruit training, such as field
craft, are being de-emphasized. Do you agree or disagree
with this?   5 4 3 2 1

λ68. It is wrong to detain people *en masse* for processing.   5 4 3 2 1

λ69. Curfews and house to house searches are often pointless. 5 4 3 2 1

λ70. Stop and search is too often done without sufficient
grounds for suspecting the person(s) stopped.   5 4 3 2 1

λ71. Which of the following tactics would you consider the
most effective in dealing with crime?
    a. random motorized patrols   1
    b. neighbourhood foot patrols   2
    c. raids/curfews/roadblocks   3
    d. responding to calls   4
    e. community service/policing   5

λ72. The military should be used for fighting crime in Jamaica:
    a. not used at all   5
    b. at a much reduced level   4
    c. at the present level   3
    d. at an increased level   2
    e. become totally involved   1

λ73. The police tend to use too much violence in dealing with
suspects (5= too much, 1 = too little, 3= just enough).   5 4 3 2 1

λ74. Citizens should be more involved in policing their
communities.   5 4 3 2 1

λ75. How do you feel about the Neighbourhood Watch
programme?   5 4 3 2 1

λ76. Neighbourhood Watch committees should have police
supervised access to firearms.   5 4 3 2 1

λ77. Community beat patrol is very important (5),
important (4), unimportant (2), very unimportant (1).   5 4 3 2 1

λ78. The role of the Neighbourhood Watch should be
restricted to being "the eyes and ears of the police".   5 4 3 2 1

λ79. Advanced police technology is the most important thing
needed by the JCF to reduce crime.   5 4 3 2 1

λ80. The acquisition of better surveillance equipment is the
most important thing needed to improve the JCF's
intelligence capability.   5 4 3 2 1

λ81. Community policing will make the police easier targets
for criminal violence.   5 4 3 2 1

Attitudes to Police Deviance

λ82. Most members of the JCF are corrupt.   5 4 3 2 1
λ83. Most members of your unit are corrupt.   5 4 3 2 1
λ84. Most members of the JCF officer corps are corrupt.   5 4 3 2 1
λ85. Most senior officers are corrupt.   5 4 3 2 1
λ86. Every one has a price.   5 4 3 2 1

λ87. On a scale of 5 to 1 (where 5 = high, and 1 = low), how
do you rate the level of tolerance of corruption in your
immediate work centre?   5 4 3 2 1

λ88. What do you think of the following as major reasons for
police corruption?

  a.   poor salaries   5 4 3 2 1
  b.   the efforts by the public to bribe the police   5 4 3 2 1
  c.   police frustrations with the inefficiency and
corruption of the justice system   5 4 3 2 1
  d.   pressure from one's peers within the Force   5 4 3 2 1
  e.   pressure from supervisors and officers   5 4 3 2 1
  f.   other   5 4 3 2 1

λ89. Which of the following do you think is most effective
    method of controlling corruption within the Force:
    a. increased salaries   1
    b. better recruits   2
    c. better quality officers   3
    d. harsher sanctions against members of the public
        who attempt to bribe/corrupt police personnel   4
    d. a better system of accountability   5
    e. other   6

Use of Force

λ90. Have you ever been shot at by gunmen?
    Yes 1   No 2   (if no, skip to λ92)
λ91. When was the last time you were shot at?
    a. within the last 6 mths   1
    b. within the last year   2
    c. within the last three years   3
    d. more than 3 years   4
λ92. Have you ever been shot and hit by gunmen?
    Yes 1   No 2
λ93. Have you ever shot at a suspect?
    Yes 1   No 2   (if no, skip to λ95)
λ94. When was the last time that this occurred?
    1–6 months   1
    7–12 months   2
    1–3 years   3
    3+ years   4
λ95. How many arrests did you make during the period
    January–June?
    none   1
    1–2   2
    3–5   3
    6+   4
λ96. Of these how many cases were brought before the courts? _____
λ97. How many convictions secured?   _____

Attitudes to the Process of Reform

λ98. Have there been any significant changes within your
    department since Commissioner MacMillan took office?
    Yes 1   No 2   (if no, skip to λ100)

λ99. Have these changes been mainly positive (5) or
negative (1)? 5 4 3 2 1

λ100. MacMillan is doing a very good (5), fair (3), very
poor (1) job? 5 4 3 2 1

λ101. How do you rate his handling of corruption within the
Force? Very good (5), fair (3), very poor (1). 5 4 3 2 1
If fair to poor, why?
   a. violation of due process 1
   b. act on weak evidence 2
   c. victimize cops because of their lifestyle 3
   d. other (name)_____ 4

λ102. In your experience, do you think the following have
got better (5), worse (1) or remained the same (3) since
the new commissioner of police?
(For [c.] and [d.]: decreased = 5, increased = 1.)
   a. discipline within the Force 5 4 3 2 1
   b. ability to control crime 5 4 3 2 1
   c. party activism within the Force 5 4 3 2 1
   d. political manipulation of the JCF 5 4 3 2 1
   f. public support for the JCF 5 4 3 2 1
   g. promotions at the officer level 5 4 3 2 1
   h. promotion at the other ranks 5 4 3 2 1
   i. accelerated promotion 5 4 3 2 1

λ103. Would you approve or disapprove of an extension of
his contract for an additional two years? 5 4 3 2 1

Notes

Introduction

1. See *Daily Nation* 3 September 1990.

2. This is already the case in Trinidad and Tobago. However, Maureen Cain, in her recent paper, reports that in the Trinidadian context, these companies are reluctant to exercise their police powers. "Violence and private policing in the Caribbean" (paper presented at the annual meeting of the Law and Society Association, St Louis, Missouri, 29 May–1 June 1997).

3. Carl Miller was then parliamentary secretary in the Ministry of National Security.

4. *Daily Nation* 3 September 1990.

5. The community policing experiment in Houston, Texas in the 1980s under the leadership of Lee Brown is particularly interesting and instructive. Skolnick and Bayley [1986] document its early and most promising stages in their book *The New Blue Line* referred to here.

6. Where corruption among state and police officials is endemic, they are usually seen as serving the narrowest of interests – their own.

7. Public confidence in the JDF, however, remained high. The government was therefore forced to rely increasingly on the JDF in a police role for joint patrols with the police (JCF).

8. Elsewhere I discuss the implications of this for the democratic process more fully.

9. According to the *White Paper on Comprehensive Tax Reform* of 1985, only 40 percent of tax revenues were being collected.

10. This is well documented in the *Report of the Commission of Enquiry into Electoral Malpractices: Local Government Elections* [Duffus 1989], and later in *Report on Election Malpractices: General Elections* by the Jamaica Labour Party [1993].

11. In keeping with their status, and a recognition of the difficulties of getting them into this forum, senior officers were interviewed individually.

12. These scales are defined in chapter 6.

13. Profiles of these communities are given in chapter 5.

Chapter 1 – The Changing Structure of Crime in Jamaica

1. Data supplied by the Tourism Product Development Company, Kingston, Jamaica.

2. *Daily Gleaner* 16 February 1995.

3. Violent crime is disjunctively defined as criminal homicide, rape, shooting, robbery, felonious wounding and assaults. Property crime is similarly defined as burglary, break-ins, larceny from persons or dwellings, praedial larceny, larceny of and from motor vehicles and larceny from "other sources", and fraud. The latter is excluded in the use of this category in the official sources. Victimless crimes such as drug-defined crimes are excluded from both categories.

4. Prior to this, such sharp increases in crime rates were associated with, and only with, the electoral effect.

5. See *Daily Gleaner* 28 March 1995.

6. This is based on a data set of 1,400 murders developed by the author for work presently in progress. All data on murder cited in the text are generated from this data set.

7. For the police, domestic crimes may refer to a relationship, usually that the offender is known to the victim; it may also refer to a characteristic of the precipitating incident (that it is trivial) or the motive of the offender (to eliminate a sexual competitor or to gain face). Such an omnibus and nebulous category thus inflates and misrepresents the social relations driving murder in Jamaican society.

8. This was evident from separate personal interviews with three self-identified professionals in the fields of car theft, warehouse burglary and drug trafficking. This is consistent with earlier research on the arrest practices of the police, which generated data on the patterns of repeat offending derived from a survey of some 500 prisoners held in police jails in 1995.

9. *Daily Gleaner* 25 March 1994.

10. For a discussion of garrison politics, see "Garrison communities in Jamaica 1962–1993: Their growth and impact on political culture" by Mark Figueroa (paper presented to the symposium Democracy and Democratization in Jamaica: Fifty Years of Adult Suffrage, University of the West Indies, Mona, Jamaica, 6–7 December 1994).

11. Report of the Narcotics Division of the JCF. Unpublished.

12. JCF superintendent, personal communication.

13. Capt. X, manager of a private security company, interview by author (Kingston, Jamaica, September 1995).

14. See *Daily Gleaner* 26 February 1992.

15. See *Daily Gleaner* 25 July 1997.

16. The political "communities" are included in this, as party affiliation is such a strong identifier and determinant of inclusion and exclusion, and thus a generator of conflict. It is for these reasons that Jamaicans refer to their political parties as "tribes".

Chapter 2 – Police Organization

1. In their recent book *Fixing Broken Windows, Restoring Order and Reducing Crime in our Communities*, George Kelling and Catherine Coles [1996] argue that a close association obtains between public disorder and crime and that the energies of the police should be properly focused on controlling disorder if they wish to reduce

serious crime. On this theory, one could argue that a reason for the great increase in serious crime since Independence is the reduced efforts of the police in controlling disorder. Of course, as was shown in chapter 1, given the complex character of crime in Jamaica, such an explanation would seem somewhat simplistic. And it should also be borne in mind, as stated here, that the colonial police had a more political interpretation of the problem of disorder.

2. Despite the order, which indeed reflects the priorities, the focus on detection rather than prevention, with regard to crime, has in effect meant that only serious crimes are treated seriously.

3. This estimate is based on the outcomes of all completed murder cases during the years 1992 and 1994. It includes cases in which the charges were reduced to manslaughter by a process of plea bargaining. Some 48 percent of all "cleared-up" cases put before the courts ended in convictions, and only 41 percent of reported murders were cleared up. The trial outcomes were computed by the author from the records of the director of public prosecutions.

4. Commissioner Trevor MacMillan, personal communication, 1994.

5. Commissioner Trevor MacMillan, interview by author, 1996.

6. The "old police" force had existed before this, but it was not until then that police work became a full-time occupation.

7. The concept of paramilitarism is more fully explored in the later discussion of the JCF's style of policing.

8. This is evident in the typical annual report of the JCF. Without the resources to operate in this way, the JCF is usually demoralized and at a loss.

9. JCF corporal in the Mobile Reserve, interview by author, Kingston, Jamaica, April 1995.

10. Official data from the JCF Computer Centre returned 0.2 percent. But, while this output was generated at the time of the survey, the data entry was done much earlier.

11. Dismissals for abandoning the job are excluded.

12. Interview by author, 1995.

13. Interview by author, 1995.

14. Interview by author, 1996.

15. Assistant commissioner, interview by author, 1995.

16. Interview by author, 1996.

Chapter 3 – Rank and Money in the Bank: Corruption in the JCF

1. The legal battles associated with the resistance will be discussed later in chapter 8.

2. The survey measures of the prevalence of corruption are very crude. This is not primarily a technical problem, as the anticipated evasiveness and masking could be minimized by the use of "randomized response techniques" [see Hosseini and Armacost 1993]. This technique would have been more appropriate in a survey focused exclusively on corruption and administered under less threatening circumstances.

3. JCF commissioner of police, personal communication, July 1995; and personal correspondence with a member of the Narcotics Division who has investigated such cases in the USA and who first informed the author of this practice in February 1995.

4. Police videotape of the event; and assistant commissioner of police, interview by author, Kingston, Jamaica, 1995.

5. *Daily Gleaner* 2–5 December 1996.

6. JCF corporal attached to the Mobile Reserve, interview by author, 1995.

7. This includes all cases referred to the police for investigation and action by the Police Public Complaints Authority.

8. *Daily Gleaner* 29 December 1996.

9. The rate of offending by the police was computed by the author from the records of the Police Complaints Division of the JCF. As with the rates for the society as a whole, the crime rates for the police are underestimates. The risks to the complainant in reporting police crime are clearly greater. Moreover, brutality and violent conduct not resulting in criminal charges are excluded in calculating the rate of police offending.

10. Commissioner Trevor MacMillan, interview by author, 1995.

11. In my interviews with recruits in 1991, and again in 1994 when the Force was less tolerant of corrupt behaviour, this was still evident among them.

12. This was discussed in the focus groups and confirmed in a number of personal interviews.

13. Observation, author's field notebook.

14. A former member of the unit, personal communication, 1996.

15. JCF superintendent, interview by author, 1995; and acting commissioner of police, interview by author, 1995.

16. JCF superintendent, interview, 1995.

17. JCF Charge Book, entry dated 15 June 1990.

18. JCF corporal, reconstructed interview by author, 1995.

19. Focus Group, meeting with author, 28 March 1994.

Chapter 4 – The Somnolent yet Aggressive Watchman: The JCF's Style of Work

1. Of course, the exercise of police discretion quickly removes any semblance of equal treatment of all.

2. The revision of the constitution that is now being debated is likely to give a less qualified recognition of individual rights.

3. Deputy superintendent of police, interview by author, 1995; and senior superintendent of police, interview by author, 1995. Also during the course of the fieldwork, in more informal settings, a number of police persons of different ranks related personal experiences of this sort.

4. Observation, author's field notebook.

5. This figure not only depicts the general trend in work norms, but accentuates it. As a general procedure, uniformed officers are required to hand over cases of violent victimization to detectives. Arrests by uniformed constables are thus often attributed to them.

6. At the time of writing, the first case in recent times had entered the trial stage. This involved the failure of the police to promptly respond to repeated distress calls from citizens during what turned out to have been the rape and murder of a pregnant woman [see *Daily Gleaner* 24 August 1995].

7. The duration between each major joint police-military operation may be taken as a measure of the cycle. In the last three years, with the exception of

Operation Buccaneer, an antinarcotics operation that has been in progress for more than 20 years, there have been four such operations – Ardent, Shining Armour, Crest and Operation Dovetail; while in the previous six years there were fewer of such operations.

8. A representative sample of 141 prisoners in police lock-ups in the city of Kingston were interviewed as part of a pilot study of the arrest practices of the police.

9. Data collected by the author with the assistance of students for a project that is still incomplete. This is a crude underestimate as some of the prisoners who are accused of serious crime are held on remand in the prisons.

10. These include killings committed while off duty. The investigative process is usually less constrained in dealing with these.

11. See *Daily Gleaner* 14 August 1995.

12. JCF sergeant in charge at the Half Way Tree police jail in Kingston, interview by author, Kingston, Jamaica, 1995.

13. JCF sergeant in charge of the patrol unit at the Mobile Reserve, interview by author, Kingston, Jamaica, 1994; and deputy superintendent of police, Mobile Reserve, interview by author, Kingston, Jamaica, 1995.

14. *Daily Gleaner* 7 October 1992.

15. *Daily Gleaner* 16 October 1992.

16. *Daily Gleaner* 23 October 1992. Operation Shining Path was similarly occasioned by the murder of an American tourist, Norris Rayham, in June 1994. For a report on this, see *Daily Gleaner* 23 October 1994.

17. *Daily Gleaner* 9 October 1992.

18. *Daily Gleaner* 8 October 1992.

19. See *Daily Gleaner* 8 October 1992; 18 October 1992.

20. This was the Wilton Gardens versus Tivoli Gardens "war" of 1994.

21. See *Daily Gleaner* 2 June 1991.

22. *Daily Gleaner* 26 October 1992; 24 March 1996.

23. See *Daily Gleaner* 24 March 1996.

24. See *Daily Gleaner* 25 March 1996.

25. *Daily Gleaner* 11 March 1994.

26. See *Daily Gleaner* 2 August 1995.

27. *Daily Gleaner* 11 March 1996.

Chapter 5 – Police and Community: Policing the Inner City

1. Interview by author, 1995. The phrase itself may be roughly translated to mean one has to aggressively search for opportunities and be prepared to rob.

2. In the case of Clementville, another satellite garrison in western Kingston, the tribute to the dons of their colonizing garrison was paid in girls.

3. The name Renkers is taken from the creole word *renk*, meaning literally stink. As the name of the gang, it is intended to connote an emphatic "bad". It is a rather colourful example of normative inversion.

4. This phrase means that a woman should take responsibility for her man's material needs and that this should rank in order of importance second only to his sexual needs.

5. The word *cosification* is coined from the Spanish word *cosa*, meaning thing.

6. This was a national survey of the levels of fear of violent crime, commissioned by the Ministry of National Security and Justice. The number of observations in

the inner city communities was, however, somewhat low ($N = 80$). To be more conclusive a booster sample would have been required.

7. Here the term victimizing crime is used in a more restrictive sense than earlier in the text. It is taken to mean cases where the power balance between the offender and the target of the attack is uneven. Thus death, which is the outcome of gang battles, would not be regarded as victimizing but rape clearly is.

8. Data from JCF records on the research community called Alexanderville.

9. Ibid.

10. Interview by author, Normanville, Jamaica, 9 October 1995.

11. Female resident, interview by author, Normanville, Jamaica, 9 October 1995.

12. As noted earlier, this coexists with underpolicing, that is, an unresponsiveness to the policing needs of the citizens of the area.

13. Former gang leader, interview by author, Kingston, Jamaica, 1995.

14. Observation, author's field notebook, 1995.

15. Community leader, interview by author, 1995.

16. JCF superintendent of police, interview by author, 1995.

17. Observation, author's field notebook.

18. They, however, have a longer history. The records show their appearance in the rural parish of St Thomas just prior to the Morant Bay Rebellion of 1865. They have persisted and may be found in at least one of the deeper inland districts of the island.

19. Observation, author's field notebook.

20. JCF superintendent to Commissioner Trevor MacMillan, 1994.

Chapter 6 – Attempts at Reform

1. Hon K.D. Knight to Commissioner Trevor MacMillan, 24 August 1993.

2. The "old police force", which was formed in 1834, was the precursor to the JCF.

3. This could be regarded as an incipient "treasury police".

4. Observation, author's field notebook.

5. Estimated by the author in association with police administrators from the Personnel Division of the JCF.

6. See *Daily Gleaner* 1 October 1994.

7. Commissioner Trevor MacMillan, interview by author, 1995.

8. Commandant of the Police Academy, interview by author, 1995; and superintendent of the Police Staff College, interview by author, 1996.

9. Commissioner Trevor MacMillan, interview by author, 1995.

10. Estimated by the author in collaboration with representatives of the Services Branch of the JCF.

Chapter 7 – Attitudes to Reform

1. In this analysis we are particularly interested in a structure matrix. Varimax rotation tends to minimize the number of variables that have high loadings on a factor, thereby enhancing the interpretability of the factors.

2. The operational definitions are given as a note to Table 4.2.

Chapter 8 – Resistance to Reform

1. *Daily Gleaner* 13 July 1993.

2. The dynamics of change can and do often alter the perspective of honest reformers. In a personal interview with the author shortly after the termination of this tenure, Colonel MacMillan indicated that he had arrived at the conclusion that nothing short of a new police force was required.

3. *Daily Gleaner* 12 October 1993.

4. *Daily Gleaner* 13 October 1993.

5. Commissioner Trevor MacMillan, interview by author, 1995; and a senior superintendent posted at the Police Staff College, interview by author, 1995.

6. JCF detective superintendent of police, personal communication, 1997.

7. *Daily Gleaner* 2 November 1993.

8. Commissioner Trevor Macmillan, personal communication, 1995.

9. JCF constable, interview by author, 1995.

10. JCF senior superintendent of police, personal communication, 1995.

11. See *Daily Gleaner* 10 April 1994; 1 May 1994.

12. *Daily Gleaner* 31 October 1994.

13. Senior superintendent, interview by author, 1996.

14. Interview by author, 1996.

15. *Daily Gleaner* 30 May 1996.

16. *Daily Gleaner* 8 April 1997.

17. Personal communication, April 1997.

18. *Daily Gleaner* 8 November 1993.

19. *Daily Gleaner* 12 October 1993.

20. *Daily Gleaner* 5 May 1994.

21. *Daily Gleaner* 12 March 1994.

22. *Daily Gleaner* 13 October 1993.

23. *Daily Gleaner* 4 April 1994.

24. I was allowed to examine the official correspondence in which the data were reported.

25. JCF superintendent of police, interview by author, 1995.

26. *Daily Gleaner* 19 October 1996.

27. *Daily Gleaner* 10 October 1993.

Chapter 9 – Conclusion

1. *Daily Observer* 22 May 1997.

2. For a discussion of the Maritime Counter Narcotics Agreement, see an article by Stephen Vascianne entitled "The PM at sea: American search in Jamaican waters", that was published in the *Daily Gleaner* 20 October 1997.

3. "Order" here does not mean the opposite of chaos, not predictable ways of behaving based on culturally conditioned codes. It is not meant in this socio-logical sense but, rather, in a more political sense as the concrete order, the particular order.

Bibliography

Primary Sources

Charge Book, Jamaica Constabulary Force (JCF).
Criminal Intelligence Division, Jamaica Constabulary Force (JCF).
Police Service Regulations, Jamaica Constabulary Force (JCF).
Statistics Unit, Jamaica Constabulary Force (JCF).

Newspapers

Daily Gleaner
Daily Nation
Daily Observer

References

Ahire, P. 1991. *Imperial Policing*. London: Open University Press.
Ali, K. 1992. "Scotland Yard watch Trinidad police." *Caribbean Week* 3, no. 26.
Allen, D. 1980. "Crime and treatment in Jamaica." In *Crime and Punishment in the Caribbean*, R. Brana-Shute and G. Brana-Shute, eds. Gainesville, FL: Center for Latin American Studies.
Alpert, G., and R. Dunham. 1988. *Policing Urban America*. Prospect Heights, IL: Waveland Press.
Americas Watch. 1986. *Human Rights in Jamaica*. New York: The Americas Watch Committee.
Anderson, P., and M. Witter. 1994. "Crisis, adjustment and social change: A case study of Jamaica." In *Consequences of Structural Adjustment A Review of the Jamaican Experience*, E. Le Franc, ed. Kingston, Jamaica: Canoe Press, University of the West Indies.
Annual Report of the Contractor General. 1993. Kingston, Jamaica: Government Printing Office.
Auten, J. 1985. "The paramilitary model of police and police professionalism." In *The Ambivalent Force: Perspectives on the Police*, A.S. Blumberg and E. Niederhoffer, eds. New York: Holt, Rinehart and Winston.
Baldwin, J. 1987. "Why accountability?" *British Journal of Criminology* 27, no. 1.

Barnett, L. 1977. *The Constitutional Law of Jamaica*. London: Oxford University Press.

Bayat, J. 1993. *The State in Africa: The Politics of the Belly*. London: Longman.

Bayley, D. 1992. "Comparative organization of the police in English speaking countries." In *Modern Policing*, M. Tonry and N. Morris, eds. Chicago: University of Chicago Press.

———. 1994. *Police for the Future*. New York: Oxford University Press.

Beckford, G. 1972. *Persistent Poverty: Underdevelopment in Plantation Economies of the Third World*. New York: Oxford University Press.

———. 1984. "The struggle for a relevant economics." *Social and Economic Studies* 33, no. 1.

Beetham, D. 1991. *The Legitimation of Power*. New York: MacMillan; Atlantic Highlands, NJ: Humanities Press.

Belize. 1992. *Abstract of Statistics*. Belize City: Government of Belize.

Bennett, R., and J. Lynch. 1996. "Towards a Caribbean criminology: Problems and prospects." *Caribbean Journal of Criminology and Social Psychology* 1, no. 1 (January).

Bent, J. 1994. Memorandum to Commissioner T. MacMillan.

Best, J., and D. Luckenbill. 1989. "The social organization of deviants." In *Deviant Behaviour: A Text-Reader in the Sociology of Deviance*, D.H. Kelly, ed. New York: St Martins Press.

Blau, P., and M. Myer. (1987). *Bureaucracy in Modern Society*. New York: McGraw-Hill.

Blom-Cooper, L. 1990. *Guns for Antigua: Report of the Commission of Inquiry into the Circumstances Surrounding the Shipment of Arms from Israel to Antigua and Transshipment on 24 April 1989 en Route to Columbia*. London: Duckworth.

Blumberg, A.S., and E. Neiderhoffer (eds.). 1985. *The Ambivalent Force: Perspectives on the Police*, third edition. New York: Holt, Rinehart and Winston.

Boyd, D. 1988. *Economic Management, Income Distribution, and Poverty in Jamaica*. New York: Praeger.

Braithwaite, J., and W. Braithwaite. 1980. "The effect of income inequality and social democracy on homicide." *British Journal of Criminology* 20, no. 1.

Brogden, M. 1977. "A police authority: The denial of conflict." *Sociological Review* 25.

———. 1982. *The Police: Autonomy and Consent*. London: Academic Press.

———. 1987. "The emergence of police: The colonial dimension." *British Journal of Criminology* 27.

Brook, L. 1993. "Police discretionary behavior: A study in style." In *Critical Issues in Policing*, R. Dunham and G. Alpert, eds. Prospect Heights, IL: Waveland Press.

Brown, A., and H. Brewster. 1974. "A review of the study of economics in the English-speaking Caribbean." *Social and Economic Studies* 23, no.1.

Brown, L. 1994. "Crisis, adjustment and social change: The middle class under adjustment." In *Consequences of Structural Adjustment: A Review of the Jamaican Experience*, E. Le Franc, ed. Kingston, Jamaica: Canoe Press, University of the West Indies.

Bryman, A., and D. Cramer. 1990. *Quantitative Data Analysis for Social Scientists*. London: Routledge.

Buchanan, P. 1986. *Community Development in the 'Ranking' Economy: A Socio-Economic Study of the Jamaican Ghetto*. Kingston, Jamaica: P. Buchanan.

Buendia, H.G. 1989. *Urban Crime: Global Trends and Policies.* Tokyo: United Nations University.

Buttler, A. 1992. *Police Management.* Aldershot: Dartmouth Publishing.

Cain, M. 1979. "Trends in the sociology of police work." *International Journal of the Sociology of Law* 7.

———. 1996. "Policing there and here: Reflections on an international comparison." *International Journal of the Sociology of Law* 24, no. 4.

Carnegie, A. 1991. "Police powers in the West Indies: Some constitutional aspects." *Caribbean Law Review* 1, no. 2.

———. 1993. "Police powers in England and Wales: The courts and the changes of PACE." *Caribbean Law Review* 3, no. 2.

Chadee, D. 1996. "Race, trial evidence and jury decision making." *Caribbean Journal of Criminology and Social Psychology* 1, no. 1.

Chevannes, B. 1992. "The formation of garrison communities." Paper presented at symposium, Grassroots Development and the State of the Nation, in honour of Professor Carl Stone, Faculty of Social Sciences, 16–17 November, University of the West Indies, Mona, Jamaica.

Chevigny, P. 1991. "Police deadly force as social control: Jamaica, Argentina, and Brazil." *Criminal Law Review* 1, no. 3.

———. 1995. *Edge of the Knife: Police Violence in the Americas.* New York: The New Press.

Chuck, D. 1980. "The role of the sentencer in dealing with criminal offenders." In *Crime and Punishment in the Caribbean*, R. Brana-Shute and G. Brana-Shute, eds. Gainesville: Center for Latin American Studies.

Clammer, J. 1998. "Framing the other: Criminality, social exclusion, social engineering in developing Singapore." In *Crime and Social Exclusion*, C. Finer and M. Nellis, eds. Oxford: Blackwell Publishers.

Clarke, M. 1987. "Citizenship, community, and the management of crime." *British Journal of Criminology* 27, no. 4.

Collins, R. 1995. "Three faces of cruelty: Towards a comparative sociology of violence." In *Readings in Comtemporary Sociological Theory: From Modernity to Post-modernity*, D. McCurrie, ed. Englewood Cliffs, NJ: Prentice Hall.

Colman, A., and P. Gorman. 1982. "Conservatism, dogmatism and authoritarianism in police officers." *Sociology* 16.

Crandon, I., R. Carpenter, and A. McDonald. 1994. "Admissions for trauma at the University Hospital of the West Indies." *West Indian Medical Journal* 43.

Curry, J. 1932. *The Indian Police.* London: Faber and Faber.

Danns, G. 1982. *Domination and Power in Guyana: A Study of the Police in a Third World Context.* New Brunswick, NJ: Transaction Books.

Day, G., and J. Murdoch. 1993. "Locality and community: Coming to terms with place." *Sociological Review* 41, no. 1.

de Albuquerque, K. 1984. "A comparative analysis of violent crime in the Caribbean." *Social and Economic Studies* 33, no. 3.

———. 1996. " 'Give me a five dollar': The drug menace in the Eastern Caribbean." *Caribbean Weekly* 7, no. 8.

Deosaran, R. 1989. "The psychology of the young offender: Towards appropriate strategies." In "New directions in Caribbean social policy," M. Cain, ed.

Unpublished conference proceedings, Institute of Social and Economic Research, University of the West Indies, St Augustine, Trinidad.

————. 1992. "The jury on trial: The court of psychology." In *Social Psychology in the Caribbean. Directions for Theory and Research*, R. Deosaran, ed. San Juan: Longman Trinidad.

Diederich, B. 1984. "The end of West Indian innocence: Arming the police." *Caribbean Review* 13, no. 2.

Duffus, H. 1989. *Report of the Commission of Enquiry into Electoral Malpractices: Local Government Elections*. Kingston, Jamaica: Government Printing Office.

Easton, D. 1965. *Systems Analysis of Political Life*. New York: John Wiley.

Economic and Social Survey (ESS). Various years. Kingston, Jamaica: Planning Institute of Jamaica.

Ehrenfield, R. 1992. *Evil Money: Encounters along the Money Trail*. New York: Harber Business.

Ellis, H. 1973. "Accommodation of violence: A study of attitudinal systems and their relevance to crimes and violence in Jamaica." MSc thesis, University of the West Indies, Mona.

————. 1992a. *Identifying Crime Correlates in a Developing Society: A Study of Socio-economic and Socio-demographic Contributions to Crime in Jamaica, 1950–1984*. New York: Peter Lang.

————. 1992b. "Crime and control in the English-speaking Caribbean: A comparative study of Jamaica, Trinidad, Tobago and Barbados 1960–1980." In *Crime and Control in Comparative Perspectives*, H. Heiland, L. Shelly, and H. Katoh, eds. New York: Walter de Gruyter.

Emsley, C. 1983. "The origins and development of the police." In *Controlling Crime*, E. McLaughlin and J. Muncie, eds. London: Sage.

Enloe, C. 1976. "Civilian control of the military: Implications in the plural societies of Guyana and Malaysia." In *Civilian Control of the Military: Theory and Cases for the Developing Countries*, C. Welch, ed. Albany: State University of New York Press.

Erickson, R. 1982. *Reproducing Order: A Study of Police Patrol Work*. Toronto: University of Toronto Press.

————. 1989. "Patrolling the facts: Secrecy, publicity and police work." *British Journal of Sociology* 40, no. 2.

Evans, G., A. Heath, and M. Lallijee. 1996. "Measuring left-right and libertarian-authoritarian values in the British electorate." *British Journal of Sociology* 47, no. 1.

Eyre, A. 1984. "The Effects of political violence on the population and urban environment of Kingston, Jamaica." *Geographical Review* 74, no. 1.

Fielding, N. 1984. "Police socialization and police competence." *British Journal of Sociology* 35, no. 4.

————. 1994. "The organizational and occupational troubles of community policing." *Policing and Society* 4.

Figueroa, M. 1994. "Garrison communities in Jamaica 1962–1993: Their growth and impact on political culture." Paper presented at symposium, Democracy and Democratization in Jamaica: Fifty Years of Adult Suffrage, Faculty of Social Sciences, 6–7 December, University of the West Indies, Mona, Jamaica.

Foucalt, M. 1977. *Discipline and Punish: The Birth of the Prison.* New York: Pantheon Books.

Fraser, A. 1979. "Public order in the Commonwealth Caribbean." *West Indian Law Journal* (May).

Goldstein, H. 1977. *Policing a Free Society.* Cambridge, MA: Balliger.

———. 1979. "Improving policing: A problem-oriented approach." *Crime and Delinquency* 25.

———. 1987. "Toward community-oriented policing: Potential, basic requirements, and threshold questions." *Crime and Delinquency* 33, no. 1.

Goulbourne, H. 1984. "On explanations of violence and public order in Jamaica." *Social and Economic Studies* 33, no. 4.

Gottfredson, M., and T. Hirschi. 1990. *A General Theory of Crime.* Stanford: Stanford University Press.

Granovetter, M. 1985. "Economic action and social structure: The problem of embeddedness." *American Journal of Sociology* 91.

Greene, J. 1989. "Police and community relations: Where have we been and where are we going?" In *Critical Issues in Policing: Contemporary Readings,* R. Dunham and G. Alpert, eds. Prospect Heights, IL: Waveland Press.

Grey, O. 1994. "Discovering the social power of the poor." *Social and Economic Studies* 43, no. 3.

Griffith, I. 1994. "Security and the drug trade." *Caribbean Affairs* 7, no. 4.

Gunst, L. 1995. *Born Fi Dead.* New York: Henry Holt.

Guyana Police Force. 1990. *Annual Report.* Georgetown, Guyana: Guyana Police Force.

Habermas, J. 1995. "What does a crisis mean today? Legitimation problems in late capitalism." In *Readings in Contemporary Sociological Theory: From Modernity to Post-Modernity,* D. McCurrie, ed. Englewood Cliffs, NJ: Prentice Hall.

Haferkamp, H., and H. Ellis. 1992. "Power, individualism and the sanctity of human life: Development of criminality and punishment in four cultures." In *Crime and Control in Comparative Perspectives,* H. Heiland, L. Shelly, and H. Katoh, eds. New York: Walter de Gruyter.

Hagan, J. 1994. *Crime and Disrepute.* London: Pine Forge Press.

Hagan, J., and B. McCarthy. 1992. "Street life and delinquency." *British Journal of Criminology* 43.

Hall, S., et al. 1978. *Policing the Crisis: Mugging, the State and Law and Order.* New York: Holmes and Mier.

Handy, C. 1985. *Understanding Organizations.* Harmondsworth: Penguin.

Harriott, A. 1992a. "Survey of community based organizations in Jamaica." Unpublished report.

———. 1992b. "Vigilante justice: Problems of crime management in Jamaica." Paper presented at symposium, Grassroots Development and the State of the Nation, in honour of Professor Carl Stone, Faculty of Social Sciences, 16–17 November, University of the West Indies, Mona, Jamaica.

———. 1994. "Race, class and the political behaviour of the Jamaican security forces." PhD diss., University of the West Indies, Mona, Jamaica.

Hayek, F. 1960. *The Constitution of Liberty.* Chicago: University of Chicago Press.

Headley, B. 1982. "Structural correlates of dependent capitalist development and increase in criminality in Jamaica." PhD diss., Howard University, Washington, DC.

————. 1994. *The Jamaican Crime Scene: A Perspective.* Mandeville, Jamaica: Eureka Press.

Heckscher, C., R. Eisenstat, and T. Rice. 1994. "Transformational processes." In *The Post-Bureaucratic Organization: New Perspectives on Organizational Change,* C. Heckscher and A. Donnellon, eds. London: Sage Publications.

Held, D. 1989. *Political Theory and the Modern State.* Stanford: Stanford University Press.

Herst, M. 1991. "Review of the Jamaica Constabulary." Unpublished report.

Heywood, A. 1994. *Political Ideas and Concepts.* London: Macmillan.

Hill, A. 1995. "Militant tendencies: 'Paramilitarism' in the British police." *British Journal of Criminology* 35, no. 3.

Horton, C. 1995. *Policing Policy in France.* London: Policy Studies Institute.

Hosseni, J., and R. Armacost. 1993. "Gathering sensitive data in organizations." In *Improving Organizational Surveys: New Directions, Methods and Applications,* P. Rosenfeld et al., eds. London: Sage.

Hutter, B. 1986. "An inspector calls: The importance of proactive enforcement in the regulatory context." *British Journal of Criminology* 26, no. 2.

Incardi, J. 1993. *Criminal Justice.* New York: Harcourt Brace College Publishers.

Inter-American Development Bank. 1997. *Columbia: Country Profile.* Washington, DC: Inter-American Development Bank.

Jamaica Constabulary Force (JCF). 1961. *Police Service Regulations.* Kingston, Jamaica: Government Printing Office.

————. 1990. *Force Standing Orders* 2248, 5 July.

————. 1992a. *Force Standing Orders,* second edition, Vols. 1 and 2. Kingston, Jamaica: Government Printing Office.

————. 1992b. "Intelligence brief for prime minister." Unpublished document.

————. 1992c. "Intelligence brief for commissioner." Unpublished document.

————. 1992d. "Operation Ardent: A review."

————. 1993–94. "Draft police management review." Unpublished draft report.

————. 1994. "Draft annual report 1994."

————. circa 1994. "Operation Crest: A review presentation."

————. 1995. *Force Standing Orders* 2518, 7 August.

————. Various years. *JCF Annual Report.* Kingston, Jamaica: JCF.

Jamaica Labour Party (JLP). 1993. *Report on Election Malpractices General Elections – March 30, 1993.* Kingston, Jamaica: JLP Institute for Political Education.

Jefferies, C. 1952. *The Colonial Police.* London: M. Parrish.

Jefferson, T. 1987. "Beyond paramilitarism." *British Journal of Criminology* 27, no. 1.

————. 1993. "Pondering paramilitarism: A question of standpoints." *British Journal of Criminology* 33, no. 3.

Johnson, D. 1976. "The triumph of reform: Police professionalism 1920–1965." In *The Ambivalent Force: Perspectives on the Police,* A.S. Blumberg and E. Niederhoffer, eds. New York: Holt, Rinehart and Winston.

Johnson, L. 1988. "Controlling police work." *Work, Employment and Society* 2, no. 1.

Johnson, M. 1987. "A century of murder in Jamaica 1880–1980." *Jamaica Journal* 20, no. 2.

Jones, T., T. Newburn, and D. Smith. 1996. "Policing and the idea of democracy." *British Journal of Criminology* 36, no. 2.

Kaufman, M. 1985. *Jamaica under Manley: Dilemmas of Socialism and Democracy.* London: Zed Books.

Kelling, G., and C. Coles. 1996. *Fixing Broken Windows, Restoring Order and Reducing Crime in our Communities.* New York: The Free Press.

Kelling, G., T. Pate, D. Dieckman, and C. Brown. 1974. *The Kansas City Preventative Patrol Experiment: A Summary Report.* Washington, DC: Police Foundation.

Klockars, C. 1985. *The Idea of Police.* London: Sage.

———. 1991. "The rhetoric of community policing." In *Thinking about Police,* B. Klockars and S. Mastrofski, eds. New York: McGraw-Hill.

Knight, K.D. 1993. Letter to Commissioner T. MacMillan, 24 August.

———. 1994. Sectoral debate delivered in the House of Representatives, Jamaica.

Lacey, T. 1977. *Violence and Politics in Jamaica 1960–1970.* London: Frank Cass.

Leighton, B. 1991. "Visons of community policing: Rhetoric and reality in Canada." *Canadian Journal of Criminology* 33, no. 3.

Lewin, A. 1978. "Social control in Jamaica: Causes, methods and consequences." PhD diss., New York University, New York.

Lindo, C. 1990. "Police brutality." *Daily Gleaner* 25 February 1990.

Liverpool, F. 1995. "Fighting corruption in the police: Some strategic considerations for Guyana." Postgraduate term project, Carleton University, Canada.

Lundman, R.J. 1985. "Police misconduct." In *The Ambivalent Force: Perspectives on the Police,* third edition. A.S. Blumberg and E. Niederhoffer, eds. New York: Holt, Rinehart and Winston.

MacMillan, T. 1994. Management review of the JCF 1993.

———. 1995. Speech to the Montego Bay Chamber of Commerce and Industry (June).

Manning, P. 1974. "Dramatic aspects of policing: Selected propositions." *Sociological and Social Review* 59.

———. 1977. *Police Work: The Social Organization of Police Work.* Cambridge, MA: MIT Press.

Mansingh, A., and P. Ramphal. 1993. "The nature of interpersonal violence in Jamaica and its strain on the national health system." *West Indian Medical Journal* 42, no. 2.

Marenin, O. 1990. "The police and the coercive nature of the state." In *Changes in the State: Causes and Consequences,* E. Greenberg and T. Mayer, eds. London: Sage Publications.

Martin, S.C. 1993. "Fear of crime: Program to deal with." Unpublished paper.

Matthews, L., and G. Danns. 1980. *Communities and Development in Guyana.* Georgetown, Guyana: University of Guyana.

Maynall, P., T. Baker, and R. Hunter. 1995. *Police-Community Relations and the Administration of Justice,* fourth edition. Englewood Cliffs, NJ: Prentice Hall.

McCalla, W. 1974. "Violent delinquency and the law in Jamaica." LLM thesis, University of the West Indies, Cave Hill, Barbados.

McCarthy, B., and J. Hagan. 1995. "Getting into street crime: The structure and process of criminal embeddedness." *Social Science Research* 24.

McIntosh, S., and H. Ghany. 1996. "Fundamental rights, government and the death penalty." *Caribbean Journal of Criminology and Social Psychology* 1, no. 1.

Meeks, B. 1996. *Radical Caribbean: From Black Power to Abu Bakr.* Kingston, Jamaica: The Press University of the West Indies.

Melchers, R. 1993. "A commentary on 'Vison of the Future of Policing in Canada: Police Challenge 2000'." *Canadian Journal of Criminology* 35, no. 1.

Merquior, J. 1980. *Rousseau and Weber: Two Studies in the Theory of Legitimacy.* London: Routledge and Kegan Paul.

Messner, S. 1989. "Economic discrimination and societal homicide rates: Further information on the cost of inequality." *American Sociological Review* 54.

Miller, C. 1997. Speech at the annual dinner of the Society for Industrial Security, Kingston, Jamaica.

Mills, G. 1992. "Conflict between ministers and civil servants." In *Issues and Problems in Caribbean Public Administration*, S. Ryan and D. Brown, eds. St Augustine, Trinidad: Institute of Social and Economic Research, University of the West Indies.

Ministry of National Security and Justice. 1993. *Citizens Consultative Committees.* Kingston, Jamaica: Ministry of National Security and Justice.

Mintzberg, H. 1989. *Mintzberg on Management: Inside the Strange World of Organizations.* New York: The Free Press.

Mohammed, R. 1985. "Behaviour disorder among Jamaican adolescents." MSc thesis, Department of Social and Preventive Medicine, University of the West Indies, Mona, Jamaica.

Moore, M. 1992. "Problem solving and comunity policing." In *Modern Policing*, M. Tonry and N. Morris, eds. Chicago: University of Chicago Press.

Morris, N. 1994. "'Dangerousness' and incapacitation." In *A Reader on Punishment*, A. Duff and D. Garland, eds. Oxford: Oxford University Press.

Muir, W. 1977. *Police: Street Corner Politicians.* Chicago: University of Chicago Press.

Mullan, M. 1961. "A theory of corruption." *Sociological Review* 9, no. 2.

Niederhoffer, A. 1969. *Behind the Shield: The Police in Urban Society.* New York: Anchor Books.

Noruisis, M. 1994. *SPSS Professional Statistics.* Chicago, IL: SPSS Incorporated.

Nozick, R. 1974. *Anarchy, State and Utopia.* New York: Basic Books.

Nye, I. 1958. *Family Relationships and Delinquent Behaviour.* New York: John Wiley & Sons.

O'Dowd, D. 1991. "Review of the Trinidad and Tobago police service." Unpublished report. Port of Spain, Trinidad.

O'Gilvie, N. 1984. "Getting ready: Twenty-one years of preparation." *Alert* 11.

Orrett, W. 1951. *The History of the Guyana Police.* Georgetown: The Chronicle.

Ortet-Fabregat, G., and J. Perez. 1992. "An assessment of the attitudes towards crime among professionals in the criminal justice system." *British Journal of Criminology* 32, no. 2.

Ortiz, R. 1994. "Police culture: A roadblock to change in law enforcement?" *Police Chief* 61, no. 8.

Otley, C. 1964. *An Historical Account of the Trinidad and Tobago Police Force from the Earliest Times.* Port of Spain, Trinidad: C. Otley.

Patullo, P. 1996. *Last Resorts: The Cost of Tourism in the Caribbean.* Kingston, Jamaica: Ian Randle Publishers.

Peak, K. 1994. "Police executives as agents of change." *Police Chief* 61, no. 1.

Peak, K., and R. Glensor. 1996. *Community Policing and Problem Solving.* Upper Saddle River, NJ: Prentice Hall.

Perl, R. 1994. "US-Andean drug policy." In *Drug Trafficking in the Americas*, B. Bagley and W. Walker III, eds. London: Transaction Publishers.

Police Public Complaints Authority. 1995. "Draft annual report 1994–95." Kingston, Jamaica.

Potts, L. 1982. "Police leadership: Challenges for the eighties." *Journal of Police Science and Administration* 10, no. 2.

———. 1983. *Responsible Police Administration: Issues and Approaches.* Tuscaloosa: University of Alabama Press.

Pryce, K. 1976. "Towards a Caribbean criminology." *Caribbean Issues* 11, no. 2.

Putnam, R. 1993. *Making Democracy Work.* Cambridge: Harvard University Press.

Reiner, R. 1980. "Fuzzy thoughts: The police and law and order politics." *Sociological Review* 28.

———. 1992. "Police research in the United Kingdom: A critical review." In *Modern Policing*, M. Tonry and N. Morris, eds. London: University of Chicago Press.

Reith, C. 1943. *The British Police and the Democratic Ideal.* Oxford: Oxford University Press.

Renny, A., et al. 1951. *Report of the Commission of Enquiry into the Police Force.* Kingston, Jamaica: Government Printing Office.

Report of the Director of Elections, various years. Kingston, Jamaica: Government Printing Office.

Richards, A. 1940. *Memoirs of Thirty-six Years Police Service.* Rosseau, Dominica: A. Richards.

Riechers, L., and R. Roberg. 1990. "Community policing: A critical review of underlying assumptions." *Journal of Police Science and Administration* 17, no. 32.

Roberg, R., and J. Kuyendall. 1982. "Mapping police organizational change." *Criminology* 20, no. 2.

———. 1990. *Police Organization and Management: Behavior, Theory and Process.* Pacific Grove, CA: Brooks/Cole Publishing.

Robotham, D. 1984. "The emergence of sociology in Jamaica." *Social and Economic Studies* 33, no. 1.

Sanders, A., and R. Young. 1995. "The 'PACE regime' for suspects detained by the police." *Political Quarterly* 66, no. 2.

Scarman, L. 1981. *The Brixton Disorders 10–12 April 1981: Report of an Inquiry by the Rt. Hon. Lord Scarman.* London: Her Majesty's Stationery Office.

Scott, G. 1987. *Report of Commission of Enquiry into the Extent of the Problem of Drug Abuse in Trinidad and Tobago.* San Fernando, Trinidad: Unique Services.

Seymour, M., and E. Wint. 1993. "Strategy for the revitalization of blighted areas: Report of National Inner-City Committee." Unpublished report to the Kingston Restoration Company, Kingston, Jamaica.

Sherman, L. 1987. "Deviant organizations." In *Corporate and Governmental Deviance*, D. Ermann and R. Lundman, eds. New York: Oxford University Press.

———. 1992. "Attacking crime: Police and crime control." In *Modern Policing*, M. Tonry and N. Morris, eds. Chicago: University of Chicago Press.

Singham, A. 1968. *The Hero and the Crowd in a Colonial Polity.* New York: Vail-Ballou Press.

Skolnick, J., and D. Bayley. 1986. *The New Blue Line: Police Innovation in Six American Cities.* New York: The Free Press.

Skolnick, J., and J. Fyfe. 1993. *Above the Law: Police and the Excessive Use of Force.* New York: The Free Press.

Small, G. 1995. *Ruthless – The Global Rise of the Yardies.* London: Warner Books.

Sparrow, M., M. Moore, and D. Kennedy. 1990. *Beyond 911: A New Era for Policing.* New York: Basic Books.

St Cyr, E. 1983. *The Theory of Caribbean Economy: Its Origins and Current Status.* Occasional Paper No. 4. St Augustine, Trinidad: Institute of Social and Economic Research (ISER), University of the West Indies.

STATIN. Various years. *Statistical Yearbook of Jamaica.* Kingston, Jamaica: Government Printing Office.

Stinchcombe, A.L. 1963. "Institutions of privacy in the determination of police administrative practice." *American Journal of Sociology* 69 (September).

Stone, C. 1980. *Democracy and Clientilism in Jamaica.* New Brunswick, NJ: Transaction Books.

———. 1982. *The Newer Caribbean: Decolonization, Democracy and Development.* Philadelphia: Institute for the Study of Human Issues.

———. 1987. "Crime and violence: Socio-political implications." In *Crime and Violence Causes and Solutions,* P. Phillips and J. Wedderburn, eds. Mona, Jamaica: Department of Government, University of the West Indies.

———. 1991a. "Survey of public opinion on the Jamaican justice system." Unpublished report to US Agency for International Development, Kingston, Jamaica.

———. 1991b. "Solutions." Unpublished report to US Agency for International Development, Kingston, Jamaica.

———. 1992. "Value, norms and personality development in Jamaica." Typescript.

———. 1995. Speech to Building Societies of Jamaica. In *Carl Stone Speaks on People, Politics and Development,* R. Stone, ed. Kingston, Jamaica: Rapid Printers.

Sutherland, W. 1988. "The life and times of Operation Buccaneer IV." *Alert* 13.

Sutherswaite, Y. 1975. "The legal and social implications of the Suppression of Crimes (Special Provisions) Act, and the Gun Court Act." LLM thesis, University of the West Indies, Cave Hill, Barbados.

Sykes, R., J. Fox, and J. Clarke. 1985. "A socio-legal theory of police discretion." In *The Ambivalent Force: Perspectives on the Police,* third edition, A.S. Blumberg and E. Niederhoffer, eds. New York: Holt, Rinehart and Winston.

Teten, H. 1991. *The Jamaica Constabulary Force: An Occupational Survey to Determine Selection Criteria and Training Needs.* Washington, DC: Miranda Associates.

Thomas, H. 1927. *The Story of a West Indian Policeman or 47 Years in the JCF.* Kingston, Jamaica: The Gleaner Company.

Tokatlian, J. 1994. "Drug summitry: A Columbian perspective." In *Drug Trafficking in the Americas,* B. Bagley and W. Walker III, eds. London: Transaction Publishers.

Trinidad and Tobago. 1991. *Annual Statistical Digest.* Port of Spain, Trinidad: Government Printing Office.

Trinidad and Tobago Police Service. 1994. *Annual Report of the Trinidad and Tobago Police Service.* Port of Spain, Trinidad: Government Printing Office.

Trojanowicz, R., and B. Bucqueroux. 1990. *Community Policing: A Contemporary Perspective.* Cincinnati: Anderson Publishing Company.

United Nations Commission on Crime Prevention and Criminal Justice. 1992. In *Panos Briefing* 26, no. 1 (1997).

United Nations Development Program (UNDP). 1992. *Human Development Report.* New York: UNDP.

———. 1993. *Survey of Living Conditions.* New York: UNDP.

———. 1995. *Survey of Living Conditions.* New York: UNDP.

United States Government. 1994. "The illegal drug trade: Excerpts from a global report by the US Government." *Caribbean Affairs* 7, no. 4.

Van Maanen, J. 1976. "The asshole." In *The Ambivalent Force: Perspectives on the Police,* first edition, A.S. Blumberg and E. Niederhoffer, eds. New York: Holt, Rinehart and Winston.

———. 1989. "Making rank: Becoming an American police sergeant." In *Critical Issues in Policing,* R. Dunham and G. Alpert, eds. Prospect Heights, IL: Waveland Press.

Vascianne, S. 1996. *The Privy Council versus the Caribbean Court of Appeal: Some General Observations.* Mona, Jamaica: Cultural Studies Initiative, University of the West Indies.

Waddington, P. 1982. "Conservatism, dogmatism and authoritarianism in the police: A comment." *Sociology* 16.

———. 1987. "Towards paramilitarism? Dilemmas in policing civil disorder." *British Journal of Criminology* 27, no. 1.

Weitzer, M. 1995. *Policing Under Fire: Ethnic Conflict and Police-Community Relations in Northern Ireland.* Albany: State University of New York.

Wetheritt, M. (ed.). 1989. *Police Research: Some Future Prospects.* Aldershot: Averbury.

Williams, C. 1975. "Crime in Jamaica, its causes and treatment." LLM thesis, University of the West Indies, Cave Hill, Barbados.

Wilson, J. 1968. *Varieties of Police Behaviour.* Cambridge: Harvard University Press.

———. 1975. *Thinking about Crime.* New York: Vintage Books.

Wilson, J., and J. Herrnstein. 1985. *Crime and Human Nature.* New York: Simon and Schuster.

Wolfe, L. 1993. *Report of the National Task Force on Crime.* Kingston, Jamaica: Government Printing Office.

Wolfgang, M., R. Figlio, and T. Sellin. 1972. *Delinquency in a Birth Cohort.* Chicago: University of Chicago Press.

Index